HIGHER EDUCATION IN INDIA SINCE INDEPENDENCE

CONCEPTS IN COMMUNICATION INFORMATICS & LIBRARIANSHIP (CICIL)

For a list of titles in this series, see pp. 310-12 at the end of the book

About the Author

DR. O.P. GUPTA (*b* 1947) is at present working as librarian in University Grants Commission. He holds Ph.D (Hindi) and degree in Master in Library Science. He began his career as a college librarian (1971-73); served at Central Headquarters, C.G.W.B, Ministry of Agriculture (1974-80) and since December, 1980 has been serving the UGC in various capacities.

Dr. Gupta is a scholar, writer and is associated with a number of professional and non-professional bodies and committees. He is Member Secretary to the Panel of Library and Information Science and to the committee working on Curriculum Development of Library and Information Science. His publication includes 'Dictionary of Library and Information Science' and 'Development of University Libraries after in dependence'.

Concepts in Communication
Informatics & Librarianship-42

General Editor: **S.P. AGRAWAL**

HIGHER EDUCATION IN INDIA SINCE INDEPENDENCE

UGC and its Approach

O P GUPTA
Librarian
University Grants Commission, New Delhi

CONCEPT PUBLISHING COMPANY, NEW DELHI 110059

ISBN 81-7022-447-0

First Published 1993

Published and Printed by
Ashok Kumar Mittal
Concept Publishing Company
A/15-16, Commercial Block, Mohan Garden
NEW DELHI-110059 (India)

Lasertypeset by
Microtech Advance Printing System (Pvt.) Ltd.
H-13, Bali Nagar
NEW DELHI-110015

GENERAL EDITOR'S INTRODUCTION

During the British regime our universities suffered from two major handicaps. Firstly, inadequate availability of funds was responsible for stiffling their proper growth and development and was not conducive for promotion of research and maintenance of standards. Secondly, there was the excessive control of the Government which sometimes reduced these august bodies to mere Government departments. With the attainment of Independence the scenario changed completely. The first important step, which the Government of India took in this direction, was the appointment of Radhakrishnan Commission which, by making far-reaching recommendations, heralded the rebirth of higher education in the country. The other important measure was the constitution of the University Grants Commission in 1956 on the pattern of University Grants Committee of Great Britain by an Act of Parliament. This independent body has three broad purposes before it. First is the disbursement of grants to the colleges and universities. The second is to monitor their development and progress, particularly to promote and co-ordinate the university education and to determine and maintain standards of teaching, examination and research in the universities, in consultation with the Central Government or the State Government as the case may be. Lastly, the Commission is to see that universities function in free academic atmosphere and that they may not be fettered either with the political or bureaucratic handicuffs. However, the general duty of the Commission as laid in its constitution, is to take, in consultation with the universities or other bodies concerned, all such steps as it may think fit for the promotion and co-ordination of university education and for the determination and maintenance of standards of teaching, examination and research in the universities. In order to perform its functions the Commission has been empowered to enquire into the financial needs of the universities, allocate and disburse grants to them, recommend to any university, the measures necessary for the improvement of university education and to advise the university upon the action to be taken for the purpose of implementing such recommendations and perform such other functions as may be prescribed or deemed necessary for the Commission for advancing the cause of higher education in India.

Since its creation the Commission has striven hard to fulfil the role assigned to it. It has produced a large number of reports which are the results of the deliberations of the review committees set-up by it from time to time to enquire into specific issues and problems of university education as well as working of a particular university or universities and also of the conferences, seminars and workshops sponsored by it to discuss the various aspects of higher education.

Dr. O.P. Gupta, who has had a long association with the working of the Commission, has rendered a useful service to the cause of higher education by bringing out the present publication, which, for the first time, highlights the broad features of these reports and the main points made in them for the benefit of researchers, university teachers, administrators and decision-makers. More so because this publication has also traced in brief the historical development of university education in the country from ancient times to the present day and has described in detail the powers and functions of UGC, its organisational structure and composition.

S.P. AGRAWAL

PREFACE

Indian Nation's modern education is a planned revolution to achieve all round development. In free India the University Grants Commission (UGC), New Delhi, since its inception, has been playing a vital role in maintaining the standards of University Education in the country. It distributes Central funds among universities and colleges to ensure their speedy and balanced growth. In order to discharge its duties the Commission formulates policies based on the advise of academicians and scholars. The deliberations and recommendations of scholars/experts are recorded in the various forms of UGC publications so as to bring these ideas and the programmes to the notice of the academic community.

There is, however, startling dearth of bibliographical tools in our country as far as the departmental publications are concerned. Due to one or the other reasons, many of the publications of the government departments, autonomous institutions, etc. do not find their due place in bibliographical tools. The Commission's publications are the most sought after documents by teachers and research scholars alike. Newly emerged institutions are badly in need of such publications which contain pioneer policies on almost all the UGC ongoing schemes. As such a need for a comprehensive bibliographical document comprising UGC publications as well as similar other publications on higher education was felt.

It gives me pleasure in bringing out this publication which is a record of trends developed in higher education during last four decades. It is neither a survey nor history of higher education. It may, however, be said that it is just like a progressive record on schemes in the field of higher education implemented by the Central Government.

The publication has been designed in four sections with introduction to give a view of higher education. Section I provides history, background and organisational structure of the UGC. Section II consists of annotation of the UGC publications and a bibliography of the articles published in UGC's *Journal of Higher Education*. Section III contains appendices consisting of selected references, books and journals on education published in India and abroad. Section IV consists indices to operate the text.

I must place on record that the first attempt was taken on partial fulfilment of dissertation during Master of Library Science Studies at Aligarh Muslim University.

I must put on record the valuable guidance and suggestion of Dr. S.P. Agrawal, former Director of NASSDOC, which made possible the present shape of the document. I am, thankful to Prof. Noorul Hussan Khan, Librarian, Aligarh Muslim University whose constant encouragement put me to work. I am also thankful to my friends and professional colleagues who encouraged in the venture.

I am extremely grateful to my wife who has been a constant source of encouragement.

Thanks are also due to Concept Publishing Company who very kindly took up the publication and brought out with immense care.

It is hoped that the publication will be useful to educational planners, administrators and researchers. The interest of the scholars will be encouragement to the efforts and suggestions for improvement will be welcomed gratefully.

O.P. GUPTA

CONTENTS

ABBREVIATIONS

AIU	Association of Indian Universities
AVRC	Audio-Visual Research Centre
CAS	Centres of Advance Study
Chair	Chairman
COHSSIP	College Humanities and Social Science Improvement Programme
Comp.	Compiler
COSIP	College Science Improvement Programme
CSIR	Council of Scientific and Industrial Research
COSIST	Committee for Strengthening of Infrastructure in Science and Technology
DSA	Department for Special Assistance
EMRC	Educational Media Research Centre
FIP	Faculty Improvement Programme
IARI	Indian Agricultural Research Institute
ICSSR	Indian Council of Social Science Research
INFLIBNET	Information and Libraries Networking
n-d.	No date
NEP	National Education Programme
P.	Page
POA	Programme of Action
SC/ST	Scheduled Caste/Scheduled Tribe
UNESCO	United Nations Educational Scientific and Cultural Organisation
UGC	University Grants Commission

LIST OF APPENDICES

SECTION I

HISTORY, BACKGROUND AND ROLE OF UGC IN THE DEVELOPMENT OF HIGHER EDUCATION

INTRODUCTION

India has always worked for peace and peaceful coexistence, treating the whole world as one family. To promote friendship and equalise all the groups of Indian Society to bring world culture nearer, it would be necessary to provide equal opportunity to all to access to the education. The approach will make masses familiar with the achievements of each other and will contribute for the progressive society. As a result "Education has been accorded high priority as an integral part of countries development". It has been considered as fundamental right as well as first priority of every citizen. Due to this reason a constant increase has been registered all over the country as reported in Selected Education Statistics 1988-89. Literacy rate differences from 1971 to 1991 are as under:

Literacy

Namé of the State	1971	1981	1991
1	2	3	4
Andhra Pradesh	24.57	29.94	45.11
Assam	28.15	—	53.42
Bihar	19.95	26.20	38.54
Gujarat	35.79	43.70	60.91
Haryana	26.89	36.14	55.33
Himachal Pradesh	31.96	42.48	63.54
Jammu & Kashmir	18.58	26.69*	—
Karnataka	31.52	38.46	55.98
Kerala	60.42	70.74	90.59
Madhya Pradesh	22.14	27.87	43.45
Maharashtra	39.18	47.18	63.05
Manipur	32.91	41.35	60.96
Meghalaya	29.49	34.08	48.26
Nagaland	27.40	42.57	61.30

Contd.

1	2	3	4
Orissa	26.18	34.23	48.55
Punjab	33.67	40.86	57.14
Rajasthan	19.07	24.38	38.81
Sikkim	17.34	34.05	56.53
Tamil Nadu	39.46	46.76	63.72
Tripura	30.98	42.12	60.39
Uttar Pradesh	21.70	27.16	41.71
West Bengal	33.20	40.90	57.72
Andaman & Nicobar Island	43.59	55.16	73.74
Arunachal Pradesh	11.29	20.79	41.22
Chandigarh	61.56	64.79	78.73
Dadar & Nagar Haveli	14.97	26.67	39.45
Delhi	55.61	61.54	76.09
Goa Daman & Diu	44.75	56.65	76.96
Lakhshadweep	43.66	55.07	79.23
Mizoram	57.79	59.88	81.23
Pondicherry	40.02	55.85	74.91
Total	29.45	36.23	52.11

– Census is yet to be held

With increase in literacy percentage the pupils in primary school increased four times and number of schools doubled to the previous strength, the number of universities have gone up to 144 and Deemed to Universities and Institutions of National importance up to 25 as on Appendix VIII. The country is running about 10,000 colleges to expand the quantitative educational facilities throughout the country. The greater emphasis on qualitative improvements have also been realised with modernisation. The thinkers all over the world believe that education is to provide a coherent picture of the Universe and an integrated way of life, function of the education is the guidance of adventure to the realisation of the potentialities of individual in the face of actual world of man and things. There is a great disparity between what country requires and what education offers. In particular when "democracy depends for its very life on a high standard of general, vocational and professional education. We cannot presume real freedom unless we presume the values of democracy, justice and liberty, equality and fraternity". Indian culture did not believe in compelling people to accept its way of life. It encourage each group to find out its home in India to live by its own conception of the good life. Our educational institutions must educate on the right lines and provide proper facilities to educate larger number of people.

Education

If we see the educational history of India, it will be clear that in olden days India was an educationally most advanced country of the world in making contribution to the developments of man's knowledge and culture. It's seats of learning attracted scholars from all over the world. *Vedas* and *Dharma Sutras* have discussion on Parishads or Assemblies of Brahmans. The most well organised centres of learning of the age were 'Taksasila' and 'Nalanda'. Vedas, Upnishadas, Buddhism, Journalism, Philosophy and logic were the important subjects of study. Vallabhi in Kathiawad and Kanchi in South were also great centres of learning. These were the days when teachers and pupil were in close relation. During medieval period Muslim rulers encouraged the establishment of Madarsas/Schools at various selected places in the country. The important institutions of this period were specialised in one or more branches of knowledge. The medium of instructions was mainly Arabic. A controversy to impart instructions through Arabic, Sanskrit or through English took place about 1835.

In 1844 Government resolved that for public employment in every case preference would be given to those who had been educated in Western Science and were familiar with English language. If we see twenty-five year history (1857-1882) the growth was mainly in the number of colleges and students and no university was established. The first modern university was established in 1857 at Calcutta and was followed by Bombay and Madras Universities.

After achieving political independence in 1947 a great venture of over all development of national reconstruction with the objectives of economic and social freedom of equality, justice and dignity was launched. The progress of national economy and education were recognised interdependent and essential for cultural development of the country. Apart of its many other factors: growing consciousness for reading, reach of education to untouched sections of the society, technological application and reforms suggested by the experts of various disciplines, developed a general awakening among masses. It was, therefore, realised that speedy growth of educational institutions and programmes will bring revolutionary changes in all parts of life.

These may be some of the reasons that education "continued to evolve, diversify and extend its reach to the society. Every country of the world is in practice of developing its system of education to express and to promote its unique socio-cultural identity and to meet the challenges of the times". To achieve these objectives the existing educational conditions were reviewed time to time and suggestions were made by the various field specialists to identify the variety of new challenges and new dimensions of emerging subjects.

The fundamental role of education was very well realised by the freedom struggle leaders like Mahatma Gandhi and Pt. Jawahar Lal Nehru. Gandhiji was of the view that "education should be directly relevant to the life of the people". These are some of the reasons that after independence too much stress had been put to educational reconstruction in India. Similar feeling was expressed by Maulana Azad, a great scholar, in his one of the speeches. When he said that "our special attention after independence, one of the most important was that of National Education and what may be called its system of pattern. It was realised general education available to the common people is neither adequate nor appropriate to their needs". Educational system of the country instead of making people useful members of society makes them superfluous and liability to the nation. It was, therefore, felt that our education system should reduce the wide gulf between urban and rural areas and to improve the standards of living of rural people, especially of agricultural labour and small and marginal farmers. The changes should be made to make the common people principle beneficiaries rather than the upper and middle classes. Because in Indian society even after removal of the *Princes* and *Zamindars*, the upper and middle classes were continued as the principle beneficiaries of the modern education system. The low caste poor people under deplorable economic conditions and false social constrains were not able to access to education. Due to other various reasons our most of the population remains untouched of education though education has key position in the growth and development of society.

In fact the system of education borrowed from the Britishers does not serve our purpose. We need a system which will enable common men his responsibilities and meaning of life. This work can be performed by implementing regional language as medium of instructions and by supporting the deprived Social Group's Students.

Every individual has birth right of education to develop his faculties of mind to live a full human life. Accordingly "we have to remould our system of education and so organise it that a great majority of our people, after completing their secondary education should be absorved in the various professions, institutions, handicrafts, etc. Only a small proportion should pursue higher education in the universities and their number should not exceed the capacity of the society to make good use of them."

For educational revolution several committees and commissions talked and recommendations were made, but more is still pending. Education reconstructions have been one of the most debated themes during last four decades due to its immediate effect on cultural, economic and political progress of the society. To give new direction to existing education scene Government has conducted a countrywide debate. As a result of which National Policy on Education (NPE), 1986 and Programme of Action (POA), 1986 have been developed by the Ministry of Human Resources and Development for making new initiatives towards educational reconstruction. National Policy on Education (1986) in its introduction lays emphasis on importance of education and records that 'New environment will require new designs of human resource development. The coming generations should have ability to internalise new ideas constantly and creatively. They have to be imbued with a strong commitment to human values and social justice, all this implies better education'. Policy recommended that "the role and responsibilities of the States in regard to education will remain unchanged, the Union Government would accept a large responsibility to reinforce the national and integrative character of education, to maintain quality and standards, to study and monitor the educational requirements of the country as a whole in regard to manpower for development, to cater to the needs of research and advanced study, to look after the international aspects of educational culture and human resource development, and in general, to promote excellence at all levels of the educational pyramid throughout the country. To give a serious thought Central Government has constituted a Review Committee 1990 under the Chairmanship of Acharya Ramamurthy. The Review Committee has talked for education a people movement in the best interest of common people and it should be for life.

Demands for education in general and higher education in

particular has increased tremendously in the last few decades, which is evident from the growth of students, teachers and institutions. As per the records of U.G.C. Annual report constant increase at all levels is as under:

Year	No. of Universities & Deemed Universities	Colleges	Students
1979-80	101+11	4,558	26,48,579
1980-81	112+11	4,722	27,52,437
1981-82	118+13	4,886	29,52,066
1982-83	120+13	5,039	31,33,093
1983-84	124+15	5,246	33,22,929
1984-85	125+15	5,590	34,04,096
1985-86	132+17	5,816	35,70,897
1986-87	136+19	6,512	36,81,870
1987-88	142+22	6,647	38,14,417
1988-89	144+25	6,912	39,47,922
1989-90	146+28	6,942	42,46,878
1991	147+29	7,121	44,25,247

Higher Education

Higher education provides people an opportunity to react on the critical "social, economic, cultural, moral and spiritual issues facing humanity. It contributes to the national development through dissemination of specialised knowledge and skill. It is, therefore, a crucial factor of survival". According to Amrik Singh and Sharma higher education seeks to promote excellence, adventure of ideas and research for truth. It is to cultivate new knowledge and interpret old knowledge in the light of needs and discoveries. It is also to provide the right kind of leadership in all walks of life and identify gifted youth and help them to develop their potential to the full by cultivating physical fitness, developing the powers of mind, right interests, attitudes and values. It was realised in past that to meet the growing needs of developing society, the higher education should be given some direction. The schemes, therefore, were reviewed and some new one were introduced to accommodate rapid developing modern urban economy.

The courses offered by the institution of higher learning/ universities have become almost obsolete. Since Independence continuous efforts are being made to review the higher education system, the number of commissions, notably Education Commission 1948-49, Education Commission 1964-66, National Policy on Education 1986 and Acharya Ramamurthy Review Committee (1990) have been constituted by the Government to find out a national pattern of education for the whole country, the subject is being debated in conferences and workshops.

In this direction the first serious attempt was setting up of education commission under the Chairmanship of Dr. Sarvapalli Radhakrishnan, the eminent educationist and philosopher. His report recommends the universities "have to provide leadership in politics and administration, the professions, industry and commerce. They have to meet the increasing demand for every type of higher education, literacy and scientific, technical and professional, etc. They must enable the country to attain, in as short a time as possible, freedom from want, disease and ignorance, by the application and development of scientific and technical knowledge. It is for the Universities to create knowledge and train minds who would bring together the two, material resources and human energies. If our living standards are to be raised a radical change of spirit is essential" "the universities as a maker of the future cannot persist in the old patterns, however, valid they may have been in their own day with the increasing complexity of society and its shifting pattern. Universities have to change their objectives and methods, if they are to function effectively in our national life". The first Prime Minister, Pandit Jawaharlal Nehru, therefore, in his special convocation at Allahabad University expressed "A university stands for humanism, for tolerance, for reason, for the adventure of ideas and for the search of truth. It stands for the onward march of the human race towards even higher objectives. If the universities discharge their duty adequately, then it is well with the nation and the people".

Since the higher education is full of varieties, the Government of India felt the need for a comprehensive review of higher education system with a view to reconstruct it in the light of our social and political needs. As a result of it another commission was set-up under the Chairmanship of Prof. D.S. Kothari.

The Education Commission (1964-66) constituted to hold a comprehensive review and to advise the Government on National pattern of education and general principles and policies for the development of education at all stages and in all aspects. The

Commission recommended "radical reconstruction of education is essential for economic and cultural development of the country for national integration and for realising the ideal of a socialistic pattern of society. It was of the view that the education system must produce young men and women of character and ability committed to national services and development". Only then a sense of common citizenship, culture and National integration will prevail. Accordingly, Government resolved to promote free and compulsory education to all to fulfil the assurances of Constitution Article 45.

The present system of higher education includes various types of institutions, universities and colleges. The universities are of various types – Central, State and Deemed, etc. Central Universities are established by an act of Parliament whereas State Universities are by an act of State Legislature. The colleges are also of two types — Private and Government. In private colleges some are affiliated to universities and some are working without affiliation. Recently UGC has granted autonomy to a number of colleges. The academic institutions are increasing with the increasing population to extend teaching, research and examination facilities to the population surrounded to these.

University Grants Commission

To determine and maintain standards for promotion and co-ordination of education of various types of universities and colleges, University Grants Commission was established as statutory body under the Act of Parliament in 1956. It was authorised to enquire into the financial requirements of the universities and colleges and to make appropriate grants to these. It advises on the establishment of new universities and other matters pertaining to the standardisation of higher education in India. The detailed powers, functions and composition are on Appendix-VI. In its working commission consults the universities as well as experts of various fields for which subject panels are drawn, normally for a period of two years. It is in practice of formulating guidelines for the schemes introduced in consultation with the committee appointed to discuss the subject problems. The Committees are suppose to make systematic and objective assessment of the problem to suggest various measures of improvements.

To meet the requirements the working of the UGC has been

reviewed by the persons with an intimate knowledge and experiences of the functioning of the UGC as well as University system of the country. In pursuance of the recommendations made by the Public Accounts Committee of Parliament, Government appointed a committee on August 31, 1974 under the Chairmanship of Dr. V.S. Jha to review the policies and programmes of the UGC, carried out since its inception. The review evolved certain parameters to make effective efforts for implementing various schemes. One of the important findings of the review report was an urgent need of monitoring and evaluation of various schemes or activities of the UGC and more close interaction between UGC, Central Government, State Government, Universities and Colleges. It also has recommendations on standards, grants, research, planning, evaluation, organisation and legal aspects. Critical evaluation of the UGC working since its inception i.e. 1956 to 1975 have been made by this Committee.

Another Review Committee (1978) under the Chairmanship of Prof. Satish Chandra was appointed on the directives of the Central Government to undertake a comprehensive review of various programmes being implemented by the UGC. The effort was to determine the impact of these programmes on the determination and the maintenances of standards of teaching, research and examination in the universities. The Committee carried out studies with the help of various sub-groups to identify schemes which have no impact on the maintenance and improvement of standards of university education, the idea was to discontinue such schemes. Similarly, it was asked to assess the quality of programmes which have been in operation for about three years or so to decide future plan of action.

To foster better standards of education and also to raise the quality and relevance, efforts were initiated during the Seventh Plan period. The science and mathematics teachings were promoted at all levels. Similarly, non-formal, open or distance learning, women education, vocational education and education for scheduled castes and scheduled tribes was specially promoted.

A variety of new challenges of social requirements put stress upon the Government to formulate and to implement a National Policy on Education for the country. The NPE (1986) and POA (1986) for higher education recommended the following programmes:

(i) Consolidation and expansion of institutions;

(ii) Development of autonomous college and departments;
(iii) Redesigning courses;
(iv) Training of teachers;
(v) Strengthening research;
(vi) Improvement in efficiency;
(vii) Creation of structures for co-ordination at the State and National level; and
(viii) Mobility.

The programmes are being implemented by University Grants Commission and progress is being reported to Parliament through its Annual Report which mainly contains information on the following issues :

Budget—	Plan Non-plan Sub-plan Additional Special
Enrolment—	New universities Colleges Departments Centres Institutions Autonomous colleges
Faculty Improvement Programme—	Seminars Symposias Workshop Conference Refresher course National lectures Emeritus fellowship Teacher fellowship
Programmes—	Super Conductivity Mass Communication Research Programme COSIST NET

Curriculum Development
Subject Panels
Computer Facility
Cultural Exchange with other countries
Sports facilities
Adult Education
Special Fellowship for SC/ST
Coaching Classes
Women studies

A brief review of some of the ongoing programmes of UGC will give an emerging picture of higher education scenario:

1. It distributes Central Government Grants among the universities and colleges which fulfil the guidelines available in this regard. Plan proposals are invited on predesigned guidelines and are discussed to decide the pattern of assistance during the Plan period.
2. The Commission (UGC) has a number of quality improvement programmes. To attract bright and talented researchers. The Commission is holding Junior Research Fellowship examinations since 1984. For improving the quality of teachers a qualifying test before their recruitment has been introduced. No. of University Test Centres (Appendix-XII) have been set-up to conduct these examinations. Institutional arrangement, teachers fellowship under faculty improvement programmes, refresher courses and funding of research projects are being made. The funds are also made available to meet travel expenses of the teachers for attending International Conferences etc.
3. The Commission gives assistance for infrastructural development in the university system. Assistance provided on percentage basis for academic buildings, staff quarters, student hostels, equipments, books and journals and such facilities required to promote the quality of education. The proposal of universities and colleges are finalised on the recommendations of the visiting committees constituted by the Commission.
4. The proposals of new universities to declare fit to receive Central Grants under Section 3 of the UGC Act and to colleges under Section 2(f) of the UGC Act, are finalised after

evaluating these on the guidelines formulated for the purpose.

5. The Commission is providing financial assistance to the development of the following Centres:

(a)	Centre of West Asian Studies	AMU, Aligarh
(b)	Centre for Studies on Nepal	BHU, Banaras
(c)	Chinese and Japanese Studies	Delhi Uni.
(d)	Centre for South East Asian Studies	Calcutta Uni.
(e)	Centre for African Studies	Bombay Uni.
(f)	Centre for Soviet Studies	Bombay Uni.
(g)	Centre for South and South East Asian Studies	Madras Uni.
(h)	Centre for Urban Development and Regional Planning	Osmania
(i)	Centre for Economics of East European Studies	Gokhale Instt.
(j)	Centre for South Asian Studies Centre	Rajasthan
(k)	Centre for Indo-China Studies	Shri Venkateswara
(l)	Centre for Gulf Studies	JNU
(m)	Centre for Soviet Studies	JNU
(n)	Centre for Latin American Studies	Goa Uni.
(o)	Centre for SAARC Studies	Andhra
(p)	Centre for Central Asian Studies	Kashmir.

6. Information Centres — The National Information Centres involving the use of computers have been established at Bangalore, Bombay and Baroda to provide service in specialised areas as under:

Bangalore	: Up-to-date abstracting service in the areas of Physics, Bio-Sciences, Chemistry, Mathematics and Earth Sciences.
Bombay	: Sociology, Gujarati, Woman Studies, Home Sciences, Library Science and Special Education.
Baroda	: Economics, Political Sciences, Education and Psychology.

The objective of the centres are to improve the information access to the teachers and students and to provide for bibliographic support to make available the latest documentation in the respective disciplines. The centres provide current awareness, information and reference services.

More and more steps have been taken to support research programmes of individual teachers as well as departments. To create research facilities in university system a cadre of Research Scientists in all subjects and at the level of lecture, reader and professor have been introduced.

7. Centres of Advances Study — Since 1963 special assistance has been provided to some of the promising departments as on (Appendix-VII) on the basis of their work and existing facilities etc. These centres are intended to encourage 'the pursuit of excellence' and to raise the quality of research.
8. In the field of educational development role of electronic medium like TV is very much recognised. The Commission is providing colour TV sets to selected colleges under mass communication programme. Two-hour programmes are being telecasted daily through INSAT IB on Doordarshan Network. It has important programmes like 'countrywide classroom' and 'save the planet'. The Commission has set-up nine AVRCs and four EMRCs in universities and colleges for training and production of TV software. These programmes are promoting distance education effectively.
9. A network programme — INFLIBNET to interlink university libraries and information centres of Deemed Universities and Institutions of national importance have been developed and forwarded to the Ministry of Human Resource Development for approval. In programme advanced computer and communication technologies will be used effectively to share the resources of the libraries. Computer facilities have been extended to 104 universities and 481 colleges up to the end of 1988-89. Under the programme INFLIBNET centre has been set-up at Ahmedabad to co-ordinate the institutions participating in it.
10. Academic Staff College The U.G.C. has approved 48 universities to set-up ASC to provide facilities for orientation of lectures who has eight years' continuous service in universities and colleges. About 150 University departments/Institutions for organising subject oriented refresher courses in Science, Humanities and Social Sciences during 1990-91 for in service

teacher with more than five years of continuous service have also been identified. The schedule of refresher courses/orientation programme are notified time to time.

11. Scheme of Special Assistance – Since 1973 allocations are made to selected universities and departments for infrastructural facilities. Grants are also made for museum, visual arts, studies, computer centres and jubilee grants etc. The departments which are receiving special assistances as on (Appendix-X) are taken in consideration through evaluation.
12. Since 1986 UGC initiated steps to modernise curriculum to achieve uniform standards. The surveys of all the existing syllabi have been conducted and number of groups of experts of the field discussed to suggest revision. The Commission so far has received model curricula in 20 disciplines. These models have also been discussed at National Level workshops.
13. Autonomous Colleges – The UGC has approached to the universities to make provisions in their acts and statutes to accommodate the concept of autonomous colleges. As a result of continuous efforts as on Appendix-IX colleges have been granted autonomous status. Guidelines have also been prepared to recognise autonomous departments. The Commission (UGC) has initiated to work on accreditation as on Appendix-XIII. It has also advocated for setting up of State Council of Higher Education as on Appendix-XIV. Apart of it a great deal of work has been carried out to promote distance education in various disciplines. The institution as on Appendix-XI are imparting instructions through distance education programme.

The brief account of the schemes and programmes run by UGC leads to the higher education scenario of India. In subsequent sections, subject growth and trends in last four decade will be depicted. In documents, where the deliberations are recorded in the form of the reports, to forward the recommendations for effective applications and to know growth rate, summary annotations of such reports will be helpful in knowing the initiatives taken by the University Grants Commission.

History Development

As we all know the history of higher education system in India has its roots in the provincial educational growth. In the beginning of this century Provincial Governments adopted the practice of giving grants-in-aid to institutions imparting higher education in the country even with the establishment of the first modern universities in 1857. During this period the powers and the composition of the university bodies were regulated by the State and the development of education was left with the private enterprises. The universities and colleges were free to develop their own resources to improve their work. But in actual practice these institutions were not able to secure much financial support from private sources. And were getting a part from fees paid by students. These had to depend largely on Government grants which were not always readily in their reach.

In India education has provincial concern, by Article 246 given to Central Government the function of co-ordination and determination of standards in institution for higher education or research including scientific and technical institutions. The first move towards setting up an all-India universities organisation was made in 1924 when Government of India called together representatives of the fourteen universities of India in a conference at Shimla. This conference developed the Inter-University Board of India, now the Association of Indian Universities. In fact, as early as in 1945 on the recommendation of the Committee set-up by the Central Advisory Board of Education report on Post War Educational Development in India (Sargent Committee Report, (1943) the Government of India appointed "University Grants Committee" of four part time members to advice the Government on grants to be paid to the Central Universities — Aligarh, Banaras and Delhi. The Committee was consisting of four members in 1946 and in 1947 its membership was increased and it was authorised to deal with the universities of the country. But no funds were placed at its disposal, and its role was purely advisory. The functioning of this Committee by one or other reasons was ceased in 1949.

Education Commission 1948-49 under the Chairmanship of Dr. Radhakrishnan was set-up to report on Indian university education and to suggest improvements suitable for present and future educational requirements of the country.

It was the first time when education was treated as the most important factor for achieving rapid economic growth and technological progress of the modern changing world. The education became the focal point of planning. Education Commission (1948-49) along with other contribution is firm in the opinion that the efficiency or speed can only be achieved with the adequate Central financial supports, in addition to their own resources. Thus adequate amount as Central subsidy to all universities and colleges was realised.

The Commission (1948-49), therefore, recommended the formulation of a Committee or Commission on the general model of the University Grants Committee of the United Kingdom with a full time Chairman and other members who were to be appointed from the outstanding educationists known for their wisdom and integrity. The Minister of Finance and Education should also be represented on this body for allocating grants to universities.

As we all know that the universities in India are established under the Acts of State Legislation, except the Central universities which are concern of Central Legislation. The Government of India to co-ordinate these two or keep up the standards of university education, adopted systematic measures and proposed the establishment of a Central Council of University Education. A Bill of this approach was circulated to all the State Governments and Universities/Institutions for their opinion. After a series of conferences and consultations the idea of setting a Central Council of University Education was abandoned and the proposal of setting up a University Grants Commission on the lines of the recommendations of the Education Commission (1948-49) was placed before Parliament in September 1954. While the Bill was under preparation, in 1952, the Government issued a resolution for setting up an Interim University Grants Commission to advice the Government on the allocation of grants-in-aid from public funds to the Central universities and to other universities and institutions of higher learning whose cases of grants might be referred to the Commission by the Government.

The University Grants Commission in its present form started functioning on 28th December 1953, with an autonomous status under an act of Parliament in 1956 with defined responsibilities with the first Chairman, Dr. Shanti Swarup Bhatnagar, and Shri Samual Mathai as first Secretary. Thus it was established by a resolution of the Ministry of Education to deal with university affairs for the propose of allocation and disbursement of grants to universities as well as for the purpose of co-ordination and maintenance of standards of university education in India.

In its early days the Commission was functioning to implement the programmes initiated by the Ministry. But from Fourth Plan onward, one may see the changing role of the UGC. The UGC is different both in character and functions from other autonomous organisations. It is functioning to discharge constitutional functions of the Central Government viz., co-ordination and maintenance of standards of higher education. As statutory body extends its advise to the universities, colleges, State Governments and to the Government of India on the issues relating to higher education. Keeping in view these objectives and also to produce skilled manpower in scientific and technical fields. The UGC has initiated many systematic steps to revolutionise the university education.

Location

In its beginning the office of the University Grants Commission (UGC) was in Mandi House, later it was shifted to the building of the Council of Scientific and Industrial Research, called Old Mill Road. Later in 1963 the Commission put to the present building i.e. at Bahadur Shah Zafar Marg, New Delhi.

The Commission has privilege, of outstanding scholars as its members. The following scholars have served as Chairman since its inception:

Shanti Swaroop Bhatnagar
Humayun Kabir
Hridaya Nath Kunzru
C.D. Deshmukh
V.S. Krishna
D.S. Kothari
George Jacab
Satish Chandra
Madhuri R.Shah
Yash Pal
Man Mohan Singh
G. Ram Reddy

The UGC Act has been amended time to time in 1970, 1974 and 1984 to implement the reviewed Government policies. In its starting the work load was not too much because the number of universities, their requirements and Government funds were limited but all these factors in last four decades have multiplied in many folds. The grant provision during 1988-89 under non-plan 19,433.01 lakhs and in plan was 14,508.58 lakhs. With this enhancement even the challenges of the modern technology and growth in all spheres of academic activities cannot be fulfilled; some other measures to be initiated to tackle the problem.

One of the significant development of the century is the recognisation of the education as fundamental right. The scientific progress and education would become an extremely important thrust area in 21st Century. Education is supplying necessary manpower in even critical areas of development. The impact of massive investment and attention are visible now in all sectors of life. It is good for human resource development for future growth and full awareness of social and human values for building a strong character to lead a better responsible social life. Aims and objectives of university teaching have been identified in brief are "Transmission of the intellectual and ethical heritage of humanity to the young's enrichments of their heritage and extension of the boundaries of knowledge; development of personality".

Important Functions and Powers

The UGC is making efforts to improve higher education in the country through various schemes. In one hand it provides financial assistance to the universities established by Central and State Acts, institutions deemed to be university under Section 3 of UGC Act, and college approved under 2(f) of the UGC Act for the improvement of standard of education, provision of essential facilities, equipment and for promotion of the welfare of students and teachers. And on the other hand the Commission also undertakes new projects and modifies current procedures in the light of experience and future needs. The quality of university education in India depends on the standards maintained by the universities and colleges, therefore, the UGC is making effort to improve their staff, equipment, libraries, laboratories and other facilities. For the promotion and co-ordination of university education and for maintenance of standards of teaching, examination and research in universities the UGC Act 1956 Chapter III, Section 12 — Powers and functions of the Commission reads as under —

It shall be the general duty of the Commission to take, in consultation with the universities or other bodies concerned, all such steps as it may think fit for the promotion and co-ordination of university education and for the determination and maintenance of standards of teaching, examination and research in universities, and for the purpose of performing its functions under this act the Commission may —

(a) Enquire into the financial needs of universities.

(b) Allocate and disburse, out of the funds of the Commission, grants to universities established or incorporated by or under a Central Act for the maintenance and development of such universities or for any other general or specific purpose.

(c) Allocate and disburse, out of the funds of the Commission, such grants to other universities as it may be deem (necessary or appropriate for the development of such universities or for the maintenance, or development, or both of any specified activities of such universities) or for any other general or specified purpose.

Provided that in making any grant to any such university, the Commission shall give due consideration to the development of the university concerned, its financial needs, the standard attained by it and the national purpose which it may serve.

(cc) Allocate and disburse out of the fund of the Commission, such grants to institutions deemed to be universities in pursuance of a declaration made by the Central Government under Section 3, as it may deem necessary, for one or more of the following purposes, namely:

(i) For maintenance of special cases
(ii) For development
(iii) For any other general or specified purpose

(ccc) Established in accordance with the regulations made under this Act, institutions for providing common facilities, services and programmes for group of universities or for the universities in general and maintain such institutions or provide for their maintenance by allocating and disbursing out of the fund of the Commission such grants as the Commission may be deemed necessary.

(d) Recommends to any university the measures necessary for the improvement of university education and advise the university upon the action to be taken for the purpose of implementing such recommendations.

(e) Advise the Central Government or any State Government on the allocation of any grants to universities for any general or specified purpose out of the consolidated fund of India or the consolidated fund of the State as the case may be.

(f) Advise any authority, if such advise is asked for on the establishment of a new university or on proposals connected with the expansion of the activities of any university.

(g) Advise the Central Government or any State Government or university on any question which may be referred to the Commission by the Central Government or the State Government or the university, as the case may be.

(h) Collect information on all such matters relating to university education in India and other countries as it thinks fit and make the same available to any university.

(i) Require a university to furnish it with such information as may be needed relating to the financial position of the university or the studies in the various branches of learning undertaken in the university, together with all the rules and regulations relating to the standards of teaching and examinations in the university respecting each of such branches of learning.

(j) Perform such other functions as may be prescribed or as may be deemed necessary by the Commission for advancing the cause of higher education in India or as may be incidental as conducive to the discharge of the above functions.

The UGC Act authorises the Central Government on the advice of the Commission to declare by notification in the Official Gazette that any institution for higher education other than a university, shall be deemed to be a university for the purpose of this Act, and on such a declaration being made all the provisions of this Act shall apply to such institution as if it were a university.

College can be brought within the purview of UGC Act, if they are affiliated to, or from constituent members of or are run directly as university college by a university in accordance with the provisions of its Act, and statutes and regulations made under that Act. The Commission proposes its Five-Year Plans to implement the Central Government policies. The programmes are widely discussed at various levels, conferences, seminars, workshops and group meetings organised for the purpose time to time. For implementing Central Government programmes, the UGC has evolved its own mode of operations. The grants-in-aid are provided on the basis of the recommendations of its Review Committee, Visiting Committee and other such Committees formulated to consider the proposals and recommendations.

Organisational Set up

As laid down in the UGC Annual Report 1987-88 secretarial composition and working pattern can be represented in brief by the following chart:

Chairman
↓
Vice-Chairman
↓
Secretary
↓
Additional Secretaries and equivalent
↓
Joint Secretaries
↓
Deputy Secretaries
↓
Under Secretaries
↓
Section Officers
↓
Supporting Staff

The Secretariat of the Commission is headed by a Secretary. He is assisted by the Officers of the level of Additional Secretaries. It is organised on the pattern of Sections, Divisions and Bureaus. The basic unit is a section which is headed by a Section Officer and is supported with adequate staff comprising Assistants, U.D.C., L.D.C./Typist, normally numbering between five and eight, depends on the workload of each section. Usually, for two sections there is a supervisory officer who is either an Under Secretary or an Education Officer or an Officer of equivalent rank. Normally four or five Sections constitute a Division. In some cases a Division is headed by a Joint Secretary. But, normally a Division is headed by a Deputy Secretary or an Officer of equivalent rank.

The main function of the Sections and Divisions are generally administrative. The Secretariat Officer normally works as Member Secretary to the Committee formulated by the Commission. The assistance is extended by the Secretariat to all the committees and groups working on the subject assigned to these. The staff and officers of the Commission at the level of Sections and Divisions can only forward the matters with their comments and decision in matters are only taken at the appropriate levels.

The work of a group of Joint Secretaries/Deputy Secretaries/ other officers of equivalent rank is supervised by one of the officers of the rank of Additional Secretary.

For specialised items of work, which are generally of a specified duration, or for specific assignments, the Commission engages consultants. These consultants advise the Commission on matters pertaining to data-based systems of management, mass communication, educational technology and Physical education and Sports, etc.

According to Section 10 of the UGC Act, the Commission appoints a Secretary and other employees as necessary for the efficient functioning of the Commission. These appointments are made on the basis of the recruitment rules approved by the Central Government. The manner of appointment includes direct, promotion, deputation and contractual appointments. In service conditions Government of India rules are opted. The organisational structure is reviewed on the recommendations received from various study groups constituted for the purpose.

Composition

According to the UGC Act, 1956 (as modified up to Ist October, 1984) Chapter II, Section Five, the Commission shall consist of —

(1) (i) a Chairman
(ii) a Vice-Chairman, and
(iii) the other members to be appointed by the Central Government.

(2) The Chairman shall be chosen from among persons who are not officers of Central Government or of any State Government.

(3) Of the other members referred to in clause (iii) of Sub-Section (1)—
(a) two shall be chosen from among the officers of the Central Government, to represent that Government;

(b) not less than four should be chosen from among persons who are, at the time when they are so chosen, teachers of universities; and

(c) the remainder shall be chosen from among persons —
   (i) who have knowledge or experience in agriculture, commerce, forestry or industry;
   (ii) who are members of the engineering, legal, medical or any other learned profession, or
   (iii) who are Vice-Chancellor of University or who, not being teachers of universities are in the opinion of the Central Government educationists of repute or have obtained high academic distinction.

Composition of the Commission as on May, 1992.

Dr. G. Ram Reddy — Chairman
Prof. S.K. Khanna — Vice-Chairman
Representaive of the Ministry of Human Resource Development, (Deptt. of Education) Govt of India,
Secretary (Expenditure), Ministry of Finance, Govt. of India.

Prof. Ram Lal Parikh,
Vice Chancellor,
Gujarat Vidyapeeth,
Ahmedabad

Dr. Bipin Chandra
Professor of History
Jawaharlal Nehru University
New Delhi

Prof. Pranab Kumar Sen
Professor of Philosophy
Jadavpur University
Calcutta

Prof. A.S. Nigavekar,
Deptt. of Physics
University of Poona
Pune

Prof. D.R. Gadekar
Professor of Geology
M.S. University of Baroda
Vadodara

Prof. Basheeruddin Ahmad
Vice-Chancellor
Jamia Millia Islamia
New Delhi

Shri Subhash Yadav
Director NAFED
New Delhi

Prof. D.P. Singh
Former Professor and
Head Deptt. of Public Administration
University of Lucknow
Lucknow

The appointing authority for the above members is the Central Government and the members are appointed for a period of two-years term. The Chairman, Vice-Chairman and Secretary are the full time salaried employees of the Commission.

REFERENCES

Monographs

1. Ministry of Education, Education Commission 1964-66 – Report, New Delhi, Govt. of India, 1971.
2. Ministry of Education, Education Commission 1948-49 – Report, New Delhi, Govt. of India, 1950.
3. University Grants Commission, Standards of University Education, New Delhi, 1965.
4. Ministry of Education, Committee on Model Act for Universities, New Delhi, Government of India, 1964.
5. Ministry of Human Resource Development, National Policy on Education –, New Delhi, Government of India, 1986.
6. Ministry of Human Resource Development, Programme of Action: National Policy on Education, New Delhi, Government of India, 1986.
7. University Grants Commission – Annual Report 1988-89, New Delhi, 1990.
8. Ministry of Information and Broadcasting, speeches of Maulana Azad 1947-58, New Delhi, 1987.
9. Ministry of Human Resource Development, Selected Education Statistics, 1988-89, New Delhi, 1990.
10. University Grants Commission, Review Committee on UGC Programme – Report, New Delhi, 1981.
11. Ministry of Education and Social Welfare, Review Committee on the University Grants Commission, New Delhi, 1977.
12. Ministry of Information and Broadcasting, India 1988-89, a reference annual, New Delhi, Publication Division, 1989.
13. Education for our people: A Policy frame for the Development of Education 1978-87, Bombay, Allied, 1978.
14. University Grants Commission, Development of Higher Education and Research in the Universities 1980-85, New Delhi, 1986.

Articles

1. The University Grants Commission. S.R. Dongerkery, *Educational India* 19(6) Dec. 1952, pp. 172-73.
2. University Grants Commission. Sushil Kumar Sen, *Journal Education* 2(2) Dec. 1954-Feb. 1955, pp. 61-68.
3. Union University Grants Commission and State University Grants Committee. Nirmal C. Bhattacharyya. *Journal Education* 4(3-4) Mar. 1956 — Aug. 1957, pp. 117-22.

4. University Grants Commission (India). Affiliated colleges and the University Grants Commission; editorial. *Educational India* 23(8) Feb. 1957, pp. 257-58.
5. University Grants Committee (States, India). Union University Grants Commission and State University Grants Committee. Nirmal C. Bhattacharyya. *Journal Education* 4(3-4) Mar. 1956-Aug. 1957, pp. 117-22.
6. University education and the U.G.C. editorial. *Educational India* 24(11-12) May-June 1958, pp. 373-74.
7. Affiliated colleges and the University Grants Commission; editorial. *Educational India* 25(9) Mar. 1959, pp. 351-52.
8. Implementation of U.G.C. Scheme: Memorandum submitted to Dr. C.D. Deshmukh, Chairman, University Grants Commission. *Journal Education* 7(1) Sep-Nov. 1959, pp. 42-49.
9. University Grants Commission: Approved scheme: New pay scales for college teachers. *Journal Education* 7(1) Sep-Nov. 1959, pp. 20-41.
10. Third Report of University Grants Commission. *Journal Education* 7(2) Dec. 1959-Feb. 1960, pp. 101-07.
11. A memorandum on the U.G.C. Scheme and the present situation. *Journal Education* 9(1) Sep-Nov. 1961, pp. 42-49.
12. University Grants Commission. D.C. Sharma. *Indian Education* 4(2) Jan. 1965, pp. 6-9.
13. The role of the University Grants Commission in the development of the Indian universities. S.R. Dongerkery, *New Frontiers in Education* 3(2) Aug. 1973, pp. 32-56.
14. University Grants Commission (India). NAEP and the University Grants Commission. M.L. Mehta, *Prasar* 7(1-2) April-July 1980, pp. 11-26.
15. 25 years of UGC : Dilemmas and difficulties. K.L. Joshi, *Journal Higher Education* 6 (1-3) 1980 81, pp. 63-68 refs.
16. The University Grants Commission : A personal view. Samuel Mathai, *Journal Higher Education* 6 (1-3) 1980-81, pp. 55-61.
17. Role of the University Grants Commission in framing the policy of higher education. A Mathew, *Journal Higher Education* 9(2) Aug. 1983, pp. 177-95 refs.
18. New year gift from UGC. *Student Action* 2(8) Ja 1984, pp. 5-11.
19. Development of Higher Education, by S.K. Khanna, *University News*. 27(38) 1989, pp. 2-4.

SECTION II

ANNOTATION TO THE UGC PUBLICATIONS

ANNOTATED BIBLIOGRAPHY OF UGC PUBLICATIONS

Library and Information Science

(1) University and College Libraries (1965), p.228.

This is the report of the University Grants Commission appointed review committee under the Chairmanship of the distinguished Library-scientist Dr. S.R. Ranganathan. It reviews the problems concerned with the Organisation and Development of University and College Libraries. It also consists the proceedings of the Seminar 'from publisher to reader, work flow in University and College Libraries held from 4th to 7th March, 1959. It has addresses and working paper of the seminar followed with an index.

(2) Library Science in Indian Universities (1965), p.86.

This is the report of the review committee appointed by the University Grants Commission to review standards of teaching and research in Library Science in the universities. This was an organised attempt under the Chairmanship of Dr. S.R. Ranganathan to assess the library consciousness in the country. The Committee collected information through a questionnaire from the Library Science departments and made recommendations on curriculum, admission qualifications, minimum qualifications for teaching posts etc. Existing facilities of teaching and research with new sectors of research are reviewed.

(3) Development of Library Facilities in Universities and Colleges (1968), p.52.

The publication gives the commission's view point that the library has become an important means of communication and advancement of knowledge. It reviews the provisions made for promotion of library facilities to the increasing enrolment in educational institutes. The report is also an assessment of the progress made on the recommendations of the University Education Commission (1964-66). Publication includes the recommendation of UK-UGC Committee on libraries. The tentative estimate for Fourth Plan proposals have been included. The main text is followed by eight appendices and one chart to furnish the statistical information about universities and colleges. A survey report along with recommendations on University of Delhi is included in the end.

(4) Committee on Revision of Pay Scales of Librarians and Directors of Physical Education in Universities and Colleges – Report. Part B (1986), p.49.

This publication is a report of the UGC appointed committee on Dec. 24, 1983 under the Chairmanship of Professor R.C. Mehrotra, to consider the revision of pay scales, career/professional development and service conditions of Librarians and Directors of Physical Education in Universities and Colleges. It has five chapters for presenting brief history along with the role and responsibilities of Librarians and Directors of Physical Education in Universities and Colleges. The Committees recommendations on revision of pay scales are followed by three appendices, for presenting existing prescribed qualification, qualifications for future recruitment and formula for fixation of pay for Librarians and Director of Physical Education in the Universities and Colleges.

(5) Development of an Information and Library Network — Report of the Inter Agency Working Group (1988), p.xxii, 473.

This document sets out a project proposal for the establishment and development of an Information and Library Network, in short called as INFLIBNET in the country during the Eighth-Five Year Plan (1990-95). Report contains recommendations, glossary of terms, references and number of appendices and minutes of the meetings of various committees, statistical information collected from the universities and a good number of illustrations.

Journalism

(6) The Status of Journalism and Communication Education in India — Report (1981), p. 124.

The report is outcome of the committee worked under the Chairmanship of Professor K.E. Eapen, for evaluation of the recommendations of many important committees and workshops held on the subject. It records some important recommendations for future prospects of the Journalism. Brief description under various headings for journalism training programmes in universities has been included. The committee was constituted by the UGC panel on Mass Communication. The main text of the report is followed by three appendices containing information collected from the universities.

Psychology

(7) Psychology in Indian Universities — Report (1963), p. iii, 71.

The report has examined the existing facilities in the universities for teaching and research in the field of psychology and allied subjects. The Committee has made several valuable suggestions and recommendations for improvement of courses of study and promotion of research. The Review Committee on Psychology was appointed under the Chairmanship of Dr. B. Kuppuswamy in March, 1961. The main text is followed by ten appendices to include the syllabus of B.A./B.Sc. and M.A./M.Sc. classes and for approved topics of doctoral dissertations during 1963-65.

(8) Psychology in Indian Universities (1968), p. v, 71.
The publication is not available for annotation.

(9) Rath (R). Reorientation of Teaching and Research in Psychology in the Indian Universities (1979), p. 264.

The publication is the outcome of four regional workshops in psychology sponsored by the UGC in order to formulate guidelines for reorienting the syllabus and research in the subject. The six appendices for details of recommendations including some model deliberations offered by psychologists with new and revolutionary lines of thinking and approach with regard to various aspects of the syllabus and research are included. It has the name of members of panel on psychology during 1974-76, 1976-78, 1978-80.

(10) Status of Psychology in Indian Universities (1982), p. 34.

The report deals with the status of psychology as an academic discipline in Indian Universities. It gives brief history development and salient features, orientation of teaching and research in psychology with the references of all the reports published so far on the subject. The Sub-Committee of the UGC Panel on psychology has offered comments and suggestions on the trend of student enrolment, teacher-student ratio and areas of specialisation etc. The main text is followed by nine appendices for various issues like data on strength of staff in UTD/UC, courses of study areas of specialisation and research activities, journals published, institutions and professional organisations, engaged in teaching and research in psychology.

Philosophy

(11) Philosophy in Indian Universities — Report (1966), p. 108.

The publication is a report prepared by the Review Committee appointed by the University Grants Commission under the Chairmanship of Prof. N.A. Nikam. It has a brief historical account to present position of 36 university departments of Philosophy. The objectives of teaching, research and the role of philosophy in education are discussed and the summary of observations and recommendations are recorded. Syllabus for B.A. and M.A. for optional and compulsory papers, and topics of doctoral dissertations are included in ten appendices.

(12) Philosophy Teaching in India (1978).
The report is not available for annotation.

Social Sciences

(13) Sociology in Indian Universities — Report (1966), p. iii, 72.

This is the report of the Review Committee appointed by the UGC to review the development and existing facilities of Sociology in India. Report also consists committee's observations and recommendations, summary on teaching and research objectives of sociology. The main text is followed by six appendices for questionnaire issued to Indian Universities for pattern of papers at B.A. and M.A. for procedure for admission to research courses and for topics of doctoral dissertations in Sociology.

(14) The Status of Teaching of Sociology and Social Anthropology — Report, Part II (1979), p iii, 259.

It is the Second part of the status report on the teaching of Sociology and Social Anthropology prepared by the Committee constituted under the Chairmanship of Prof. M.S.A. Rao. It contains six regional reports and suggestions thereon. In the end bibliography is given.

(15) The Status Report on Anthropology (1982), p. 131.

It is the report in which the panel of Anthropology has examined the organisational and academic aspects of the anthropology departments of the different universities. It contains the guidelines of the UGC constituted committee under the Chairmanship of Prof. S.R.K. Chopra, for the development of anthropology during the Sixth Plan. The report has an appraisal of the courses of study in the different universities. The important aspects—eligibility of admission, system of teaching and evaluation at the master's degree level, research and training at M.Phil and Ph.D level, research projects and infrastructure and equipment has been discussed in detail. It has three annexures and two appendix for statistical information.

(16) The Status Report on the Teaching of Sociology and Social Anthropology (1982), p. vi, 188.

The report deals with the status of teaching and research in Sociology as an academic discipline in Indian Universities. It gives the historical background of the growth of sociology departments in the universities – both the pre-independence and post-independence periods. An attempt has also been made to delineate the emerging trends in respect of areas of specialisation, and to explore the various measures of development which would make teaching and research in sociology more useful and socially relevant. The report has been prepared by a sub-committee of the panel on sociology. The first part is devoted to discussion of the major trends in the discipline of sociology and also to the gaps which needs special attention and the new directions for strengthening teaching and research. Second part gives departmental profiles and thrust areas in which departments grouped on a zonal basis for a better and co-ordinated view of development.

Political Science

(17) Political Science in Indian Universities — Report (1967), p. 116.

This is the report of the Review Committee on Political Science appointed by the University Grants Commission under the Chairmanship of Professor V.K.N. Menon. The Committee has discussed and examined the standard of teaching and research in political science in Indian universities and suggested measures for improvement. Committee's report and recommendations are followed by eleven appendices giving information on various issues. B.A./M.A. syllabus for compulsory optional papers, titles of doctoral dissertations approved during 1961-62 and 1962-63 are included.

(18) Iqbal Narayan. Revision of Political Science Syllabi — Report (1978), p. 135.

Report contains the deliberations of the five zonal workshops and embodies the national courses involved on the issue of the revision of the political science syllabi. It has trend analysis of the syllabi of US Universities. The report has eight chapters on various issues; like syllabi at B.A., M.A. and M.Phil course, research areas and methodology etc. In the end seven appendices includes information on the revision of political science syllabi working paper, list of participants of various UGC zonal workshops and samples of syllabi and report of ICSSR working group on research methodology in political science.

(19) Political Science in India : State of the Discipline and Agenda for the future, compiled by Iqbal Narayan and P.C. Mathur (1982), p. 68.

The status report is based on the data collected from the various universities in response to the questionnaire circulated by UGC panel on political science and public administration. It is designed in seven chapters — starts with general introductory remarks to general survey of various parameters of the discipline, supplemented by recommendations and suggestions. Also deals with pattern of modernisation of the political science courses in various universities.

Economics

(20) Modernisation of syllabi in Economics — Report (1979) p. vii, 57.

The report contains deliberations on modernisation of economics syllabi and a review of teaching of economics in Indian universities. It also has recommendations of Seminar on Teaching of Economics. In the end it has list of participants of different five workshops.

(21) Status Report on Economics Teaching in India (1983), p. vii, 20.

The report contains information on the panel reports of UGC (1978-81), Review Committee and other related reports (1963-74). The status report gives the state of economics studies and facilities available in Indian Universities. These studies were carried out through a questionnaire of the UGC panel on Economics. Various aspects of the subject: Courses offered, student enrolment, faculty strength, teacher-student ratio, library facilities, research programme thrust areas and other related issues have been discussed in brief. It also has twenty-five tables for statistical representations.

(22) The curriculum development centre in Economics — Report (1989), p. 332.
See annotation part of the entry No. 52(A).

Legal Education/Law

(23) Towards a Socially Relevant Legal Education: A Consolidated Report (1979), p. iv, 96.

This publication is in three parts. Part one is a working paper for the UGC Regional Workshop in law 1975-77 by Upendra Baxi, Professor of Law, Delhi University. Second part is a report of the UGC workshops on socially relevant legal education and part three comprises three appendices which deals with recommendations arrived at the UGC workshops, list of participants and list of members of the UGC panel of Law 1947-77.

(24) Status of Teaching and Research in the Discipline of Law. (1981), p. 69.

It is the report of the committee appointed by UGC panel on law. It contains the classified and organised information on various aspects collected from 30 universities by the committee. The universities are grouped in five regions. Thus the attempts to present an all-India as well as region-wise picture of legal education in the country. Some recommendations for the improvement of legal education and for the disposal of the Sixth Plan grants have also been made. It also has six tables to cover classified information on strength of student and teachers ratio, qualification of full time teachers, library requisitions and expenditure along with the research in progress.

(25) Status of Teaching and Research in the Discipline of Law. (1981), p. iv, 69.
Publication is not available for annotation.

Defence Studies

(26) Committee on Defence/Strategic Studies — Report (1987), p. iv, 24.
Publication is not available for annotation.

Social Works Education

(27) Social Work Education in Indian Universities (1965), p. 100.

This report of the Review Committee contains the studies on need for developing an integrated approach to the formulation of courses of study in social work and re-orientation of field work programmes. It contains useful suggestions for improvement of social work training in the universities and non-university institutions in the country. The Committee worked under the Chairmanship of Dr. Radhakamal Mukherjee. It is a general survey of social work in India and contains recommendations of the Committee. Eight appendices include information about institutions visited by the committee, uniform syllabus for social welfare courses, course outline, publications by the departments and titles of doctoral dissertations.

(28) Review of Social Work Education in India, Retrospect and Prospect — Report (1980), p. 239.

This report presents survey of social work education in India and significant recommendations for its development. It also has norms for professional education, suggestions for setting up of field service projects and autonomy for social work institutions. Also has recommendations for the promotion of research and emphasis on need to enhance institutional facilities and capabilities and funds for poorly equipped libraries of these institutions. Followed by three appendices consisting of list of institutions for social work education tables and list of persons with whom discussions were held. It has comprehensive index in the end.

(29) The curriculum development centre in Social Work Education — Report (1990), p. 456.
Annotation may be seen in entry No. 52(A).

Education

(30) General Education — Report (n.d.), p. v, 89.

It is the report of the experts Committee appointed by University Grants Commission under the Chairmanship of Shri S. Govindarajulu, in 1958 to go into the whole question of general education in Indian Universities. The Committee discusses number of principles on which general education can be introduced in Indian higher education. It has the record of the various views, suggestions and recommendations for imparting general education. The main text is followed by seven appendices for various aspects — syllabus for natural sciences etc. In the end it has a comprehensive bibliography on the subject.

(31) Review Committee on Education — Report (1966), p. 94. Publication is not available for annotation.

Adult and Continuing Education

(32) Regional Conference on Continuing Education — Report, Hyderabad (1976), p. 76.

The volume devoted to intensive deliberations held on continuing education in Seminars and Workshops organised in the various parts of the country. It contains seven papers on the subject contributed for the conference by the reputed scholars. The text is followed by the list of participants and programme of the conference.

(33) Regional Conference on Adult and Continuing Education Simla (1976), p. 68.

The publication contains addresses of B.S. Jogi, Mohan Sinha Mehta, S. Chakravarti and Statement of decisions adopted by the conference. It has the papers on rural university by Ravi J. Mathai, and also on various aspects of continuing education by various eminent authors, the role of university in society traditionally and today, by Mrs. Kamalini H. Bansali and universities and people's education for development in India by C. Kishore Saint. In the end list of participants in regional conference on adult and continuing education is included.

(34) The Seminar on Continuing Education, Poona (1976) p. 47.

This volume is a report of the Poona Seminar which contains keynote address; Continuing Education — The imperative of our times by M.S. Mehta. It has recommendations followed by three papers :

(i) University and Community Continuing Education in Indian Universities, by Nicolas Haines;

(ii) Some thoughts on Adult Education as an Academic discipline, by James A. Draper; and

(iii) Adult Education as a Field of University Study by A.J.A. Nelson.

The list of the participants is added in the end.

(35) Revised Guidelines on Adult and Continuing Education and extension (1982), p. 19.
The publication is not available for annotation.

(36) UGC working Group on Point No. 16 of the New 20-point Programme of the Government of India — Report (1983), p. 77.

It is the report of the joint working group of the University Grants Commission and Ministry of Education and Culture constituted in September 1982 to review the UGC programmes on adult education extension through universities/colleges, and also to suggest a dynamic programme on point No. 16 of the new 20-point programme of the Government of India, under the Chair Dr (Mrs) Madhuri R. Shah. Report contains recommendations of the Committee and six tables along with eleven annexures on various aspects.

(37) Adult Education and Extension Programmes Guidelines. (n.d.), p. 16.

It contains the guidelines for Adult Education and Extension Programmes along with four annexures: showing format of projects, norms of literacy and numeracy and suggested financial pattern for department/centre of adult education and for extension in universities.

(38) Guidelines on Point No. 16 of the New 20-point Programme: Eradication of Illiteracy and Spread of Universal Elementary Education (1983), p. 69.

The publication lays emphasis on essential education to all citizens, irrespective of their age, sex and class. It has suggestions for approaching to achieve this objective by inter-sectoral co-operation and inter-agency co-ordination. It also has a brief discussion for various other related areas – organisational set-up, training, teaching, incentives and programmes. Main text is followed by fifteen annexures presenting formats, expenditure pattern, statistical conclusions with regard to literacy level in India as per 1981 Census and Adult Education Programme reports of different types.

(39) Training Manual for Adult Education Functionaries (1985), p. 85.

The publication contains foreword written by Dr. Madhuri R. Shah and a report of the group appointed by the UGC to develop a training programme for adult education functionaries for implementing Point No. 16 of the New 20-point Programme of the Government of India. It has guidelines for training and five appendices for guidance for formulation of proposal, list of State resources centres in India and an action plan. Illustrations are also given on various studies.

(40) New Guidelines on Adult and Continuing Education and Extension Programmes in Universities and Colleges (1988), p. 81.

The publication is an approach to review the development programmes run by the UGC in universities and colleges. Review of the UGC activities and universities recorded separately. It also contains the guidelines for the pattern of UGC financial assistance, and institutional and individual incentives. In ten annexures information, on guidelines issued by UGC in different years, core support to universities, support for training, area-based programmes, support, different formats of reports and Government of India guidelines on mass programme for functional literacy is made available.

Audio-Visual

(41) Audio-visual Aids in Higher Education — Report (1969), p. 72.

This is the report of the Committee appointed by the University Grants Commission on audio-visual aids for higher education, including programmed learning. It has reviewed the present position, scope and development of audio-visual aids in India. It has observations and recommendations of the committee followed by ten annexures for various information collected by the committee.

Medium of Instruction

(42) Medium of Instruction — Report (1961), p. 123.

This is the report of the working group appointed by the University Grants Commission to consider all aspects of the question pertaining to the change of the medium of instruction for English to an Indian language. It also contains four appendices to include the proceedings and introductory remarks by Dr. C.D. Deshmukh, summary of replies received from universities in connection with the adoption of Indian language as medium of instruction in the universities and recommendations on the proposals of Delhi University.

Physical Education

(43) The Committee on Physical Education — Report (1967), p. 30.

It is the report of the Committee appointed by the UGC in December 1965 to examine the facilities of physical education and standards of games and sports in Indian Academic Institutions and also to recommend measures to improve the standard and level of performance of student activities. The report consists the background paper on which Committee was appointed and the terms and reference, statistics gathered on various aspects and observations and recommendations made on the importance of physical education, compulsory physical education, national fitness scheme and other related aspects — specialised coaching, qualifications and status of physical education teachers, organisational pattern of Department in Universities and Colleges. It has two appendices in the end for the questionnaire used for collecting information and assumptions made for working out the total estimates on the proposed programme.

Population Education

(44) Lecture Series on Population Education, compiled by the Department of Family Welfare (1982), p. 103.

The publication gives a demographic picture of India and study of various features and population control measures and policies. It contains the population studies of the neighbouring countries.

Higher Education

Autonomous Colleges

(45) Criteria, Guidelines and Pattern of Assistance to Autonomous Colleges (1973), p. 4.

The publication contains objectives and consequences of affiliation system along with criteria for selection of Autonomous College. It also discusses their relationship with the university and has brief note on procedure for conferment of autonomous status and pattern of assistance.

(46) Revised Guidelines on the Scheme of Autonomous Colleges (1987), p. 59.

The brochure deals with identification of criteria, need, objectives, monitoring, evaluation and accountability of autonomy. It also contains the discussions on the issue of relationship with parent university, other issues discussed are recorded under the headings: award of degrees, status, governance of autonomous colleges and pattern of financial assistance etc. In sixteen annexures different formats, charges, composition of various committees, UGC guidelines on structuring courses and on actual training days etc. and the programme of action as approved by the Government of India in 1986 for development of autonomous colleges, design of courses and orientation of teachers, are designed.

Autonomous Department

(47) Guidelines for Scheme of Autonomous Departments/ Institutes/Centres/Schools within the 'University set-up (1989), p. 12.

The publication contains brief account of guidelines on the various aspects — need, objections, criteria of identification, status, function, relationship and accountability of autonomy of departments/

institutes/centres/schools within the university set-up.

Building — Hostels

(48) Panel on University Buildings Hostels — Report (1960), p. 24.

The report is the compilation of the hostel building panel on various hostel building issues. It includes many inspection reports of different types of hostels and recommendations for improving hostel facilities etc. The main text is followed by two appendices for cost analysis and for proforma for hostel buildings. In the end illustrations are added.

(49) Teacher's Hostels — Report (1964), p. 6.

It is the report of the Building Advisory Committee which looked into the problem of the residential accommodation for staff and students. It contains the norms for space and equipment with the specified purpose. The main text is followed by two appendices for blue print of different types of accommodation.

Residential Quarters

(50) Committee on Residential Accommodation for Students and Teachers — Report (1965), p. 25.

This report contains the study of all aspects of the problem of residential accommodation for students and teachers. With general background, value of hostel life, improvement in hostel facilities for rural areas, women students and students homes are the subject of discussion. Summary recommendations on future policy and programmes are included. Appendix contains estimated expenditure required for the purpose.

Courses/Curriculum

(51) The UGC Delegation to Study Evening and Correspondence Courses in the USSR — Report (1969), p. 38.

The report reviews the systems of evening and correspondence courses run in school and higher education in USSR. The report has record of the foreign visits and of deliberations among Indian scientists and scholars who participated to study the development of the subject. The report starts with the description — history and emergence of idea — evening and correspondence courses in USSR and includes observations and recommendations in the light of USSR experience on the subject.

(52) Revised Guidelines for Restructuring of Courses of first Degree level in the Faculties of Arts, Social Sciences and Science in Universities and Colleges (1983), p. 22.

The publication contains a list of subject panel reports (1978-83) along with University Grants Commission revised guidelines for restructuring of courses of first degree level in the faculties of Arts, Social Sciences, and Science in universities and colleges. It also has five annexures giving information on subjects which could be introduced at the first degree level. List for recommended books is given in the end.

52(A) **Curriculum Development Centre Reports**

The Commission has taken up a project to enhance the quality and standards of education and also to promote excellence in teaching. The task was assigned to number of centres on various subjects located at various universities. The courses and curricula has been modernised and reports are being brought out. The publications will be of great help to the academic bodies and scholars. These publications are the outcome of the deliberations of the subject experts at various levels. The document contains the course contents for each unit, lecture schedule, broad outlines of tutorials, problem solving exercises, practical and project at a glance picture. In the end of every document minutes of the UGC group discussions on that subject are included. So far following subject reports are brought out and for other subjects the exercise is in progress.

(53) The Curriculum Development Centre in Chemistry Report (1988), p. 257.

(54) The Curriculum Development Centre in Hindi — Report (1988), p. 487.

(55) The Curriculum Development Centre in Docial Work Education — Report (1990), p. 456.

(56) The Curriculum Development Centre in Urdu (1989), p. 305.

(57) The Curriculum Development Centre in Visual Art and Design — Report (1989), p. 142.

(58) The Curriculum Development Centre in Geography — Report (1989), p. 278.

(59) The Curriculum Development Centre in Sanskrit — Report (1989), p. 773.

(60) The Curriculum Development Centre in English — Report (1989), p. 371.

(61) The Curriculum Development Centre in Commerce — Report (1989), p. 370.

(62) The Curriculum Development Centre in Economics — Report (1989), p. 332.

(63) The Curriculum Development Centre in Performing Arts — Report (1989), p. 270.

(64) The Curriculum Development Centre in Bio Physics — Report (1989), p. 188.

(65) The Curriculum Development Centre in Bio Chemistry — Report (1989), p. 87.

(66) The Curriculum Development Centre in Mathematics — Report (1989), p. 387.

(67) The Curriculum Development Centre in Law — Report, Vol. I (1990), p. 105.

(68) The Curriculum Development Centre Law — Report, Vol. II (1990), p. 756.

(69) The Curriculum Development Centre in History — Report (1990), p. 410.

(70) The Curriculum Development Centre Foreign Language (1990), p. 222.

(71) The Curriculum Development Centre in Philosophy (1990), p. 448.

(72) The Curriculum Development Centre in Zoology (1990), p. 657.

Enrolment

(73) University Development in India: Basic Facts and Figures 1972-73 to 1976-77, Part I Section-A Universities, Colleges and Enrolment (1979), p. xi, 579.

The publication is on statistical information on Indian Universities. It has been designed in six headings and with number of tables to group the relevant information. This is the 12th issue in this series and splitted after it into two parts: A and B.

(74) University Development in India: Basic Facts and Figures 1972-73 to 1976-77, Part I: Section-C Postgraduate and Research Enrolment (1981), p. 950-1289.

This section of the series publication contains enrolment data at the postgraduate and research levels which has been arranged both universitywise and subjectwise as well as statewise in the different universities, with separate figures and university departments/ university colleges and affiliated colleges.

(75) University Development in India: Basic Facts and Figures 1977-78 to 1981-82: Part I Section-A Universities, Colleges and Enrolment (1984), p. xiv, 817.

It is the thirteenth compilation of the series of the information and statistics division of the University Grants Commission provides summary of statistical information about the Indian Universities which gives trends and changes occurring in higher education. It covers the statistics for the years from 1977-78 to 1981-82. The tables are arranged under universities and universities under States and States are arranged in alphabetical order.

(76) University Development in India: Basic Facts and Figures 1982-83: Part I, Section-A, Universities, Colleges, Enrolment and Teaching Staff (1987), p. 341.

It contains statistical information for the years 1981-82 and 1982-83 on All India basis for universities statewise distribution of universities and institution deemed to be universities with their location, year of establishment, type and territorial jurisdiction etc. Colleges related information of teaching departments, enrolment levelwise, foreign students, women students and staff position facultywise is given in various tables.

(77) University Development in India: Basic Facts and Figures 1982-83; Part I, Section-B (1990), p. 268.

The publication is in two parts. Part I is devoted to postgraduate and research enrolment in the faculties of Arts, Science and others. Part II contains teaching staff in the faculties of Arts, Science and others.

Examination Reform

(78) Evaluation in Higher Education: A Report of the Seminars on Examination Reform Organised by the University Grants Commission under the Leadership of Dr. Benjamin S. Bloom (1961).

The volume highlights some of the deficiencies in our present system of examinations. Remedial measures have also been proposed. The specific objectives of teaching in various fields of knowledge have been identified and suggested that test materials may be proposed to assess the objective of teaching. It has working papers containing some observations on examination in India, question papers, syllabi and a programme of action on examination improvement, addresses given by Dr. C.D. Deshmukh, Professor Samuel Mathai, Dr. R.P.

Paranjpye, Dr. Balbhadra Prasad, Dr. P.J. Phillip, Mr. B.H. Zaidi and selected references on educational evaluation are available. It has lists of delegates to the Seminars held at Osmania, Poona, Patna, Aligarh Universities and also programmes of the seminars.

(79) Examination Reform Report (1962), p. 115.

The present report has underlined the fact that teaching, learning and examination actually constitute a unity of functions. The report dealt at some length with the technical aspects of examinations. It has also emphasised the fact that any reform in examination would be unavailing without a corresponding reform in the teaching and learning processes. Report contains solutions and suggestions for some of the current problems of the examination system of Indian Universities. The Committee worked under the Chairmanship of Shri S.R. Dongerkery to take up these matters with students, teachers and in the conference of Vice-Chancellors. In the end it has 15 appendices.

(80) Three Studies in Examination Technique, by H.J. Taylor (1964), p. 33.

This publication contains studies on an Examination of Examiners, Supplementary Examinations and grace marks. The main attention in this publication is 'how can the conventional examination be modified' and the design of more efficient and objective method of testing is achieved. All the three papers deal with experiment on marking, particular examination problem and to decide which candidates should pass.

(81) Examination Reform in Central Universities — Report (1969), p. v, 29.

This report is prepared by the UGC appointed committee under the Chairmanship of Prof. F.C. Auluck to study the examination system of Central Universities. It has made recommendations for examination reform.

(82) Principles and Mechanics of the Semester System (1971), p. 78.

This report is the outcome of the UGC appointed Committee 1957 which underline the fact that teaching, learning and examinations constitute a unity of functions and committee suggested various measures for reform of the examination system. It gives survey of the existing arrangement and recommends measures for improvement of standards of teaching and research and suggests model syllabus.

(83) Examination Reform a Plan of Action : Endorsed by the University Grants Commission (1973), p. 20.

This document contains guidelines suggested about the examination system at various educational levels. It also has information about the name of members of the working group of the Ministry of Education and Social Welfare who worked on examination reform, internal assessment, marks and grades, national examination, and question banks. In the end selected bibliography on examination reform is included.

(84) Examination Reform a Plan of Action, and the Recommendations of the Zonal Workshops (1976), p. iv, 44.

The volume is in three sections; Section I deals with examination reform: A plan of action and various issues regarding the system of grading etc. Section II contains recommendations of zonal workshops and Section III deals with principles and mechanics of the system of grading in the universities (based on the recommendations of the zonal workshops).

(85) Guidelines on Coaching Classes for Competitive Examinations for Weaker Sections amongst Minority Communities (1984).

The bróchure contains useful information in brief on all possible aspects of the programme. It has seven annexures to keep relevant formats and information about various examinations.

(86) Revised Guidelines on Coaching Classes for Competitive Examinations for Weaker Sections amongst Educationally Backward Minority Communities (1988), p. 19.

The guidelines on the scheme of coaching classes for minorities are framed in pursuance of point No. 11 of the Prime Minister's 15-point programme, and the National Policy on Education (1986). According to this scheme students belonging to weaker sections amongst educationally backward minority communities would be accountable on an all-India basis. The text is devoted to discuss various issues: Aims and objectives organisation, location of centres, activities, training, admission, motivation, financial pattern, regional resources centres and release of grants etc. Seven annexures for including, model advisory committee, staffing and financial pattern of coaching centres, format for progress report and format for proposal to start coaching centre etc. are included.

(87) UGC Guidelines Regarding the Minimum number of Actual Teaching days Programme of Examination Reform and Workload for Teachers in Universities and Colleges (1989), p. 9.

The brochure has first five pages as circulars vide which these guidelines were sent to the Ministry and the Universities. Last four pages are devoted to the guidelines to determine working hours and workload of teachers. Minimum programme of examination reform has been suggested in brief.

Examination Results

(88) M.A. & M.Sc. Examination Results, 1955-60; Statewise Classification (1962), p. 69.

The document has M.A. and M.Sc. results for the year 1955-60 arranged alphabetically Universitywise.

(89) University Development in India: Basic Facts and Figures, 1972-73 to 1976-77: Part II Section-A Examination Results; 1973 Annual + 1972 Supplementary and 1974 annual + 1973 supplementary (1980), p. vi, 393.

It contains the statistical information compiled by the UGC on the basis of returns received from the universities. In this issue, results for 1972-73 and 1973-74 subjectwise have been shown for M.A./M.Sc. Examinations. Seven appendices have also been added at the end showing the out-turn data in the different fields, for ten years and in certain cases for five years.

(90) University Development in India: Basic Facts and Figures 1972-73 to 1976-77. Part II Section-C Examination Results: 1976 Annual + 1975 Supplementary (1981), p. 789-1215.

It contains detailed statistics relating to Doctorate degrees awarded during 1975-76 and examination results relating to 1976 Annual and 1975 supplementary examinations. Various tabular statement for information on doctoral degree award have been presented facultywise, subjectwise, universitywise and statewise. Separate statements are presented for M.A., M.Sc. and women students.

(91) University Development in India: Basic Facts and Figures: Part II Examination Results 1977 (1977 Annual and Supplementary) (1983), p. xiii, 363.

The volume contains statistical information compiled by statistical section of the UGC regarding examination results including doctorates awarded from Indian universities and institutions deemed to be universities during the year 1977. It has been designed in six sections and four appendices giving Ph.D. output, examination results at a glance (1950-77) and woman education strength.

(92) University Development in India: Basic Facts and Figures: Part II Examination Results 1978 (1978 Annual and Supplementary) (1984), p. 296.

This is the third publication in the series which contains factual outturn of graduates and postgraduates from the Indian Universities and institutions deemed to be universities. The publication groups the statistics in five sections in number of tables.

(93) University Development in India: Basic Facts and Figures 1982-83: Part II, Examination Results – 1980 (Annual and Supplementary). (1990), p. 203.

Publication is in two sections. Section I contains examination results 1980 of graduate and post-graduate, facultywise, and section II has examination results 1980 of women graduates and post-graduates.

Plan Discussion

(94) Guidelines for Preparation of Development Proposals for Improvement of Undergraduate Educational Facilities in Affiliated Colleges during the Fifth Five Year Plan period (1974), p. 6.
Document is not available for annotation.

(95) Guidelines to the Universities for Preparations of Proposals for the Sixth Plan (1981), p. 15.
Publication is not available for annotation.

(96) Guidelines for the Sixth Plan Visiting Committees to Universities (1982), p. iv, 4.
Publication is not available for annotation.

(97) Guidelines: Seventh Plan Development Proposals of universities (1986).
Publication is not available for annotation.

(98) Guidelines to the Universities for Preparation of Development Proposal for the Seventh Plan (1986), p. 54.

This volume is formulated to implement the programme of action for the new education policy. It contains guidelines for formulating of Seventh Plan development proposals and also for special assistance programmes of teaching and research. It has eight annexures for proforma models and pattern of assistance.

(99) Seventh Plan Discussions with Universities (1987).

Document consists the plan proposal of the various universities along with deliberations of the experts and UGC officers on the subject.

(100) Development of Higher Education: Seventh Five Year Plan, 1985-90: Draft Proposals (n.d.), p. xi, 80.

The document contains intensive deliberations of the UGC

constituted working group for advising in the preparation of draft proposals for the development of higher education during Seventh Five Year Plan (1985-90). The publication has preamble followed with the names of the working group and the approach paper discussed by the group.

Pay Scales and Service Rules

(101) Some Problems of University Administration — Report of the Committee Appointed by the UGC following the Report of the Santhanam Committee on Prevention of Corruption (1967), p. 22.
Document is not available for annotation.

(102) Central Universities Retirement Benefit Rules 1967: Corrected up to 31 December 1977 (1978), p. iv, 89.

The volume contains General Provident Fund-cum-Pension-Cum-Gratuity rules and contributory provident fund-cum-gratuity rules for the Central Universities and Indian Institute of Sciences, Bangalore. It has twelve annexures for various forms.

(103) Guidelines for Continuous Internal Evaluation (1982), p.26.

It contains guidelines for continuous Internal evaluation – objectives, mechanics and objectivity in evaluation. In four appendices the aspects – tools, minimum programmes, monitoring and scaling of calibration of Marks/Grades of continuous Internal Evaluation are included.

(104) Role and Responsibility of Teachers (1981), p.59.

This volume is based on the deliberations of the working group which has worked on the role and responsibility of teachers. It includes papers of individual scholars who contributed on specific topics – Assessment of the teacher in Higher Education, by Dr.(Smt.) Madhuri R. Shah, participation of teachers in Adult Education, Educational Extension and Community Development, by Dr. Malcolm S. Adiseshiah, Assessment of teacher and teaching by Dr. J.N. Kapur and Assessment of the teacher, by Dr. A.M. Ghose.

(105) Revision of Pay Scales of Teachers in Universities and Colleges – Report (1986), p. vii, 139.

This report is prepared by the UGC appointed committee to review the scales of pay of teachers in universities and colleges under the Chairmanship of Professor R.C. Mehrotra. The report contains recommendations on emoluments and conditions of service and other benefits for the welfare of teachers. It has suggestions on eligibility, qualifications and incentives in the form of advance increments for research degrees and it also has deliberation on other various related issues in brief in six chapters followed with eight appendices.

(106) Committee on Revision of Pay Scales of Librarians and Directors of Physical Education in Universities and Colleges – Report (1986), p.49.

The publication is a report of the UGC appointed committee on Dec. 24, 1983 under the Chairmanship of Professor R.C. Mehrotra to consider the revision of pay scales, career/professional development and service conditions of librarians and Directors of Physical Education in Universities and Colleges. The report has five chapters for presenting brief history along with role and responsibilities of librarians and Directors of Physical Education in Universities and Colleges. The Committee recommendations on revision of pay scales are followed by three appendices for presenting existing prescribed qualifications, qualifications for future recruitment and formula for fixation of pays for librarians and Director of Physical Education in the Universities and Colleges.

(107) The Expert Committee on the Minimum Qualifications and Workload etc. for Librarians and Directors of Physical Education in Universities and Colleges – Report (1987), p.47.

This report is brought out by a Committee appointed by UGC under the Chairmanship of Professor R.C. Mehrotra, on Dec. 24, 1983. The report has three chapters for background work as well as for recommendations regarding qualifications, evaluation, workload, code of conduct, professional training etc. for librarians and Directors of Physical Education. The main text is followed by six appendices for list of Sub-Committee members who designed the format for evaluation and professional training programme for librarians and Directors of Physical Education.

(108) Committee of Accreditation and Assessment Council – Report (1987), p.13.

The report has the composition of the Committee and sub-committee constituted to develop a mechanism for accreditation and assessment of higher education. The draft document prepared for setting up of Accreditation and Assessment Council indicating therein the objective, functions, structure and the methodology of assessing the performance of educational institutions is available as Annexure II.

Research

(109) University Development in India: Basic Facts and Figures 1972-73 to 1976-77: Part I Section-D Postgraduate and Research Enrolment (1982), 1664-1291.

It contains data for enrolment at the postgraduate and research level. The information is designed both subjectwise and statewise in different universities, with separate figures for university departments and colleges. Twelve appendices contain information about enrolment 1950-51 to 1976-77 and teaching staff in university teaching departments and affiliated colleges.

(110) Support for Science Research in the Universities (1974), p.15.

The brochure contains guidelines along with application forms for major and minor research projects in science subjects.

(111) UGC's Policy and Programme for Improvement of Research in the Universities (1984), p.14.

This brochure contains a summarised account of Commission's role and activities in regard to standard of education and research in universities.

(112) Support for Research in Science (1985), p.vi, 16.
Document is not available for annotation.

(113) Development of Higher Education and Research in the Universities 1980-85 (1986), p 86.

Publication is in eleven sections. Section one deals with origin and role of the University Grants Commission. The other sections are devoted to Guidelines for Sixth Plan programmes — maintenance and co-ordination of standards, restructuring of courses and examinations, Faculty development, support for research, utilisation of INSAT for Higher Educational and Regional Co-operation etc. The findings are supported by illustrations and statistics wherever necessary. The main text is followed by three appendices for Development of Higher Education in India: A policy frame, on-going programmes of the University Grants Commission, and Guidelines to Universities for preparation of proposals for the Sixth Plan.

Faculty Improvement Programme (FIP)

(114) Faculty Improvement Programmes Pertaining to Teachers in Affiliated Colleges (n.d.), p. 7.

The brochure contains guidelines on the scheme along with number of proformas and application forms for participation in the scheme.

(115) Faculty Improvement Programmes Pertaining to Teachers in Affiliated Colleges (1974), p. 12.
Publication in not available for annotation.

College Humanities and Social Sciences Improvement Programme (COHSSIP)

(116) Regional COHSSIP Conferences — Summary Report, 1977-78 (1980), p. 76.

Report provides an analysis of the recommendations of the five regional conferences organised during December 1977 to March 1978 to prepare guidelines for the operation of the College Humanities and Social Sciences Improvement Programme. It contains the deliberations of large number of teachers, principals, and other specialist/expertise of undergraduate education in the country.

(117) Hand Book of Information on College Humanities and Social Sciences Improvement Programme — (COHSSIP) (1983), p. 11.

The publication contains the objectives, selection criteria and present position of COHSSIP programmes undertaken by colleges. It has annexures containing Statewise and universitywise breakup of COHSSIP colleges and application form on the scheme.

College Science Improvement Programme (COSIP)

(118) Teaching Materials Developed for the use of Classroom and Laboratories and Undergraduate Science Instruction (1982), p. 52.

The objective behind the compilation of this publication was to give wide publicity so that the developed facilities could be used in better way. It includes the information about syllabi and courses of study, laboratory facilities, equipment, workshop, library and other teaching materials. The information is in tabulated form.

COSIST

(119) UGC Programme on Science and Technology Infrastructure Development (COSIST) in Universities : An outline (1987), p. 13.

The document is brief outline on the scheme and comprehensive information brochure on department supported under COSIST arranged subject-wise. Annexure II is the format for the report to be filled by the officer visiting the department.

(120) Progress Report of COSIST Supported Departments (1988), p. 52.

The publication contains the brief of the self-assessment of some of the departments to which communication was sent under the COSIST programme up to 1987 asking the impact of the programme on teaching and research in the concerned disciplines. The departments are discussed under subject headings like Bio Science, Chemistry, Earth Sciences, Physics, Engineering and Technology. In the end brief report of the monitoring and evaluation committee is available.

STATISTICS

(121) University Statistical Digest (1962), p. 18.

The publication is compilation of UGC Statistics Section and contains statistical information on University Education and other related matters. The universities as on 1.1.1962 are listed in Appendix-1.

(122) University Development in India : A Statistical Report, 1961-62, p. 76.

The publication contains in brief latest facts and figures pertaining to university education and study of some of the trends in Indian universities. It also has number of illustrations to present the information, a map showing universities in India up to June, 1962 and list of universities with year of establishment, type, population and information about colleges etc.

(123) University Development in India: Basic Facts and Figures, 1962-63, p 69.

It gives the summary of Statistical information about the Indian Universities along with number of illustrations.

(124) University Development in India: Basic Facts and Figures, 1963-64, p. 106.

The publication provides useful summary of important statistical information about the Indian Universities. The basis of information is the returns received by UGC from the universities and colleges.

(125) University Development in India: Basic Facts and Figures, 1964-65, p. 175.

It presents summary of important statistical information pertaining to the University education. Part II of this publication gives the number of doctorates awarded by Indian Universities during 1960-61, 1961-62, 1962-63 and 1963-64. Figures have been presented University-wise and faculty-wise. For arts and science faculties, a subjectwise break-up has also been given.

(126) University Grants Commission : Some Facts and Figures (1966), p. 23.

Document is based on tabulated information on enrolment, teaching staff, degrees awarded in science and technology and required educated manpower in India. It also has note on constitution and functions of the Commission, list of Universities, Institutions deemed to be Universities and the number affiliated colleges of each university followed with illustrations.

(127) University Development in India: Basic Facts and Figures, 1965-66, p. viii, 266.

It contains summary of statistical information pertains to Indian Universities for the period 1965-66 and the name of the Commission members. It has ten appendices for presenting growth of institutions and enrolment etc.

(128) University Development in India: Basic Facts and Figures, 1966-67, p. viii, 276.

The document prepared by statistical section of the UGC on the basis of the returns received from the various Universities and colleges. It contains briefly latest facts and figures pertaining to University education during 1964-65 to 1966-67.

(129) University Development in India: Basic Facts and Figures, 1967-68, p. viii, 324.

It is a compilation of statistical information for the period 1967-68 on various issues relating to higher education: teaching department, University, College, Woman students etc. It has eleven appendices for various types of data.

(130) University Development in India: Basic Facts and Figures, 1968-69, p. vi, 467.

This publication provides summary of statistical information about the Indian Universities for the period 1966-67, 1967-68 and 1968-69 along with fifteen appendices for various types of data.

(131) University Development in India: Basic Facts and Figures, 1969-70, p. vi, 482.

It consists all-India statistical information for the year 1969-70 pertaining to University education. Followed with fifteen appendices to present various statistical information in various forms. In the end it has statewise list for various types of institutions.

(132) University Development in India: Basic Facts and Figures, 1970-71 (1974), p. vi, 516.

It is UGC's periodical publication containing statistical information on Indian Universities. The information is based on the returns received from the various Universities and Colleges for the year 1970-71.

(133) University Development in India: Basic Facts and Figures, 1971-72 (1976), p. vi, 545.

This publication contains statistical information on various issues of higher education based on the figures for 1971-72. The cases where information was not received the previous available information have been used. It has ten appendices and followed with explanatory notes for the abbreviations used in the report.

(134) University Development in India: Basic Facts and Figures: Part III Doctorate Degree Awarded 1979-80 to 1983-84 (1988), p. 163.

The publication contains seven tables for each year for presenting the statistics in desired format. Tables are grouped in chronological order.

(135) University Development in India: Basic Facts and Figures 1972-73 to 1976-77: Part-I Section B, Staff University Department, University Colleges and Affiliated Colleges (1980), p. xi, 581-948.

The publication contains number of tables on statistics of staff both faculty-wise as well as designation-wise, in the different universities with separate figures for university departments/university colleges and affiliated colleges. It also has data on postgraduate and research enrolment.

Standard

(136) Standard of University Education — Report (1965), p. viii, 282.

It is the report of the UGC appointed Committee under the Chairmanship of Dr. Sidhanta in 1962. The report contains study on standard of teaching and research in relation with growth of student, teacher and Institutions. Other important issues like standards Admission policy, courses of study, undergraduate education, postgraduate studies and research, science education. Improvement of teaching, medium of instruction, Examination reform and organisation of Universities are discussed in brief. It contains summary recommendations along with various information designed in 36 appendices.

Student

Indiscipline

(137) Problem of Student Indiscipline in Indian Universities — Report (1960), p. 25.

It is a report on the problem of student indiscipline submitted by the UGC appointed Committee under Chairmanship of Dewan Anand Kumar. It also has article 'The Students' Union, by F.T. Bennett as appendix I and main recommendations of the Committee as appendix II.

(138) The Committee on Students Welfare and Allied Matters — Report (1967), p. 35.

The volume is the report of the Committee worked under the Chairmanship of Dr. T. Sen on student indiscipline. The Committee has identified common factors responsible for student unrest, the study is carried out in the light of US Education Foundation findings on the question of student welfare. Report suggests ways and means to improve student morale. The main text is followed by three appendices — causes of student indiscipline and remedies suggested by Professor Humayun Kabir, recommendations of the Seminar on Student Welfare organised by the Education Commission in collaboration with the world university in Delhi University in Aug.-Sept. 1965 and questionnaire for students.

Welfare

(139) Committee on Health Services for Students and Staff in Universities and Colleges (1967), p. ii, 28.
Publication is not available for annotation.

Women Studies

(140) Guidelines for the Development of Women's Studies in Indian Universities and Colleges (1986), p. 7.

The publication contains guidelines on the aims and objectives, activities — teaching/research/training, organisation. Pattern of assistance, formulation of proposals and monitoring committee etc. for the development of women's studies in Indian Universities and colleges.

Others

(141) Education and the Universities, D.S. Kothari (1961), p. 20.

It contains an address delivered by Dr. D.S. Kothari at the

Vice-Chancellors' Conference held at New Delhi on 28-29th October 1961. Various aspects – cost of Education, Expansion and Standards, student wastage, Entrance and Scholarship tests, Three-year degree scheme, General Education, improvement of syllabi, assessment of student work, seminar and summer schools, Centres of advanced study, Academic mobility and need for new Universities has been discussed in brief. In the end it has illustrations presenting statistical data on different issues.

(142) Some Aspects of Secondary Science Education, D.S. Kothari (1962), p. 9.

It contains some aspects of Secondary Science Education discussed by Dr. D.S. Kothari at the Sixth annual Conference of the All India Science Teachers' Association, held at Udaipur on 26th Dec., 1961.

(143) Science and the Universities, D.S. Kothari (1965), p. 30.

It contains the Presidential address given at the fiftieth session of the Indian Science Congress Association, Oct. 7, 1963. A review of various issues related with Science growth and science in rich and poor countries are available in it.

(144) Handbook of Universities in India (1963), p. 275.
Publication is not available for annotation.

(145) Committee on Sitting up a University for the North Eastern Region of India – Report (1965), p. 50.

It is the report of the Committee appointed by University Grants Commission and Ministry of Education jointly in Dec. 1963 under the Chairmanship of Professor A.R. Wadia, to examine all aspects of opening University in North Eastern Region. The Committee visited and identified area and also contacted with public, Government and Educationists, and made recommendations after studying the different problems of hill and plains along with population density of the North Eastern Area. The main text is followed by five appendices for related information.

(146) The Committee on Colleges – Report (1967), p. 44.

It is the report of the Committee appointed by UGC in Sept., 1962 to advise the commission on the general policy to be followed for developing colleges and to make suggestions regarding the effective utilisation of the limited available resources. It has suggested ways and means of improving the standards of collegiate education. The main text is followed by two appendices containing affiliation conditions laid down by University of Andhra and procedure for Grant-in-aid to the Colleges in Delhi.

Advance Study Centre

(147) Centres of Advance Study in Indian Universities (1967), p. 77.

Document has a brief note on the twenty-six centres of advance study in various fields in Science, Social Science and Humanities. The studies are supported with photographs. The main text is followed by seven appendices: List of commission members as on 1.4.1967, names of members of committee on centres of advance study, Assessment committee for CAS and names of the Scientists and Scholars who visited centres under this programme.

(148) UGC delegation to the USSR – Report (1968), p. 40.

Report contains the observations of the UGC delegation to the USSR on Review of the System and structure of education in Soviet Union, observation about Moscow University, other Institute of Moscow, Leningrad, Indian Students in Leningrad and other Academic Institutions alongwith language policy and Mathematics in Russian Universities. It has two appendix containing statistical information.

(149) Education Surges Teaching Linked to needs, by D.S. Kothari (1970), p. 8.

It is a special report appeared in the *Times* (London) supplement on India which gives a picture of Indian Higher Education. The publication is as reproduction of aforesaid report.

(150) On the Threshold of India's Citizenhood, by C.D. Deshmukh (1962), p. vii, 393.

This volume is the collection of the convocation addresses given by C.D. Deshmukh when he was Chairman of the UGC. These are illuminating discussions of some of the most outstanding and complex educational problems of the time.

(151) In the Portals of Indian Universities, Convocation and other Addresses, by C.D. Deshmukh (1959), p. 336.

The publication is the collection of a few of the addresses delivered by Shri C.D. Deshmukh during 1956-58 after he became the Chairman of the UGC. The addresses contain some of thoughts of Shri Deshmukh on various aspects of education in India. These not only reflect thinking of Shri Deshmukh but also the trends of opinion, discussion in the commission and in the University as a whole on matters of importance.

(152) Committee on Governance of Universities and Colleges – Report, Part-I Governance of Universities (1971), p. 96.

This report, stressing the importance of effective participation of teachers and students in decision-making and governance. It has brief information on Acts, Statutes, ordinances and regulations, visitor and the Universities, Authorities, other University bodies, Organisation of teaching departments, University administrators etc. It also contains information about committees on Governance of Universities, and colleges.

(153) Committee to Enquire into the Working of the Central Universities – Report (n.d.) p. 177.

This is the report of the Committee appointed by University Grants Commission to inquire into the working of the Central Universities. It contains the names of the members and terms References. The report consists of five chapters: (1) To examine whether the Central Universities are fulfilling the objectives set for them in their Acts and Statutes. (2) To examine the general state of discipline, (3) Adequacy of the machinery to deal with the grievances of students and staff,

(4) The desirability of evolving a code of conduct for political parties to their involvement in the University affairs, (5) Measures of reform for promoting an academic atmosphere on the Campuses. Different related aspects have also been enumerated in the nine Annexures.

(154) Review Committee on UGC Programmes – Report (1981), p. 208.

The report is the outcome of the UGC appointed review Committee under the Chairmanship of Prof. Satish Chandra. It consists the review submitted by Sub-Committee on ongoing UGC Schemes and programmes. Committee's observations and recommendations on the centres of advance study, Department of Special assistance, college science improvement programme and Financial assistance to teachers for research work are available. The main text is followed by thirty-four annexures for information collected from the Universities and Colleges.

(155) The University Grants Commission Act, 1956 (3 of 1956): As Modified up to the Ist October, 1984 (1985), p. ii, 17.

The publication is in four chapters containing number of sections in each. Chapter Ist deals with preliminary of the act and second Chapter has details about commission's establishment, composition and other various important related aspects where in Chapter third powers and functions of the commission are laid down. And in last 4th Chapter miscellaneous issues are summarised.

(156) UGC Committee on the Involvement of the Universities and Colleges in the Promotion of National Integration – Report (1986), p x, 144.

The report is in three parts – Part I: Introduction, Part II: National Integration and the University System. Part III: Conclusions and recommendations followed with eleven Annexures. Annexure I is the statement on National Integration (approved by Minorities Commission of India), Annexure II is on National Integration – the internal Defence of India by Srimati Indira Gandhi, Prime Minister, III is the presidential address by M.H. Beg, and IV is All India National Integration Convention, New Delhi (Jan. 12-14, 1984), V is the extract of Fifth Minorities Commission report, VI is opinions and suggestions of the Chairman on future of the Minorities Commission of India, VII – National Integration Samities and Councils and guidelines for programmes, Annexure VIII is a proposal for the Institute of Studies in National: Bhikhu Parekh and in Annexure XI: UGC Committee on National Integration and BHU Act Section 4 (a).

Scheduled Castes and Scheduled Tribes

(157) Facilities to Scheduled Castes and Scheduled Tribes in Universities and Colleges (1982), p. xii, 135.

The report contains analysis in the position of actual admission and Employment of Scheduled Castes and Scheduled Tribes in Universities and Colleges during 1977-78. It has UGC guidelines and circulars issued time to time on the subject in twelve annexures and statistical information in seventy-eight appendices.

(158) Facilities to Scheduled Castes and Scheduled Tribes Universities and Colleges: Analysis on the Position of Actual Admission and Employment of SC and ST in Universities and Colleges during 1978-79, 1985, p. xvi, 363.

The report is analysis of the actual position of admission and appointments of Scheduled Caste and Scheduled Tribe candidates in the year 1978-79 in Indian Universities. It contains the names of the officers/officials of UGC who were associated with the study. In ten annexures UGC guidelines on various issues related to SC/ST are available. It also contains 146 appendices for presenting statistical information in various forms.

(159) University System and Extension as the Third Dimension – Report (1987), p. 200.

The Review Committee report contains observations on the areas of non-formal education like, Adult Education, Continuing Education, Population Education, Community Education, Environmental Education, National Integration, Legal literacy, Rural development, Science for the people etc. In view of these observations, some immediate operational measures have also been suggested. The Report is in four parts, the last part has fifteen appendices covering various lists, models, formats and statistical profiles containing some of the thought of Shri Deshmukh on various aspects of education in India. These not only reflect thinking of Shri Deshmukh but also the trends of opinion, discussion in the commission and in the University as a whole on matters of importance.

(160) Development Programmes Sponsored by the UGC (1964), p. 31.

It has account of the UGC Schemes initiated to improve higher education in the country through plans. Information about major development schemes at present under implementation is furnished in this brochure. It enumerates issues related to the universities, colleges, teachers, students and research scholarships and fellowships.

(161) Development of Higher Education in India: A Policy Frame (1978), p. 16.

The publication is to suggest a policy frame for the development of higher education in India over the next ten to fifteen years. Section II deals with development of education and Section III on development of higher education in India.

(162) Hand Book of teaching facilities in Higher Education, 1984-85 (1987), p. 131.

It contains information on the teaching facilities available in the departments of Universities in the country during 1984-85. The disciplines are arranged alphabetically according to Faculty under the Universities. The information is in five broad groups – Arts faculty, Science faculty, language (Indian and foreign), Religious studies/ Religious culture/Area studies/Theology, other faculties and Miscellaneous.

Affiliation of College

(163) UGC Guidelines on Terms and Conditions of Affiliation of Colleges by a University (1988), p. 19.

The publication contains the guidelines framed on terms and

conditions of affiliation of colleges by a University and a copy of the letter vide which these were circulated. The main text is followed by appendices for Gazette notification part III-Section 4 and norms for laboratory, lecture room and Library.

Teachers

(164) The Task Force on Performance Appraisal of Teachers – Report (1988), p. 2.

Publication contains the report of the task force on performance appraisal of Teacher and Appendices for list of members of task force and proforma appraisal report I & II.

(165) The Task Force on Code of Professional Ethics for University and College Teachers — Report (1989), p. 6.

The report of the task force is discussing various aspects. Goals of higher education in India, teachers rights and responsibilities with students, Guardians, fellow colleague and with Society. It has the list of members of the task force on code of professional Ethics for University and College teachers.

Survey Report

(166) Third All-India Educational Survey Higher Education 1973-74 (1978), p. 503.

The publication is first extension survey report on higher education based on UGC programmes. It has the statistics about number of Institutions, their enrolment, hostels and library facilities in different States and Union Territories. The volume has separate statistics for rural and urban students districtwise in different States and Union Territories. It has brief note for progress of higher education during 1963-64 to 1973-74 and three sections with seven appendices for various informations.

Institution – Bibliography

(167) List of Colleges under Section 2(f) of the UGC Act as on 1st August, 1964.

The publication gives the names of the various types of colleges affiliated to the Universities which have been brought under the perview of UGC Act 1956 in accordance with the regulations framed under Section 2(f). The publication is being updated every year.

Directory – Indian Research

(168) Directory of Scientific Research in Indian Universities (1974), p. 623.

The directory covers research projects in the field of science, engineering, technology, agriculture and medicine carried out in the Universities, IIT's and other educational Institutions in India. The research Projects have been broadly grouped under seven sections: Physical Sciences/Bio-Sciences/Engineering/Agriculture/ Management and Transport/chemical technology and manufactures, Industries, building and architecture. Each section has been divided into smaller groups and entries in the groups have been arranged alphabetically by the title of the project. Each entry contains information: about the title of the project, names of the investigator, name of the University department or Institution, name of the Sponsoring body, if any, duration of the project and in brief other description. The publication is available with sales department, publication division.

(169) India: Pocket book of University Education (1972), p. 259.

The publication is brought out to serve as a compact source on higher education and Universities in India. It includes the national policy on education (1968) and a summary of chapters dealing with higher education in the report of the education commission (1964-66).

(170) Dr. Zakir Hussain Memorial Lectures. Sept. 4-5, 1970, University of Delhi (n.d.), p. 26.

The publication is an article – Agricultural Transformation and Opportunities for a Learning Revolution, by M.S. Swaminathan, IARI, New Delhi.

Annual Accounts

(171) University Grants Commission – Annual Accounts, 1984-85 (n.d.), p. 102.

The publication contains main summary of accounts and details of expenditure schemewise under plan and non-plan of UGC for the period 1984-85. The Hindi version of the text is followed with it.

(172) Presidential address – 1990; Science in Society by Yash Pal, Seventh Annual Session, Indian Science Congress Association, at Cochin, p. 28.

The lecture was delivered in Science Congress meeting held at Cochin on the theme Science and Society. It reviews the impact of science and technology on Society.

(173) Yash Pal – An Open letter to fellow Academicians and Friends of Academia (1987), p. 9.
Publication is not available for annotation.

(174) Education Commission (1964-66) Summary of Recommendations on Higher Education (Chapter XI-XVI), (1967), p. vi, 74.
Publication is not available for annotation.

(175) Schemes of National Associateships (1978), p. III, 6.
Publication is not available for annotation.

(176) Scheme of Career Awards for Young Scholars in Humanities and Social Sciences (1981), p. vi, 8.
Publication is not available for annotation.

(177) Seminar on National Integration (1961), p. iv, 127.
Document is not available for annotation.

(178) Centres of Advances Study in Indian Universities (1972), p. 119.

The document has brief note on the thirty centres of advance study in various disciplines in Indian Universities. The main text is followed by eight appendices for including information on the committees various assistances and for the names of Indian and British CAS visitors. It also has twenty-three plates.

Centre of Advance Study

(179) Centres of Advanced Study in Indian Universities (1972), p. 119.

It contains a brief note on the Centres of Advanced Study in different subjects – Science, Physics, Chemistry, Botany, Zoology, Geology, Mathematics, Astronomy, Biochemistry in Humanities and Social Sciences: Economics, History, Philosophy, Sanskrit, Linguistics, Education and Sociology. It has eight appendices containing information about the Committees on Centres of Advanced Study, UNESCO assistance for their development programme, British Assistance etc. In the end the list of CAS visitors of various countries is given.

(180) University Service and Instrumentation Centres (1981), p. 16.
Publication is not available for annotation.

Science Instrumentation Centre

(181) Guidelines for University Science Instrumentation Centre (1984), p. 32.

The volume contains information about the objectives and functions of University Science Instrumentation Centres and Regional Instrumentation Centres. It also has nine Annexures for proformas, guidelines and for the list of University Science Instrumentation Centres.

(182) Guidelines for University Science Instrumentation Centres (1986), p. 11, 32.
Publication is not available for annotation.

(183) Guidelines for University Science Instrumentation Centre (1990), p. 57.

The first two pages are denoted to the needs and objectives of the

USIC programme and rest of the publication is divided into three parts. Part I deals with levels, functions, status, organisation and service conditions etc. of the USIC where the Part II deals similar aspects of Regional Instrumentation Centres (RICs). Part III is implementations of USIC programme and the guidelines followed with 10 annexures containing related information.

Summer Institutes

(184) Summer Institutes (1965), p. 35.

It contains information about the Summer Institute programmes for School and College teachers, six appendices giving information of the orientation seminars and Evaluation Conferences held during 1963-65 and list of teachers from US Universities and Colleges associated during 1963-65. It also has a list of text book, Reference books, Equipment and films used and brief note on UNESCO Coupons Scheme.

Commerce

(185) The Curriculum Development Centre in Commerce Report (1989), p. 370.
This annotation may be seen as in entury No. 52(A).

Linguistics

(186) Status of Linguistics in Indian Universities: Report (1982), p. iv, 46.

This report is outcome of the Panel of linguistics based on answers received from heads of linguistics/language departments to a questionnaire circulated in 1977. It has the names of the members of the panel on linguistics (1978-80) and a brief note on status of linguistics in Indian Universities. It has nine tables to present statistical information on universities where linguistics is taught, enrolment for different courses, strength of teaching staff, library holdings and expenditure incurred on books and journals and syllabi for M.A. linguistics. Four appendices, for survey of existing departments, copy of questionnaire and the list of universities where linguistics is taught, are followed.

Natural Sciences

Mathematics

(187) Mathematics in Indian Universities – Report (n.d.), p. 98.

It is the report of the UGC appointed Review Committee to assess the standard of teaching and research and also to suggest modification in syllabuses in order to raise the general level of academic attainment and research in mathematics in the Universities. It has brief historical sketch of mathematical research in India, Model Syllabi for B.A./B.Sc. and M.A./M.Sc. Courses, recommendations of the Committee for examination system and of future programmes etc.

(188) Mathematics Reforms Committee – Report (1966), p. 24.

It is the report of the UGC Committee formulated under the Chairmanship of Dr. D.C. Pavate to suggest measures for the improvement of the standard and quality of mathematics in Universities and Colleges in the country. The report contains significant suggestions for reviewing and revising the syllabus and system of examinations. It has appendix – on record of discussions with Academician, Prof. Alexandrov, Rector, Leningrad University, regarding revision of mathematics course.

(189) Mathematics in India Meeting, the Challenge: Proceedings of the Conference on Mathematics Education and Research, Bangalore (1973), p. 71.

It contains the deliberations of the conferences with the major problems identified in the field of mathematical education and research in the country. It also contains the detailed recommendations of the conference on all aspects of teaching and evaluation, curriculum development, preservice and in-service teacher training, centres and institutes of mathematics. The academic restructuring, grading system, talent research and nurturing of talent, application of mathematics etc.

(190) The Curriculum Development Centre in Mathematics – Report (1989), p. 387.
Annotation may be seen as in entry No. 52(A).

Statistics

(191) Statistics in Indian Universities – Report (1970), p. 140.

It is the report of the Review Committee appointed by UGC in April, 1967 under the Chairmanship of Professor R.S. Verma to examine the existing facilities in Indian Universities for teaching and research in the field of statistics and to make recommendation for the improvement of courses of study in the field. The references of Committee visits, meetings and discussions on problems relating to education and research in statistics are recorded. The Committee has reviewed growth of statistics-teaching and research in India. The main text is followed by six appendices for information collected by the Committee from the institutions engaged in the advanced study of statistics.

(192) Status of Statistics in India (1985), p. 74.

This report is the effort to supplement the UGC publication "statistics in Indian Universities". It contains early history of descriptive statistics, its role and importance in Interdisciplinary work, with teaching and research. Remarks and recommendations for pure and applied statistics are followed by four appendices containing list of research journals in India, University statistics departments, National Research Institutes and list of experts who associated for preparation of this status report.

Physics

(193) Physics in India Challenges and Opportunities: Summary of Proceedings of the Conference on Physics Education and Research. Sponsored by University Grants Commission, National Council for Science Education, US National Science Foundation and US Agency for International Development. Srinagar, 1970 (1973), p. 46.

The volume contains deliberations of the Conference, participated by

Indian Physicists from Universities, National Laboratories and Research Institutes to exchange ideas with their foreign colleagues. It reviews the state of Physics in India and recommends specific steps for improvement of Physics teaching and research also identify areas of research with reference to national needs. It finds that U.S. and Indian Physics problems are common in many respects. The publication contains the names of foreign and Indian delegates and the summary of recommendations. It gives brief account of Physics education; teaching, evaluation, research and identify following areas to change the prevailing conditions in the subjects such as, Science Teaching Centre/Regional libraries/Indian Journal of Physics Education/Research Journal/Indian Physics Association.

(194) The Curriculum Development Centre in Biophysics – Report (1989), p.188.
Annotation may seen as in entry No. 52(A).

Chemistry and Allied Sciences

(195) Chemistry in Indian Universities – Report (1963), p. 107.

It is the report of the Review Committee in chemistry appointed by UGC in May, 1960 under the Chairmanship of Professor T.R. Seshadri. Committee lays emphasis on improvement of courses of study and re-orientation in the method of research in chemistry in Indian Universities. Report contains suggestions regarding model syllabi indicating the extent of training to be provided at various levels of University education, assessment of student performance, examination pattern and training for research degrees. The text is followed by appendix for enrolment and major areas in chemistry for research, identified by the Committee.

(196) Chemistry Design for Innovation: Summary of Recommendations of the Conference Sponsored by UGC, National Council for Science Education and National Science Foundation (USA). Srinagar and Bangalore, 1969, p. 116.

The publication is on the deliberation of the Conference to assess the status of the Chemistry and Chemical education in India and to formulate guidelines for future development. It also discusses the

Indian Chemical Education problems along with the faults searched in the United States. It has recommendation for change and also suggested UGC to take initiative in important activities such as teaching programmes, research support, educational facilities, Institutions and short training courses, development of educational materials and collaborative programmes etc. Apart from this, it has recommendations to extend support to the Instrumentation Centres and suggested that there must be a Journal like *Indian Journal of Chemical Education* to keep aware the scientists about the new happenings of the subject.

(197) The Status of Research in Chemistry in Indian Universities — Report (1979), p. 38.

The report is prepared by the Chemistry panel under the Chairmanship of Prof. R.C. Mehrotra, Vice-Chancellor, Delhi University. The report gives an objective assessment of the areas of current research and contributions made by Indian Universities and also draws attention on the existing gaps and the need for promoting newly emerging areas in chemistry. It contains a brief account on the status of research in Chemistry in Universities and other educational Institutions of the country. An analysis of research publications is given in four parts — Physical, Inorganic, Organic and Biochemistry.

(198) The Curriculum Development Centre in Chemistry Report (1988), p. 257.
For annotation please see entry No. 52(A)

Biochemistry

(199) Biochemistry in Indian Universities – Report (1963), p. 70.

It is the report of the Review Committee in Biochemistry appointed by UGC in January, 1959 under the Chairmanship of Dr. B.C. Guha. Report contains brief account of the growth of biochemistry in the country. It also outlines some proposals for further expansion and development of facilities for teaching and research. Report has recommendations for independent departments of Biochemistry.

(200) The Curriculum Development Centre in Biochemistry Report (1989), p. 87.
For annotation please see entry No. 52(A).

Photochemistry

(201) Photochemistry — A Status Report (1982) p. 142.

The chemistry panel constituted a Special Committee on Photochemistry in December 1976 for preparing a status report of photochemistry under the convenership of Dr. Jagdish Shankar. Report introduces photochemistry and identify the trends in photochemistry with inter-disciplinary advancement. It gives the present status of the subject and list of seminars and symposia on photochemistry and photobiology. Recommendations for future development are followed by a Bibliography on photochemistry from page 37 to 142.

Earth Sciences

Geology and Geophysics

(202) The Status of Teaching and Research in Geology and Geophysics in India — Report (1979), p. ix, 101.

The report provides an objective assessment of the current status of teaching and research in Geological Sciences including Geophysics and contribution in these areas made by Indian Universities and Colleges. The report also focus attention on the existing weaknesses and suggest methods by which these could be eliminated for improvement of standard of teaching and research. It contains the names of UGC Panel members of the Geology and Geophysics and number of appendices for statistical information and Charts etc.

Biological Sciences

(203) Biological Sciences and National Development Strategy for Progress: Proceedings of the Conference on Education and Research in Life Sciences, Bangalore (1971), p. 244.

This volume is the outcome of the deliberations and summary

recommendations made by the Conference on Education and research in life sciences held at Bangalore from 25th June to 2nd July 1971. It contains list of Indian and foreign delegates and studies on the various aspects — need for curriculum reform, programme for continuous faculty development, evaluation, goals and status of biological research and also some problems of biological developments. It contains 35 papers which were presented in the conference.

(204) Status Report on Biological Sciences in Indian Universities (1982), p. 54.

The Biological Science panel under the Chairmanship of Prof. A.K. Sharma undertook the task of preparing this report. The report provides an objective assessment of the areas of current research and important contributions made by Indian Universities. It pays attention to the existing gaps and need for promoting newly emerging areas in Biological Sciences. The objective of the report has been to indicate the general trend of researches in Biological Sciences in India. It has comprehensive description on almost all important aspects of Biological Science, along with recommendations on curriculum reform, training and research.

Botany

(205) Botany in Indian Universities — Report (1963), p. 82.

The report is the outcome of the UGC Review Committee in Botany formulated in March, 1959 under the Chairmanship of Prof. P. Maheswari. It pertains to teaching and research in botany in Indian Universities. The Committee has realised the need for improvement in the syllabuses and re-orientation in the method of teaching and many practical and specific suggestions for botanical research with special reference to Indian conditions. Report also has brief description on curriculum reform, develop botanical gardens, high altitude biology in the University Departments and affiliated colleges.

Science and Technology

(206) University Research in Science and Technology in Relationship to National Development: Based on an Indo-US Seminar. Srinagar and Kashmir (1980), p. iv, 160.

The volume is dedicated to goodwill and mutual cooperation between scientists and technologists of the Universities of United States and India in their further examination of various issues and experiences in the years to come. It has address by Satish Chandra and the text of comprising following papers:

1. University Research problem identification	Rais Ahmed and Ramachandra Rao
2. Research problems of US Universities	F.A. Cong
3. The Good and Bads of American Research Universities	Roger Ravelle
4. Role of University in Scientific and Technological Research for National Development.	F.A. Hamington
5. Industry University Interaction in Research in India	S. Vardarajan
6. The university as a source of appropriate technology for agriculture	John. W. Melloso
7. Universities — Industries Interactions	A.N. Bose
8. University — Industry Interactions in the United States	P.J. Lucchesi
9. Technology assessment	V.K. Gaur
10. The role of US Universities in Technology appraisal	Glenn E. Schwester
11. Research management and interaction with funding Agencies	Jagdish Shanker & R.D., Patel
12. University Extension Service	M.R. Bhidey
13. University Extension activities in National Development	Donald Boston

The main text is followed by the joint statements of Seminar working groups and biodata of foreign and Indian participants.

Home Science

(207) Guidelines for Postgraduate Programmes in Home Science (1985), p. 188.

The publication contains guidelines suggested by the Panel of Home Science for improving of teaching/research and extension education in Home Science in Indian Universities and Colleges. The panel worked under Convenership Dr. (Mrs.) Rajammal P. Devadas, the guidelines contain detailed curriculum for six major areas of Home Science, namely, human development, family resource management, food science and nutrition, food service management and dietetics, textiles and clothing and home science extension. The details regarding equipment, books, journals, laboratory space an staff are also included. Publication is in three chapters and every chapter has number of papers discussing various aspects.

The Arts

(208) The Curriculum Development Centre in Performing Arts Report (1989), p. 270.
For annotation please see entry No. 52(A).

(209) The Curriculum Development Centre in Visual Art and Design Report (1989), p. 142.
For annotation please see entry No. 52(A).

Literature

English

(210) Conference on Problems of Teaching English — Report (1957)
Document is not available for annotation.

(211) English Review Committee – Report (1965), p. 56.

The report has comprehensive study of the different aspects relating to teaching and research in English language and literature Committees recommendations in regard to BA Compulsory and optional courses in English have been followed by four appendices for summary of recommendation of the KUNZRU Committee report, summary recommendation of the English teachers conference held at Hyderabad, plan of action of UGC and suggestions for syllabuses and examinations in english language at the B.A. (Hons) and M.A. Courses in Indian Universities.

(212) Syllabus Reform in English : Reports and Recommendations of Zonal and National Workshops, 1976-77 (n.d.) p. 235.

The publication is organised into three major parts followed by a set of appendices. Part I contains the three papers which were given to the participants of all the zonal workshops as background papers. Part II contains the report of the proceedings and the recommendations of all the five zonal workshops held between September 1976 and March 1977 at various university Centres. Part III is the report of the proceedings of the national workshop followed by its recommendations. The text of the addresses of Dr. Ramesh Mohan and Professor Satish Chandra followed by a summary of the concluding speech of Dr. Jagan Mohan Reddy are included in Appendix 'A'. Appendix 'B' contains the papers presented during different sessions of the National Workshop. Appendix 'C' contains a note on a course in the use of English followed by a suggested syllabus for the written English part of this course. Appendix 'D' is the list of delegates who attended the National Workshop held at CIEFL, Hyderabad.

(213) Teaching and Research in English: A Report (1981), p. 47.

The report on the status of teaching and research in English presents statistics of the postgraduate departments of English in the country and the art of teaching English language and literature at the postgraduate level. The problems: admissions, text books and other related aspects have been covered in the introductory part and constructive suggestions have been made. An assessment of the impact of the central Institute of English and Foreign languages on the postgraduate curricula in English also finds a place in the Introductory note. It has information about the names of the panel members of the English and Foreign language and profiles of the various departments of the Universities.

(214) The Curriculum Development centre in English Report (1989), p. 371
For annotation please see entry No. 52(A).

(215) The Curriculum Development Centre in Sanskrit Report (1989), p. 773.
For annotation please see entry No. 52(A).

(216) The Curriculum Development Centre in Hindi Report (1988), p. 487.
For annotation please see entry No. 52(A).

(217) The Curriculum Development Centre in Urdu Report (1989), p. 305.
For annotation please see entry no. 52(A).

(218) Arabic and Persian Studies in Indian Universities (1968), p iv, 16.
Document is not available for annotation.

Geography

(219) Geography in Indian Universities — Report (1968), p. 143.

It is the report of the Geography Review Committee appointed by UGC in 1965 under the Chairmanship of Prof. S.P. Chatterjee to assess the standard and status of teaching and research in various areas of the subject geography. Report contains assessment of existing facilities in the geography departments and future requirement of teaching and research. The objectives of the National Committee for geography and the Scientific Organisations engaged in Geography research are included. The main text is followed by twelve appendices for tabulated information.

(220) The Curriculum Development Centre in Geography Report (1989), p. 278.
For annotation please see entry No. 52(A).

History and Research

(221) Seminar on Postgraduate Teaching and Research in History — Report (1964), p. 70

The volume contains the proceedings and some of the papers presented at the Seminar. The working paper which was main document under discussion has been included here and also the summary of the comments of this paper. A few additional comments of general interest of historians are also included. Reports on the discussions and the final recommendations, and a brief factual information on problems : The work load of teachers and staff ratio is also available.

(222) Workshops in History of Art — Proceedings (1977), p. vi, 246. Document is not available for annotation.

(223) History Teaching in India: Perspective and Programmes for the Eighties — A Consolidated Report on the UGC Workshops on Modernisation of History Courses in the Universities — Guwahati, Mysore, Amritsar, Baroda, 1976 (1978), p. 114.

The report is based on the deliberations of the workshops and deals with all contemporary issues in the teaching of history viz. objective of teaching, contents of courses and improvement of standards of teaching and research. It informs new thinking by certain basic considerations in the restructuring of courses such as updating of courses, diversification flexibility, social responsibility, relevance, interdisciplinary approaches and practical orientation. It has five appendices for various zonal reports.

General

Annual Reports — UGC

In pursuance of the Section 18 of the University Grants Commission Act 1956, the Commission presents report of its financial activities before Parliament. These reports cover the progress of on-going programmes as well as account of new announcements. Keeping in view special feature of every report a separate annotation is included. On various aspects of higher education these reports are published records of the UGC. The most important quality of these publications may be the presentation of the trends of the higher education during the last four decades. These volumes also contain the deliberations of various Academic Groups formulated by UGC to study and to suggest the measures to be initiated for the improvement of Educational Standards of the University and College Education in the country. The information included in these volumes is of research value and also first hand in its nature.

(224) Dec., 1953 – March 1957, p. 47.

In pursuance of Section 18 of the University Grants Commission Act 1956, the Commission brought out the report of its activities under the title "Report of the University Grants Commission, December, 1953 – March, 1957". This first report covers the period since 1953, as is natural form at the outset it gives information about the inception and functions of the Commission, including interim Commission. It also provides the name of the Chairman, the members and the officers of the Commission. Along with this, it gives brief information about Universities of India, medium of instruction, salaries of University teachers, qualifications of teachers, financing of higher education in the country through University Grants Commission. It also provides statistics in enrolment of student and Institutions. Appendix contains statement showing grant paid to Universities during the year 1956-57. In the last it has twelve photographs.

(225) April, 1957 to March, 1958.

Report includes information on new Universities/Institutions, commission schemes : Medium of Instruction and Allied problems, Hindi, Salaries and Qualifications of University and affiliated College teachers, scholarships and publication grants, three-year degree course, general education, discipline in the Universities and student welfare. Apart of this it gives the brief account of the findings of the following Committees. (i) Building Committee (ii) Visiting Committee and (iii) Library Committee. And the progress of the other schemes with an account of foreign visits of the U.G.C. Officers Main text is followed by the following Appendices:

1. List of the State Universities which have implemented the scheme for improving the salary scales of University teachers.
2. Statement indicating the number of additional seats provided in different Engineering Institutions and the estimated cost thereof.
3. Statement showing grants paid to Universities during 1957-58.

(226) April, 1958 to March, 1959.

Report has review of the ongoing UGC Schemes and programmes for the year 1958-59. A brief note on the Commission's powers and functions is followed by the list of members of Building Committee, members of committees on development of Archaeology and Museology.

(227) April, 1959 to March, 1960.

Report gives the brief account of comparative studies of higher education system with other countries like Australia, Canada, Great Britain etc. The progress of development schemes — improvement of facilities in Colleges, development of Postgraduate education, medium of instructions working group, measures for improvement of standards, women's education, libraries and books, problems of discipline, teachers salaries and scholarships etc. are discussed. It also contains progress of the special programmes — foreign aid programmes, United States P.L.-480, and India wheat loan, Educational Exchange Programme. The main text is followed by number of appendices consisting of information on amount sanctioned for hostels up to 31.3.1960, Hostels and Staff Quarters approved in 1959-60, Payment made in 1959-60 for increase of salaries of teachers in Men's and Women's Colleges University-wise, Statement showing development grants paid to Universities including Central Universities during 1959-60, and Summary of grants paid during 1959-60.

(228) April, 1961 to March, 1962.

Report contains information in brief, on the new Universities and other Educational Institutions, salary scales revision of the staff of Central Universities, Information on development of higher education and research, improvement of standards of teaching, Central and State Universities examination reform, seminars, summer schools, Statistics on Information on affiliated Colleges, Student problems and teachers requirements — Pay scales, Staff quarters, Provident fund etc., and Progress of the UGC Schemes — Archaeology and Museology, Development of linguistics, special publications, University film clubs, study of languages, foreign exchange and exchange of Professors between Universities of India and West Germany. Main text is followed by seven appendices for showing statistics for grants paid for various purposes, and names of members of the various committees etc.

(229) April, 1962 to March, 1963.

The report contains information on various issues related with standardisation of higher education in universities and colleges. Statistical presentation is designed in nine appendices and with a number of illustrations. The names of the members of important committee are also available.

(230) 1963-64.

The Report gives the current trends, developments, Commission's view point and policies for providing grants to Universities and Colleges. It has brief account of suggestions of various expert committees which have studied various aspects for improving the quality in higher education. The report includes the Commission observations on the existing syllabi, programme of seminars and summer schools etc. Review for the number of on-going schemes : Pay scales and other essential amenities, provisions for the construction of staff quarters and teachers hostels, achieving the standards of education in University and Colleges has also been included. Report also contains various studies on New Universities, Central Universities, Colleges, teachers, students enrolment, scholarship and fellowship etc. The steps initiated with all sectors of University education for the development programmes in the field of medicine, agriculture, engineering and technology are recorded. Text is followed with twelve appendices and nine illustrations.

(231) 1964-65.

It gives information about the current trends in higher education and about significant expansion in institutions and standard of teaching and research. The detailed recommendations of the Committee on standards are included. The summer Institute in Science subjects organised in 1964 have also been reported. Thoughts on the aspects like Area study, General Education, Engineering and Technology, Medical Sciences, Teachers specific requirements, Student welfare, Scholarships and Fellowships have been summarised. Also a brief account of other schemes — community development and Panchayati Raj, Extension Lectures, Printing Presses, Foreign Exchange and Cultural Exchange programme is included. It acknowledges the appointment of the Education Commission under the Chairmanship of Dr. D.S. Kothari. In the end it consists 17 appendices and nine illustrations in support of the aforesaid descriptions.

(232) 1965-66.

Report contains facts and figures on the various aspects of higher education such as the steps taken by the Commission to improve standards, and study of proposal to convene a seminar on the subject. It also contains the suggestion of Standing Committee to advise Commission on area study programme. Account of grants of various schemes, Facultywise break-up of Doctoral Degree Awards and Educational efforts at various levels have been reported. New programmes — the centre of advance study, summer institutes and number of other efforts to raise tempo of education in the country have also been accounted for. It has thirteen Appendices and eleven illustrations.

(233) 1966-67.

The Report contains review of schemes of higher education for the period 1966-67, progress of centres of advance study, brief summary of the sanctions and guidelines given by UGC for the various schemes. It contains the important observations of the committee examined the problems related with student welfare and allied matters and the progress and provisions in scholarship and fellowship at various research levels in various faculties. Eighteen appendices and eight illustrations to present the available statistics on various aspects discussed in the publication are available in the end.

(234) 1967-68.

Publication has statistics on colleges, student enrolment, teaching staff etc. The information on new Institutions and development grants to Universities on different programmes in Science, Social Science and Humanities for equipment, books and journals etc. is available. Assistance provided to Central Universities recorded separately. It also has information on summer Institutes, Seminars and refresher courses, correspondence courses, area study etc. The recommendations of following committees are available.

(i) Advisory Committee of Vice-Chancellors;
(ii) Meeting with Vice-Chancellors of Southern Universities;
(iii) Review Committees;
(iv) Advisory Committee on History Programmes;
(v) Committees on Transport Economic and Transport Management;
(vi) Committee on Audio-Visual Aids in Higher Education; and
(vii) Other similar committees on various issues.

Brief account of fellowships and research scholarships has also been included in it. Text is followed by sixteen appendices and eight illustrations.

(235) 1968-69.

The Report has all the usual features and regular columns such as New Institutions, Examination Reforms, Development Programmes of teachers, students and inter-national collaborations etc., information on the steps taken for promotion and co-ordination of University education. The related problems are identified and an account of the UGC assistance programmes for improving the quality of the education is given. The development programme reviews on various aspects — International collaboration — Indo-UK Exchange programme, United States PL-480 programme, Indo-USSR Agreement of Economic and Technical co-operation, other Cultural Exchange programmes are included in it. Statistical information has been covered in twelve appendices and eight illustrations.

(236) 1969-70.

The Report has information about the policies and programmes implemented by the Commission during the reported period. Information about new Universities, Institutions deemed to be Universities, University Centres of Post-graduate studies and Examination reforms is available in brief. The subject — Medium of Education was discussed at length and recommendations have also been recorded. Subjects grants for development programmes, centre of advance study, colleges and for various programmes for teacher and student welfare, special programmes like National Lecturership and the findings of the Regional Conference of Vice-Chancellors and committee on development of computer facility are included in the report to present the progress. Main text is supported by fourteen appendices and eight illustrations showing educational statistics.

(237) 1970-71.

The Report contains studies on growth and expansion in the field of higher education for a decade. The Assessment reports of the visiting committees formulated to fund the various Universities for plan and non-plan expenditure are available. Summary of Commission's policy of promoting the publication of low-priced books, editions of standard works originally published in the USA, UK and USSR is highlighted. It contains an account of the assistance given to the Centres of Advanced Study, Colleges, Teachers Programmes — Summer Institutions, Seminars and Refresher Courses, Research publication programme and for students activities. Important information about committees and conferences constituted during the year 1970-71 by U.G.C. also included. Report contains the provisions made for utilising the services of selected teachers after their superannuation. Text is followed by thirteen appendices along with eight illustrations for statistical presentations: student enrolment, strength of teaching staff, degrees awarded during 1965-66 to 1967-68, centres of advance study, development grants paid to colleges: 1970-71 and expenditure plan and non-plan projects during 1970-71.

(238) 1971-72.

It discusses the progress of the higher education under various headings — Grants to universities, centres of advance study, Assistance to colleges programme for teachers, students, International Collaboration along with other matters. The main text is followed with thirteen appendices and seven illustrations for presenting annual statistical information on various issues of higher education.

(239) 1972-73.

The volume contains the amended UGC Act — composition, powers and functions and also the regular sections — Institutions and enrolment in Higher Education, Development of Universities and Colleges through plan and non-plan provisions, International programmes of Exchange and Collaboration, other UGC sponsored schemes — development of libraries, centres of advanced study, special assistance to selected departments, support for publication and research, area study, correspondence courses, teacher education, book publication and postgraduate centres. The publication has identified emerging problems of higher education. The main text is followed by twelve appendices and eight illustrations for statistical information.

(240) 1973-74.

Report discusses various issues such as Growth of Institutions, Enrolment of higher Education, Development of Universities, colleges and faculties along with the UGC sponsored programmes and studies on Fifth Plan proposals. The main text is supported by fourteen appendices for statistical information and for guidelines on various fields of work.

(241) 1974-75.

The report includes the Commission's efforts initiated to raise standards of universities and colleges and also brief statement about special programmes for restructuring higher education to make it more relevant for national needs. The expansion of higher education in particular undergraduate education in colleges have been taken in consideration for formulating guidelines. The other regular programmes — Rural Orientation, Vocational courses and career Advisory Bureaux, centres of advance study and department of special assistance, facilities for research and R&D work and non-formal and continuing education are discussed in brief. It has guidelines framed by the UGC for supporting universities during Fifth Plan period. The main text is followed with Eighteen appendices for statistical informations.

(242) 1975-76.

The Report has information about special measures taken for restoring normalcy in regard to academic and examination schedules. Review of the programmes such as revising and updating of syllabi, examination reforms, advanced level research, non-formal and continuing education is available. It has report on the steps initiated to extend facilities for Scheduled Caste and Scheduled Tribe. The main text is followed by eighteen appendices for statistical informations.

(243) 1976-77.

The Report reveals trends and impact of the introduction of the 10+2 schemes in number of States. It has brief note on the different schemes which are in progress for the maintenance and co-ordination of standard and the achievements of various panels working for the development of the higher education. It has mention for Correspondence courses, Adult and continuing education, Autonomous colleges, Book production norms for inclusion of postgraduate courses in science, social science and humanities in colleges and development of space research programmes. Text is followed by nineteen appendices for statistical presentation.

(244) 1977-78.

The Report reflects the trends and problems observed during Fifth Plan period and review of all the ongoing programmes of higher education run by the Universities and Colleges. It includes note on various issues — student unrest, policy framed for higher education,

Research, correspondence courses, cultural exchange, and facilities for Scheduled Castes and Scheduled Tribes. It also includes the deliberations and recommendations of two Regional Conferences of Vice-Chancellors held at New Delhi. The main text is followed by twenty-six appendices and few illustrations for presenting tabulated information on various issues.

(245) 1978-79.

The document is reflecting UGC's approach to the development of Higher Education during next plan period in the light of document — Policy frame in higher education. It reviews ongoing programmes and their impact on the standard of teaching, research and examination in the Universities. It has 37 appendices to present statistical information on UGC programmes.

(246) 1979-80.

It discusses Commission's efforts towards measures taken to ensure that there is no discontinuity in implementation of development programmes in Universities and Colleges initiated during earlier plan periods. Report contains guidelines for Sixth Plan proposals and review on the working of number of university activities. It mentions in brief on Science and Technology plan and facilities for Scheduled Castes and Scheduled Tribes. The main text is supplemented with thirty-eight appendices and with few illustrations to present statistical information collected from various universities and colleges.

(247) 1980-81.

The Report covers to all the existing sections including UGC Schemes and Studies — Growth of Institutions and students, maintenance and co-ordination of standards, cultural exchange, distance education, women education, facilities for SC/ST etc. The main text is followed by thirty-two appendices and number of illustrations, for statistics on the issues covered.

(248) 1981-82.

The Report includes the progress on various ongoing schemes and review on the findings of the subject Panels. Brief record of the steps suggested for development of library facilities in Universities and Colleges along with usual feature of reporting. The main text is followed by thirty-one appendices and few illustrations containing statistical information on various issues.

(249) 1982-83.

It contains reviews, guidelines and suggestions/recommendations on various UGC ongoing schemes during the period. It is designed in twelve sections supported with number of illustrations and thirty appendices for the statistical information.

(250) 1983-84.

It has guidelines on UGC Schemes proposed during the period, review on ongoing programmes and studies on Institutions and enrolment growth, maintenance and co-ordination of standards development of Universities, Colleges, Deemed Universities etc. Faculty improvement programme, Research fellowships and Associateships, cultural exchange, Adult and continuing education programmes and women studies etc. The main text is followed with twenty-four appendices and with illustrations containing statistical information.

(251) 1984-85.

It has continued all the twelve sections to include the review of the UGC ongoing programmes for the development of Higher Education in Indian Universities and Colleges. It has illustration and twenty-eight appendices for growth of Institutions, students enrolment, staff, doctorate degrees, centres of advanced study in science and humanities, department of special assistance, research projects and statement for grants paid to Universities and Colleges under plan and non-plan during 1984-85. Information about the Universities offering correspondence courses (1984-85) and about the computer facilities available in the Universities.

(252) 1985-86.

It presents information on quantitative growth of Institutions, enrolment of staff, maintenance and co-ordination of standards and on other various ongoing schemes is in thirteen sections. The main text is supported by thirty-six appendices and five illustrations to include related data.

(253) 1986-87.

It contains review of various ongoing UGC programmes. The findings and suggestions of various committees formulated during the period are recorded in it. As usual 13 sections along with the names of the commission members are available. It has thirty appendices and illustrations for the statistical information. Section I Part II is specially designed to highlight the progress made on New Education Policy.

(254) 1987-88.

The Report contains various aspects of higher education grouped in 15 sections. Every section has also been suitably divided into number of sub-sections to present studies in more effective manner. The first section gives quantitative growth of institutions, staff strength and accounts the following major thrust areas of the New Education Policy.

(a) Autonomous colleges;
(b) Redesigning of courses;
(c) State Councils of Higher Education;
(d) Accreditation and Assessment Councils;
(e) Alternative models of management in Universities;
(f) National qualifying test for recruitment of teachers;
(g) Making research and development broad based;
(h) Training Orientation of teachers;
(i) Improvement of efficiency;
(j) Youth and Sports; and
(k) Education for the minorities, Scheduled Caste, Scheduled Tribes, Handicapped and woman.

The other sections deal with review of subjects like Inter University Centres, COSIST programmes, standardisation, University development and other schemes such as Distance learning, cultural exchange programme and International collaborations. The last section deals with finances and organisational set up of UGC. It contains seven illustrations and seventeen photographs and number of appendices to highlight the progress of the ongoing programmes.

(255) 1988-89

The whole report is designed in 15 Sections followed with thirty-two appendices. Every Section is devoted to a particular feature such as Section I Quantitative growth of Institutions and New Education Policy. Section II is for Hi-tech areas and R&D efforts and Section III is for COSIST programmes. Maintenance and co-ordination of Standards are looked after in Section IV and Sections V, VI and VII are devoted to development of Universities and Colleges. Similarly Section IX to faculty Improvement programme and Section X to XI Student activities, Section XII to Adult Education, Section XIII to SC/ST, Section XIV to women studies and Section XV is devoted to UGC finances and organisational set-up. Thus the report is a very comprehensive review for all the ongoing programmes for one-year period. It is only authentic document on the information generated by UGC on various Academic issues.

Conferences/Workshops/Seminars

Conferences–Vice-Chancellor

(256) Vice-Chancellor's Conference, 3rd, New Delhi (1961), p. 58.

The conference volume is devoted to deliberations of the third conference of Vice-Chancellor's of Indian Universities held on 28th-29th October, 1961 in Vigyan Bhawan, New Delhi. The volume has recommendations of the Committees worked on standard of education and also on institutes of education and emotional integration. It contains addresses of Shri Jawaharlal Nehru, Shri Prem Kri, Dr. K.L. Shrimali and an article titled 'Education and the Universities' written by Dr. D.S. Kothari. The text is followed by the list of participants of the conference and illustrations presenting University education.

(257) Vice-Chancellors' Conference, New Delhi, (1962), p. 77.

Conference volume deals with the deliberations and recommendations made by the different committees on admissions, medium of instructions and related matters, on contents of education and co-ordination of research, on service conditions of college and University teachers and three-year degree course. The publication also contains the addresses of the Prime Minister, the Education Minister and the Chairman of the UGC with list of participants of the conference. In the end it has illustrations for presenting statistics on higher education and a map showing Universities in India in June, 1962.

(258) Conference of Vice-Chancellors Convened by the Ministry of Education and the University Grants Commission. 5th, New Delhi (1967), p. 66.

The volume deals with the deliberations of the fifth annual conference of the Vice-Chancellors held in Vigyan Bhawan, New Delhi, on 11th-13th Sept., 1967 for considering the report of the Education Commission with special reference to higher education. The volume also contains the addresses of the Prime Minister, the Education Minister, the Chairman of the University Grants Commission, and statement of recommendations made by the conference and the reports of the various committees. It has list of participants to the conference and illustrations for statistical information.

(259) Conference of Vice-Chancellors Convened by the Ministry of Education and Youth Services and the University Grants Commission. 6th, New Delhi (1969), p. 75.

Publication contains the deliberations of the sixth Vice-Chancellors' conference held in Vigyan Bhawan, New Delhi on April 21-23, 1969. It discusses statement of National Policy on Education (1968), examination reforms, participation of students at University level. The volume also presents addresses of the Ministry of Education and Youth Services, the Chairman of the UGC and the recommendations adopted by the conference with the reports of the various committees. In the end the list of participants is available.

(260) Conference of Vice-Chancellors Convened by the Ministry of Education, Social Welfare and Culture and University Grants Commission, 7th, New Delhi (1975), p. 216.

It is the volume of the deliberations of the seventh conference of Vice-Chancellors held at Vigyan Bhawan, New Delhi, on 30th September to 1st Oct., 1975. It has working papers on planning of higher education, quality improvement programmes and student amenities and youth development programmes. It also contains the addresses of the Prime Minister, the Education Minister, the Vice-Chairman of the UGC. The statements and recommendations made by the conference and the report of the committees along with notes considered by them are available. A list of participants is included in the end.

(261) Conference of Vice-Chancellors Convened by the Ministry of Education and Culture and University Grants Commission, New Delhi (1981).

The conference volume contains agenda papers along with recommendations of the Conference on various key issues of higher education. The volume also has addresses of the Education Minister, The Chairman, UGC, and of the members (Education, Planning Commission). In the end list of participants is given.

(262) Conference of Vice-Chancellors' Proceedings Convened by Ministry of Education and Culture and the University Grants Commission, New Delhi (1984), p. v., 84.

The Conference proceedings volume contains working papers discussed by the Conference and also the deliberations with the recommendations for implementation of various higher education programmes in Indian Universities and Colleges with support from UGC. It has the addresses of the Minister of State for Education, Culture and Social Welfare and the Chairman, UGC. The references of previous Vice-Chancellor conferences and a list for the members/delegates for conference is available in it.

(263) Conference of Vice-Chancellors, Srinagar, (1989).

The publication is in two Volumes. Volume one is Agenda

comprising four themes for discussion i.e. Infrastructural development in the University system, Development of human resource in the Universities, Colleges Academic improvements and programmes and Eighth Five Year Plan (UGC) directions. First few pages are a note from Professor Yash Pal, Chairman, UGC. Volume IV has status notes on various Academic issues: In the end it has two Annexures containing guidelines regarding, minimum number of teaching days, Examination reform and workload of teachers in universities and also on Schemes of Autonomous departments/ Centres/Schools within the University set-up.

Conference — Principals

(264) Conference of Principals — Report, New Delhi, (1964), p. 33.

The volume is the outline of the recommendations of the conference held during 8th – 9th May, 1964, of the College Principals, members of the Commission, and representatives of the Planning Commission and Ministry of Education. The conference worked under three groups under Chairmanship of Principals of the Colleges. It has addresses of the Member Planning Commission, the Chairman, UGC, and the Secretary, UGC. Separate recommendations of the Committee on improvement of Collegiate education programmes for students, teachers welfare, and conditions of affiliation and grant-in-aid rules for colleges are included. The main text is followed by two appendices for list of participants and members of the various committees.

Conference – Student Representatives

(265) Conference of Student Representatives Convened by the Ministry of Education and Youth Services and the University Grants Commission, Delhi (1969), p. 26.

Publication consists the recommendations of the three committees, carried out the work of the Conference of Student representatives, convened by the Ministry of Education and Youth Services and the University Grants Commission, held in Delhi Schools of Economics, Delhi University, on May 23-25, 1969. The Conference discussed the following items.

Student participation in University affairs/Curriculum and Examination reform/Employment opportunities and related problems/The role of student advisory and guidance bureau/ National Service Scheme and/The role of Student organisations in University life.

The main text is followed by two appendices for a note on the training and placement units in Indian Institute of Technology and for a report on vacation employment project undertaken by the University Employment Information and Guidance Bureau; Bombay, for the Summer 1968. List of participants is also available in the end.

Occasional Notes

(266) Occasional Notes. 1(1) (1968), p. 22.

The publication is an official organ to publicise the UGC Schemes and programmes. It contains information on summer Institutes and Schools, Seminars and Conferences, Centres of Advance Study, Cultural exchange programme, Research scholarship, Review committees, Institute of Himalayan Geology, International Union of Biological Sciences and Royal Commission on medical Education in U.K. etc.

(267) Occasional Notes. 1(1) (1969), p 53.

The publication is an official organ to give publicity to various schemes of the UGC. This issue contains summary recommendations on the various programmes — National Service Corps, National Service Schemes, Planning of book development in Asia and information about — National lectures. It has review of UGC Schemes and U.K. assistance to Centres of Advanced Study in Indian Universities. The main text is followed by three annexures.

(268) UGC Bulletin. 1(1) 1972, p 39.

The volume is the first issue of the publication UGC Bulletin which includes information on various UGC Schemes — National lecturership and Associateship, Award of fellowships during 1972-73, Orientation Courses, Cultural Exchange, Organisation of Seminar, Symposia conference and Workshops, and refresher courses during

1972-73. It has summary recommendations of Advisory Committee of Vice-Chancellors. Brief note on Indo-British discussions on University collaborations and Conferences on education is followed by the enrolment growth in the University of Delhi.

(269) UGC Bulletin. 1(2) 1972, p 40.

It contains brief information on the UGC programmes such as UNESCO Assistance to Centres of Advanced Study, College Science improvement programme, republication of low priced publication editions of standard works originally published in USA, UK and USSR, scheme of utilisation of services of retired teachers towards teaching of research work, organisation of seminars, symposia, conferences, workshops and orientation of refresher courses during 1972-73. Cultural exchange programmes, higher education and correspondence courses in the Soviet Union, recent trends of University development in India, support for scientific research, scheme of National Fellowships, National lecturerships award for 1972-73, summer Institute in social sciences and data on enrolment and posts etc.

Bulletin of Higher Education

(270) Bulletin of Higher Education 1(1) 1975, p. 39.

The periodical contains official information on the schemes and policies formulated by the Commission for raising academic standards or for restructuring the existing system. Guidelines on ongoing schemes — Introduction of Correspondence Courses, postgraduate courses, Reservation of SC/ST in Selection of UGC Research Associateships and Fellowships, Assistance under book bank Scheme having enrolment up to 250 to 500 students and preparation of University level books by Indian Authors, information on various programmes such as area study, support for centres of advanced study and projects sanctioned in Humanities and Social Sciences during Fifth-Five Year Plan. It also contains the recommendations of Zonal workshops on Autonomous Colleges, Examination reforms and development of postgraduate education in college during Fifth-Five Year Plan.

(271) Bulletin of Higher Education. 2 (1&2), 1976, p iv, 104.

The Bulletin carries official information about policies and schemes of the Commission. This issue has information on many important ongoing schemes and outlines of the Fifth Plan development programme for the Universities and Colleges. Also includes lists of Advanced research projects in Humanities and Social Sciences, Major Research projects in Science and titles of writing of University level books sanctioned by Commission during the Fifth Plan. It includes in the end the names of the commission members.

(272) Bulletin of Higher Education, 2(3), 1977, p vi, 51.

This issue of the Bulletin gives in brief, a midplan review of the work of the Panels in the Humanities and Social Sciences. It has recommendations of the UGC Standing Committee on the development of colleges during the plan period and recommendations on the implementation of several new programmes as part of the faculty improvement programmes. An account of selected, advanced, research projects in humanities and social sciences and Guidelines for development of centralised facilities such as workshops, University service and instrumentation centres, regional instrumentation centres, science education centres, computer facilities, regional library centres and national associateship have also been outlined. The modification in various schemes have been incorporated for publicity.

(273) Bulletin of Higher Education, 3 (1,2 & 3), 1978, p. 42.

This issue of the bulletin contains the Policy frame for the consideration of the academic community. Detailed information on the various schemes and programmes have been published in order to create a greater awareness in the Universities and Colleges.

Recommendations of the UGC Standing Committee on the development of Colleges: regarding liberalisation of grants for colleges; teacher fellowship programme; Centre of Advance Studies, Department of Special assistance in Universities; Scheme of Research Associateship; Scheme of National Associateship; Scheme of Special Visiting Professorships and Associateships; Scheme of Career award to young Scientist; Scheme of Unassigned grant to

Universities and Scheme of preparation of University level books by Indian authors are included. In the end Journal of Higher Education; Vol 2 Contents and list for priced and unpriced publications of the UGC is also available.

(274) Bulletin of Higher Education. 4(1,2&3), 1979, p 60.

The bulletin is an effort to keep teachers, students and educationists well informed about various activities and programmes of the UGC. It consists summarised report and recommendations of five committees constituted to advise the Commission regarding implementation of the policy frame, viz.

(1) Adult Education and Extension Programme.
(2) Criteria for Evaluation of Colleges.
(3) Regulation of student admission with facilities for weaker sections.
(4) Introduction of Regional language as Media of instructions.
(5) Role and responsibility of teachers.

It contains the report of the Committee on the reorganisations of courses at the undergraduate level and the recommendations of the joint consultative Committees on Agricultural, Medical and legal education. Other matters discussed are implementation of Examination reforms in the various Universities, University services and Instrumentation centres and the scheme of career awards to young scientists in Science, Engineering and Technology. Finally, the bulletin contains guidelines for the promotion of Gandhian studies in Universities. *Journal of Higher Education*, vol. 3 contents and bibliography of unpriced UGC publication issued after 1971 is included.

(275) Bulletin of Higher Education. 5(1&2) 1980, p 38.

The bulletin has official information on the following ongoing schemes of the UGC.

- Approach to the development of Higher Education in the Sixth Plan (Approved by Regional Conference of Vice-Chancellors).

- Revised Scheme for utilisation of services of Retired teachers.
- Special Assistance for Scheduled Castes and Scheduled Tribes student.
- Career Awards to young Social Scientists.
- Faculty improvement programmes scheme: UGC Committee recommendations.
- Criteria for viability of colleges.
- Travel grants to teachers from colleges for presenting their papers at International Conferences.
- Financial Assistance to full time research scholars working in Universities and Colleges for visits Abroad either in connection with the research work or for attending International Conferences.
- UGC Scheme for promoting performing arts.
- Contents of the *Journal of Higher Education*, Vol. 4, Nos. 1, 2 & 3, 1978-79.

(276) Bulletin of Higher Education. 5(3), 1981, p 35.

The Bulletin contains official information about Commission programmes: regional imbalances in the development of Higher Education, increase in the value of Junior and Senior research fellowships, Associateships in Sciences, Humanities and Social Sciences. It also contains guidelines for the appointment of visiting professor/visiting fellows/Professors of Eminence in the Universities, restructuring of courses and introduction of correspondence courses. The contents of the *Journal of Higher Education*, Vol. 5 and bibliography of unpriced publication is also available in the end.

(277) Bulletin of Higher Education, 6(1), 1981, p 28.

The issue of Bulletin contains the guidelines for assistance to Arts, Science and Commerce and multifaculty college for development during the Sixth Plan period through various UGC Schemes. It has information on University postgraduate centres, publications of learned/research work including doctoral thesis during 1980-81 and 1981-82. It has an account of travel grants to college teachers given for attending International conferences abroad for presenting their papers, activities under National Integration Samitis in Universities and Colleges. Contents of Vol. 6 of the *Journal of Higher Education* 1980-81 are followed by the list of UGC publications.

(278) Bulletin of Higher Education. 6(2&3), 1982, p 36.

Bulletin contains revised guidelines for colleges development during Sixth Plan period and for Adult and continuing education programmes. It also contains a list of UGC priced and unpriced publications.

(279) Bulletin of Higher Education. 7(1-3), 1983, p 36.

This issue of the publication publishes the revised guidelines for restructuring of courses of first degree level and for visiting professors/visiting fellows. It has information on the schemes such as Assistance for participation in International Conferences Abroad and publication of learned/Research Work. In the end it has contents of the *Journal of Higher Education*, Vol. 7 and list of UGC publications.

(280) Bulletin of Higher Education, 8(1,2&3), 1983, p. 35.

This volume contains revised guidelines for college development during Sixth Plan period. Identification of colleges located in Backward areas, Assistance for single faculty colleges for postgraduate education etc, and for visiting Professors/Fellows. It also has UGC minimum qualifications for the appointment of teaching staff in Universities. Notifications for the prescribed qualification for the appointment of teachers in different faculties and a list of unpriced UGC publication is available with it.

(281) Bulletin of Higher Education. 8(1), 1984, p. 58.

It contains review and detailed information about approved major research projects in Humanities and Social Sciences. Eight statistical tables are included to present data in various forms. In the end it has list for priced and unpriced UGC publications.

(282) Bulletin of Higher Education. 9(2&3), 1984, p. 47.

The volume has guidelines for minimum programme of examination reform, minimum number of actual teaching days in an academic year and workload of teachers in various subjects and for selection procedure for appointment of teaching staff in Universities and Colleges. It also contains a review, of major research projects in Science, Engineering and technology and UGC's policy programme for improvement of research in the Universities. Summary of the activities at the Adult Education and Centres and population education clubs is available in it. In the end eleven appendices presents statistical information on various issues of the work.

(283) Bulletin of Higher Education. 10(1&2), 1986, p. 24.

The Bulletin is an official publication which contains UGC regulations (amendment) 1985 regarding minimum qualifications for appointment of lecturers in English, revised guidelines for visiting professors and visiting fellows, Faculty improvement for Home Science teachers in colleges, setting of administrative Sub-Centres in Universities, schemes of planning forms through Universities and Colleges, Physical Conditions Unit in the Universities and a list of UGC publication, etc.

(284) Bulletin of Higher Education, 10(3), 1986, p. 61.

This issue of the Bulletin contains guidelines for development of woman studies in Universities and Colleges and pattern of duration of first degree courses followed by Universities. It also has statement about new courses introduced and new department set-up and M.Phil courses offered in the Universities during 1984-85. In the end index to Vol. 10 of *Journal of Higher education* is enclosed.

(285) Bulletin of Higher Education. 11 (1,2&3), 1988, p. 74.

The volume contains guidelines of grant for development of undergraduate education during the Seventh Plan, faculty improvement programme, travel grant scheme, teacher education and teacher training colleges, publication of learned/Research work including doctoral thesis etc. It has also rules for leave and utilisation of contingency grant under the scheme. Teacher Fellowship and recommendations made by UGC for different types of buildings. Information about new courses, new departments, courses offered through correspondence and pattern of duration of first degree courses in Indian Universities included list for UGC publications as on 1st Feb., 1988, is also included.

Journal of Higher Education

The Journal of Higher Education is published by the University Grants Commission to promote discussion of contemporary problems and policies in, as well as scholarly study of higher education. The journal is issued thrice a year: Monsoon, Autumn and Spring. Views expressed in the contributions are those of the authors and the Commission or the journal are not committed to them. This is a continued publication.

The 13 volumes have been brought out so far. A bibliography along with number of indexes for all the articles, research notes and communications appeared in volumes published so far is followed. The publication of Hindi version *(Uchch Siksha)* is in progress.

(287) Sponsored Publication:

The UGC has initiated sponsoring quarterly Journals such as Physics education, Mathematics education, Biology education and Chemistry education. These journals provide forum for exchange of ideas on innovating in teaching new curricula and educational technology. The publications are priced and available from McMillon Publishers India.

(288) Towards New Educational Management — Report (1990), p. 384.

The Committee worked under the Chairmanship of Professor A. Gnanam. The Committee resolved that higher education has an important role to play not only for Academic persuit and augmenting knowledge but also towards national development. University management has to play a crucial role to enable the system to discharge its role. The main emphasis has been put to provide a sound scientific framework for governance of Universities.

UGC Letter

'UGC letter' is a bi-monthly publication to disseminate UGC news in the academicians working in large Indian higher education system. The publication is also issued in Hindi under title "UGC Patra".

SECTION III

APPENDICES CONSISTING REFERENCES, BOOKS AND JOURNALS ON EDUCATION IN INDIA AND ABROAD

APPENDIX-I

The Articles, Research Notes and Communications Appeared in UGC's Journal of Higher Education from Vol. 1–14.

Adhaoo, S.H. and Vanjani, S.S. (1983), Agricultural Engineering Research and the Role of Agricultural Universities in India, 8(3) p. 381-84

Agarwal, Bina (1977), Exploitative Utilization of Educate Woman Power, 2. p. 185

Ahmad, Karuna Chanana (1982), From Secondary to Higher Education : Focus on Women, 9(3) p. 349

Ahuja, Chaman (1982), Theater Education in Indian Universities, 8(1) p. 97-101

Alain, Touraine (1982), Decline of Transformation of the Universities, 8(1) p. 1-8

Albert, D. (1985), Adjustable Internal Assessment, 10(3) p. 286-89

Altbach, Philip G. (1977), Scholarly Publishing in the Third World, 2 p. 295

Altbach, Philip G. (1979), The University as Centre and Periphery, 4 p. 157

Altbach, Philip G. (1986), The Foreign Student Dilemma, 2(1,2) p. 89-110

ltbach, Philip G. (1980), The Crisis of the Professoriate, 5(3) p. 317

Ambirajan, S. (1984), The Role of Humanities and Social Sciences in Engineering Education., 9(3) p. 333-48

Amrik Singh. (1981), Foundation and Role of UGC, 7(1-2)

Amrik Singh (1983), The Dynamics of Change, 9(2) p. 197-207

Anand, C.L. (1978), Professional Training of College Teachers through M.C.T. Degree Course, 3, p. 351

Anand, S.P. (1988-89), Teacher's Accountability an Analysis, 14(1-2) p. 186-91.

Anandalakshmy, S. (1984), Status of Home Science : A Summary of Views of Home Science Teachers in Indian Universities, 10(1-2) p. 120-21.

Anantha Krishnan, M.V. (1982), Purposeful Physics Curricula : A Systems Model, 8(1) p. 41-52

Anantha Krishnan, M.V. (1983), Science-technology Interaction : A Systems Model for Education, 9(2) p. 229-34

Anil Bhatt and H.C. Shukul (1977), Evaluation of Teachers by Students, 2 p. 415

Ankleshwaria, Zinah T. (1984), An Experimental Study to Investigate the Relative Effectiveness of Different Strategies to Teach Nutrition to Home Science College Students of Varying Intelligence, 10 (1-2) p. 84-89.

Anand, H.R. (1985-86), Ten Point Scale of Student Evaluation, 11(1-2) p. 199-201.

Ansari, M.M. (1988-89), Financial Health of Universities: A Diagnostic Study, 14(1-3) p. 65-86.

Aqueil Ahmad (1980), The Agricultural University as a Multifunctional System, 5(1) p. 57

Arnikar, H.J. (1976), Object Analysis of Study Courses, 1(3)

Asa Briggs (1983), The Higher Education Scene in Britain Today, 9(1) p. 47

Asoke Basu (1981), Politics of Academics : A Comparative Review, 7(102) p. 59.

Ashok Kumar and Darshan Anand (1982), A Comparative Study of the Value Patterns of Science and Commerce Undergraduates, 7(3) p. 277-79

Aswathanarayana, U. (1976), Towards Excellence in the Teaching of Geological Science at the Postgraduate Level, 1(3).

Azad, J.L. (1977), State Grants to Collegiate Institutions : A Study of Patterns and Procedures, 2. p.243

Bakhshish Singh (1979), World Conference on Correspondence Education, 4(1-3), p. 264

Bahuguna, S.D. (1977), Riding an Unbridled Horse, 2. p.267

Balachandran, Ethel, S. (1984), Certain Factors Governing the Teaching-learning Process Self-Assessment by College Teachers, 10(1-2) p. 90-94

Balu, S.A. and Chandran, G.S. (1980), Inter Examiner variability in Assessing Answer Scripts of Engineering Science, 5(2) p. 224

Bandyopadhyay, Swaraj and Bhattachaya, Swapan K. (1978), Student Unrest in an Unplanned University : A Case Study, 3 p. 381

Banerji, Meera and Krishna Mohan (1984), General English Syllabuses : A Critical Review, 10(3) p. 233-42.

Banerjee, Sushanta and Malhotra, Ashok (1978), Higher Education : Frames of Reference in Existing Literature, 3 p. 301.

Barun De (1988-89), The Heritage of Our Educational Framework, 14 (1-3) p. 1-17.

Baruah, M.K. and Sarma, M.K. (1985), Distribution of Intelligence among Students Pursuing Different Courses of Higher Education, 10(3) p. 262-70

Bhattacharjee, S. (1986-87), Effects of Projects on Teaching in Educational Institutions, 12(1-3) p. 174-76

Beena Shah (1985-86), Co-curricular Participation Caste and Educational Development, 11(1&2) p. 182-86.

Beverley Lindsay (1987-88), African-American Woman in American Higher Education, 13(1-3) p. 69-86.

Bhagia, N.M. et al. (1988-89), Role Performance of Heads of Colleges, 14(1-3) p. 139-50.

Bharat Bhushan (1984), Interactional Affect of Length Style and Handwriting in Evaluation, 9(3) p. 392-94.

Bharat Bhushan (1984), Open book Examination at Postgraduate Stage : An Investigation, 10(1-2) p. 97-100.

Bhaskara Rao (1986-87), Indira Gandhi National Open University – System and Communication, 12(1-3)p. 180-84.

Bhaskara Rao, P. (1985), The UGC Study Centres: Nature and Performance — A Case Study of Andhra University Centres, 10(3) p. 291.

Bhaskara Rao, V. (1979), Teaching and Research in Higher Education: Some Problems, 4 p. 11.

Bhattacharyya, B.K. (1983), Selection of Candidates for Professional Education, 8(3) p. 390-400

Bhattacharyya, P.K. (1978), Development of Need Based Curricula in Post-Graduate Education in Organic Chemistry, 3p. 181.

Bhattacharya, Swapan K. and Manabendra Nath Pal (1977), Management Information Systems in University Administration, 2 p. 213.

Bhatt, G.K. (1982), Profitability of Private Investment in Higher Education in Rajasthan, 8(1) p. 85-89.

Bhiday, M.R. (1980), Integration of Higher Education for Effective Vocational Training, 5(3) p. 371.

Bisht, Abha Rani (1982), Approval/Disapproval of Strike Culture : A Sample Survey of Students, Guardians and Teachers, 7(3) p. 272-76.

Bora, A.C. (1982), An Alternative Approach of Measuring Students Performance for Different Recruitments, 8(2) p. 215.

Bose, P.K. and Mukherjee, S.P. (1980), Graduate Employment and Higher Education in West Bengal, 5(3) p. 281.

Bose, P.K. (1984-85), Role of University in Pursuit of Quality Science, 10(1-2) p. 101-104.

Brahm Prakash (1978), The Demand for and Financing of Higher Education in Canada, 3 p. 345.

Chakravarty, Kumaresh (1971), Administration of Higher Education: An Overview, 2 p. 223.

Chalam, K.S. (1979), Expenditure on University Education : A Unit Cost Analysis, 4 p.201.

Chandra, A. and Khanna, Aparna H. (1983), Selected Social Norms of the Home Science Students, 8(3) p. 356-62.

Chandrakant, L.S. et al, (1982), New Perspectives for Technical Education – Industry Interaction, 7(3) p. 201-10

Chandrashekaran, M.K. (1980), Teaching Chronobiology in Indian Universities, 5(3) p. 343.

Chandrashekarappa, M.S. (1988-89), Field Work and the Social Work Trainee, 14(3) p. 157-64.

Chatterjee, Bishwa B. (1978), Unrest in Universities : The American Scene, 3 p. 65.

Chatterjee, B.B. (1983), Social Costs of Reservation in Higher Education, 9(1) p. 77.

Chaudhary, P.N. and Agrawal, K.G. (1978), Professional Obsolescence and the Role of Continuing Education, 3 p. 73.

Christopher, Orpen (1982), How much Role Conflict is there in the Job of University Lecturer : An International Comparison, 7(3) p. 260-65.

Christopher, Orpen (1983), Student Evaluation of Instructors, 9(1) p. 89

Christopher, Orpen (1987-88), Evaluation and Improvement of University Teaching, 13 (1-3) p. 47-62.

Coombs, Philip, H. (1981), Future Critical World Issues in Education: A Provisional Report of Findings, 7(1-2) p. 1.

Darji, D.R. and Sharma, D.K. (1982), Decision-making and Faculty Participation, 7(3) p. 266-71.

Das, P.C. (1980), Selection of Courses of Study by P.U. (Sc.) Students, 5(2) p. 236.

Dasgupta, Sugata (1976), Social Work Education : A Critique of the Classical Model, 1(3)

Datta, Bhabatosh (1979), Presidency College, Calcutta, 4 p. 14.

Datta, Bhabatosh (1980-81), Social Science Research: Universities and Autonomous Institutions, 6(1-3) p. 15-24.

Datt, Ruddar (1978), Higher Education and Future Educational Policy, 3(1, 2&3) p. 189.

Datt, Ruddar (1985-86), Distance Education in India, 11(1-2) p. 191-98.

Datt, Ruddar (1980-81), Cost and Efficiency of the different Techniques of Education in Delhi University, 6(1-3) p. 71-82.

Datt, Ruddar (1984), Planning and Development of Distance Education, 9(3) p. 305-10.

Dave, P.N. (1929), Can we Help Ourselves Teach Better? — A Case Study of Series of Teaching Workshops at BITS, Pilani, 4 p. 108.

David Beswick and Paul Rams (1987-88), Curiosity and Learning with Understanding in the First Year, 13(1-3) p. 29-46.

Daya Krishna (1978), Social Philosophy, 3 p. 117.

Deb, B.M., Sabata, B.K. and Biswas, A.B. (1977), Teaching, Innovation and Assessment in University Chemical Education, 2 p. 19.

Deousker, Mahesh and Kharc, M.P. (1985), Cost of Higher Education per Student, 10(3) p. 247-61.

Deousker, M.D. (1977), A Study into the Causes of Selection of Subjects by Students at Postgraduate Level, 2 p. 106.

Desai, Neera (1978), The Pattern of Higher Education of Women and Role of A Women's University, 3 p.5.

Devadatta, Dabholkar (1980-81), Striving for Height in Higher Education, 6(1-3) p. 41-50.

Devadoss, M. (1984), Power, Involvement and Organisational Effectiveness, 9(3) p. 407.

Dhanagare, D.N. (1981), Interdisciplinary Approach to Social Reality, 7(1-2) p. 97.

Dhawle, Anand S. (1978), Role of Institution Heads in Effective Utilisation of Libraries, 3 p. 278.

Dhawle, Anand S. and Ghose, Amitabha (1978-79), A Study of the Image of Indian Journals on Management and Social Sciences in the International Academic Community, 4 (1, 2 and 3) p. 313.

Dietrich, Goldschmidt (1983), The University as an Institution: Present Problems and Future Trends, 9(1) p. 65.

Dinesh Mohan (1983), Indian Education: The Anti-Cultural Involution, 9(1) p. 21.

Dube, S.C. (1980-81), Environment and the Challenge of Educational Management, 6(1-3) p. 9-14.

Dubey, V.K. and Prasad, C. (1977), Teaching, Research and Extension in Indian Agricultural Universities, 2 p. 393.

Eisemon, T. (1976), Some Predictors of Institutional Satisfaction: A Study of Engineering Faculty, 1(3).

Ekambaram, E.J. (1980), Teaching English by Correspondence, 5(2) p. 252.

Ettore Gelpi (1984), Intercultural Cooperation in Higher Education, 9(3) p. 323-32.

Fernandes, Julie B. (1988-89), Evaluation of Practical/Laboratory Examinations in Indian Universities, 14(1-3) p. 165-70.

Filella, S.J. (1978), College Teaching in India: An Academic Function : A Personal Relationship of Coaching for Examinations, 3 p. 321.

Frederick Wasser (1983), The Functional and Problems of Urban University in the West: A Comparative Perspective, 8(3) p. 375-80.

Furqan Qamar (1984), Financial Management: An Imperative to Temples of Higher Learning, 9(3) p. 403-406.

Gabriel, P.J. and Pillai, J.K. (1980-81), The Effectiveness of Modular Scheduling in Higher Education, 6(1-3) p. 128-30.

Ganesan, D. Raja (1977), Making Philosophy Utility-Oriented, 2 p. 357.

Gangrade, K.D. (1976), Intergeneration Difference — A Study in the Generation Gap, 1(3)

Garg, V.P. (1982), Private Costs in Higher Education, 8(2) p. 220.

Gargi Dutt (1980), Higher Education in China, 5(2) p. 157.

Ganguly, S.N. (1976), Social Philosophy — A Counter Definition of Philosophy, 1(3)

Garg, Kailash Chandra (1982), Peer Review in Science, 7(3) p. 321-23

Garrett, C. Jeanne and Garret, Larry N. (1980), Policy Analysis as an Adjunct Tool in the Prevention or Resolution on Managerial Crises in Higher Education, 5(1) p. 13.

George, P.T. (1984), Why Raju Fails to Learn English, 9(3) p. 399-402.

Gidadhubli, R.G. (1977), Some Aspects of Higher Education in the Soviet Union, 2 p. 149.

Gill, Sarjit Singh and Randhawa, T.S. (1984), Role of Colleges in Rural Development, 10(1-2) p. 73-76.

Girish Bala (1978), A Comparative Study of Adjustment Pattern of Girls in Co-Education Colleges and Women Colleges, 3 p. 405.

Giri, Mehtab (1980-81), The Changing Pattern of University Academic Controls over Affiliated Colleges, 6(1-3) p. 151-52.

Godbole, R.D. (1982), A Close Look at Sample 'Multiple' Choice Question of ETS., 7(3) p. 317-18.

Godbole, R.D. (1982), Is Adequate Coverage, a Strong Point of a Multiple-Choice Objective Test?, 8(2) p. 248-50.

Godbole, R.D. (1983), Merit List on the Basis of Scores is not Valid, 9(2) p. 269-70.

Godbole, R.D. (1986-87), Objective Tests (MCT) Inadequate for College and University, 12(1-3) p. 91-100.

Goel, S.C. (1977), Examination Reforms : A New Perspective, 2 p. 49.

Ghose, A.M. (1979), Modernisation of our . . . and Syllabi in the Humanities and the Social Sciences, 4 p. 75.

Gomathi, Mani (1980), A Sample Study of Evaluation of Teacher by Students, 5(2) p. 288.

Gore, M.S. (1977), Social Work Education, 2 p. 413.

Greville, Rumble (1984), The Open University of the United Kingdom, 10(1-2) p. 45-56.

Gunasekaran, K. (1980), A Survey of the Reappearance Cases in M.A., M.Sc., and M.Com. Semester Courses of the Madras University, 5(2) p. 220

Gunasekaran, K. (1982), An Experimental Study to Test the Superiority of Direct Grading Method, 7(3) p. 288-92.

Gupta, Dipankar (1982), Knowledge and the State : A Critique of Practical Science, 7(3) p. 189-200.

Gupta, J.P. (1984)), CCTV System in Higher Education : Hopes and Fears, 10(1-2) p. 114-16.

Gupta, L.P. (1979), A Study of Personality Syndromes and Cognitive Characteristics of Scheduled Castes, Backward Classes and Non-Scheduled Castes Students, 4 p. 381.

Gupta, M.P. (1980), A Critical Study of Evaluation Under Different Systems of Agricultural Education, 5(1)

Gupta, M.P. and Sandhu, N.S. (1978), An Analytical Study of Trimester System of Education, 3 p. 257.

Gupta, M.P. (1979), An Analytical Study of Semester System of Education, 4 p. 41.

Gupta, M.P. (1982), Role of Media Technology in Rural Education, 8(2) p. 239.

Gupta, Madan Lal (1983), Productivity Trends in Correspondence Education, 8(3) p. 349-55.

Gupta, M.L. (1986-87), Finance of Correspondence Education, 12(1-3) p. 159-68.

Gupta, S.K. (1982), Distance Education --- Problems of Co-ordination, Co-operation and Functional Autonomy, 7(3) p. 237-42.

Gupta, S.P. (1984), Second Examination: Effect on the Results of Science Postgraduate Students of Allahabad University, 10(1-2) p. 95-96.

Gupta, Sunita (1983), Value Structure of Higher Education and the University Teachers, 9(2) p. 254-58.

Gurumurthy, K.G. (1979), University Education and Rural Development, 4 p. 353.

Haecht, Anne Van (1980-81), Social Change and the Educational System, 6(1-3) p. 105-16.

Hara, Michael O. (1982), The Myth of Staff Development at the Tertiary Level of Education, 7(3) p. 297-302.

Haragopal, G. and Jagannadha Rao, K. (1979), Problems and Perceptions of Social Science Teachers in Higher Education, 4 p. 67.

Harikesh Singh (1979), Obscurantism Among the University Students, 4 (1, 2&3) p. 91

Hassan, Parveen Akhtar (1988), A Paradigm for the Success of Semester, 10(3) p. 290.

Higginson, J.H. (1985), Calcutta University Commission, 10(3) p. 215-24.

Hussain, M.A. (1981), Continuing Education and its Role in Human Resource Development in India, 7(1-2) p. 123.

Indapurkar, C.D. (1980), A Philosophical Analysis of Methods of Teaching at the Higher Education Stage, 5(1) p.7.

Indra Deva (1982), Latest Function of Higher Education in India, 7(3) p. 211-18.

Indira, R. (1987), Academic and Professional Carrier of Engineering College Teachers, 13(1-3) p. 115-20.

Indiresan, J. (1979), The Examinee : The Neglected Factor in the Examination, 4 p. 268.

Iyer, T.S. K.V. and Krishnamurthy, V. (1978), Examination Reform Innovations in Teaching and Learning, 2 p. 83.

Jacques Hallak (1979), Higher Education in France : Recent Trends, 5(1) p. 1.

Jaganath Pathy (1982), Progressive Students in Community Education, 7(3) p. 315-16.

Jaganath Pathy (1985-86), Social Science Research in Vietnam, 11(1-2) p. 77-88.

Jain, H.C. (1986-87), The Social Location of Knowledge, 12(1-3) p. 19-28.

Jain, M.L. (1980), Continuing Engineering Education, 5(1) p. 51.

Jaleel, Sahed and Sathiyagirirajan, S. (1979), A Study of Scientific Attitude of College Teachers, p. 387.

Jasdanwalla, Z.Y. (1977), Teaching of English, 2 p. 419

Jandhyala, B.G. Tilak (1980), Unit Cost Analysis of Higher Education in India, 5(2) p. 183.

Jayaram, N. (1978), Social Implication of Medical Education in India, 3 p. 207.

Jayaram, N. (1984), Philanthropy and Cultural Imperialism: The Foundation at Home and Abroad, 10(1-2) p. 23-28.

Jayagopal, R. and Nagarajan, V. (1977), Methodological Problems in Innovating Evaluation System, 2 p. 95.

Jayagopal, R. (1979), University and Emerging Educational Technologies for Adult and Continuing Education, 4 p. 365.

Jayalakshmi, Indiresan (1980), A Comparative Study of the Attitudes of Social Science and Engineering Students to Certain Aspects of Higher Education, 5(2) p. 233.

Jayalakshmi, Indiresan and Kanakaraj, K. (1982), Have 'Question Banks' Improved the Quality of Question Papers?, 8(2) p. 199.

Jayalakshmi, Indiresan (1984), Profile and Index of the Polytechnique — Industry Collaboration — an Empirical Study, 10(1-2) p. 29-44.

John Eggleston (1980), Developments in British Tertiary Education, 5(3) p. 301.

John, Dreijmanis (1978), From Weimar to Washington : The Plight of the Intelligentsia, 3 p. 227.

Jos, C.A. (1987-88), Co-operation and Banking Programmes of the Kerala Agricultural University, 13(1-3) p. 121-24.

Joseph, A. and Nagarajan, M. (1988-89), Teaching of Drama in the ESL Curriculum, 14(1-3) p. 171-77.

Joseph, A. (1986-87), Towards Implementing the Project Work at the Undergraduate Level, 12(1-3) p. 169-73.

Joshi, P.C. (1982), Social Science Research and the Institutes, 8(2) p. 155

Joshi, P.C. (1986-87), Social Science and the Government, 12(1-3) p. 1-18.

Joshi, A.W. (1979), What Ails the Indian University — An Essay, 4 p. 280.

Joshi, K.L. (1980-81), 25 years of UGC — Dilemmas and Difficulties, 6(1-3) p. 63-70.

Joshi, B.S. (1977), Problems of Chemical Education and Research, 2 p. 367.

Joshi, D.C. (1977), The National Service Scheme — A Venture of Faith, 2 p. 115.

Joshi, D.C. (1979), The Management of a Department of Studies in a Unitary University, 4 p. 417.

Joshi, D.C. (1978), Researches in Higher Education, 3 p. 399.

Jonathan, Goldstein (1985-86), Teaching the Indo-American China War, 11(1-2) p. 137-44.

Jha, M.L. (1977), Education and Abolition of Untouchability, 2 p. 401.

Jhunjhunwala, Bharat (1977), Management Education and Development., 2 p. 412.

Julka, Satyapal (1982), Models of Education System: Pitfalls Ignoring Socio-economic Variables, 7(3) p. 319-20.

Kamal Nayan Kabra (1978), Brain Drain — The Missing Perspective, 3 p. 221.

Kakkar, S.B. (1979), Student Attitudes Towards College vis-a-vis University, 4 p. 258.

Kalidas Deshpande (1977-78), Area Based Resource-cum- research Centre — A Role for Colleges to play, 3(1, 2 & 3) p. 89.

Kamat, A.R. (1982), Higher Education: Kothari Commission and After, 8 (2) p. 141.

Karuna Ahmad (1980), Equity and Women's Higher Education, 5(1) p. 33.

Kathiresan, K. (1985-86), Expectation of MBA Participants, 11(1-2) p. 175-81.

Khader, M.A. and Sushila Singhal (1983), Institutional Quality, Student Input and Output: Analysis of Six Indian Universities, 9(1) p. 35.

Khader, M.A. (1985), Predictors of Academic Success Analysis of School and College Achievement, 10(3) p. 201-14.

Khadria, Binod Kumar (1979), Brain Drain — The Missing Perspective: A Comment., 4 p. 101.

Khalid Ahmed Kazi and Rehana Ghadially (1980), Hopes and Concerns of Engineering Students in India, 5(3) p. 401.

Khan, Q.U. (1980), Higher Education in India — Some Issues, 5(2) p. 167.

Khan, M.Z. and Singh, D.R. (1979), College Youth, their Courses of Study and their View of Society, 4 p. 57.

Kishore Sant (1982), Universities and People's Education for Development, 8(2) p. 185.

Krishna Kumar (1977), English Studies in India, 2 p. 13.

Krishnamurthy, V. (1978), Can we Help Ourselves Teach Better : A Case Study of Series of Teaching Workshops at BITS, Pilani, 3 p. 149.

Krishnaswami, O.R. (1978), An Approach to Modernization of Commerce Courses, 2 p. 267.

Krishnaraj Maithreyi (1978), Employment Pattern of University — Educated Women and its Implications, 2 p. 317.

Kothari, V.N. et al. (1982), Access to Higher Education and Equalisation of Educational Opportunities Through Freeship: A Case Study, 8(1) p. 74-78.

Kuppuswamy, G. and Natarajan, R. (1985-86), Media in Engineering Education, 11(1-2) p. 127-36.

Kuppuswamy, G. and Natarajan, R. (1988-89), Lecture Method: Strategy for Improvement, 14(1-3) p. 87-100.

Kurien, C.T. (1978), An Open and Participatory College Administration, 2 p. 203.

Kundu, M. (1982), Teaching in a Poly-Cultural Context, 8(2) p. 191

Lakshminarayana, U.A. Vizaya Dattatreya Sarma (1980), Social Economic and Academic Awareness and Position of Collegiate Teachers — A Study, 5(3) p. 395.

Lalitha, M.S. and Sawaranjit Toor (1980), A Study of Awareness to the Indian Social Problems as Evinced by the Post-graduate Students of Bangalore University, 5(1) p. 96.

Lata Murugkar (1983), Development of Goals and Women's Higher Education, 8(3) p. 321-26.

Leela Inamdar (1982), Academy of Science, USSR Structure and Function, 8(1) p. 9-18.

Lumsden, D. Barry (1983), Preparing Future Educational Leaders to write for Scholarly Publication, 9(2) p. 279-81.

Mahajan, H.N. (1983), Question Banks and Construction of Tests and Reporting of Results for Internal Assessment and External Examination, 9(2) p. 235-44.

Maithreyi, Krishnaraj (1980), The Status of Women in Science in India, 5(3) p. 381.

Malaviya, A. (1984), Commitment and Rural Basis of Teachers for Rural Orientation of Home Science Education, 10(1-2) p. 77-83.

Malhotra, R.K. (1983), Our Research and Research Scholars, 9(2) p. 285-88.

Mandle, Vijay. V (1976), Management Education and Development, 1(3)

Manorama Barnabas (1977), Undergraduate Education under the Semester System, 2 p. 329.

Manavalan, R. (1982), Practice School Programme at BIS — New Concept in Higher Education, 8(2) p. 235.

Marjorie Fernondes (1986-87), Constraints on the use of Educational Technology in Indian Higher Education, 12(1-3) p. 177-80

Martin Carnoy (1980), Educational Innovation in the Third World, 5(2) p. 141.

Mathew, A. (1983), The Role of University Grants Commission in Framing the Policy of Higher Education, 9(2) p. 177-96.

Mathew, Zachariah (1983), Fair Access to Higher Education : Reflections on India's and China's Experience of the Past Thirty Years, 8(3) p. 311-20.

Mathur, Jayshree (1982), On Academic Freedom, 8(1) p. 110.

Mathur, Kuldeep (1977), Leadership and Organizational Structure in a University, 2 p. 233.

Mathur, Rajeswar, N. (1979), On Implementation of a Mastery Learning Strategy, 4(1&2) p. 333

Maureen, Woodhall (1980), The Use of Student Loans in the Finance of Higher Education, 5(3) p. 417.

Mehra, L.S. (1985-8€), Financing of Research in U.K., 11(1-2) p. 202-10.

Mehta, Pradeep Kumar (1978), Education and Assistance: A Case-study of Government College, Sawai Madhopur (Rajasthan), 3 p. 390.

Mehta, V.R. et al (1978), Teaching Curriculum in Agricultural Education, 3 p. 165.

Mehrotra, R.C. (1980-81), Science, Technology, Development and the Universities, 6(1-3) p. 25-40.

Mehrotra, R.C. (1982), Industry — University Interaction, 8(1) p. 19-28.

Menon, M.B. and Sahoo, P.K. (1984), Educational Technology in Higher Education, 9(3) p. 408.

Michel, Woitrin (1980), Louvain-La-Neuve (Belgium) : A New Town Built by and for a University, 5(2) p. 203.

Mishra, B.L. (1987-88), Distance Education and Management Training: The Case of GNOU, 13(1-3) p. 146-50.

Mishra, P.K. (1977), Anthropology and New Universities, 2 p. 351.

Misra, R.G. and Arora, O.P., Direct Grading vs. Grading via Analytical Marking, p. 95.

Misra, Sunil (1983), International Symposium on Problems of Development of Under-Privileged Communities in the Third World Countries, 9(1) p. 131.

Mohammad Aslam (1988-89), Undergraduate English in the Kashmir Region : A Study in Local Errors, 14(1-3) p. 192-98.

Mohanty, B. and Satapathy, C. (1983), Socio-Economic Profile of Technical Graduates in Orissa University of Agriculture and Technology, 8(3) p. 363-74.

Mohsin, S.H. (1979), Student Practice of Engineering, 4 p. 144.

Mohinder Singh (1979), Service and Maintenance of Sophisticated Scientific Instruments in Universities, 4 p. 278.

Mohan Rao, R.M. (1988-89), Rural Higher Education for Rural Development, 14(1-3) p. 53-64.

Moonis Raza and Amitabh Kundu (1980), Evaluation in Higher Education, 5(3) p. 359.

Moonis Raza and Aggrawal, Yash (1985-86), Higher Education: Regional Dimension Figures are at page 225 to 234, 11(1-2) p. 1-38.

Moonis Raza and Marjorie Fernandes (1987-88), Functions of Teachers in Higher Education, 13(1-3) p. 3-28.

Moorthy, S. Radhakrishna (1980-81), The Need for Autonomous Boards of Undergraduate Courses, 6(1-3) p. 153-54.

Mosha, Hereme J. (1985-86), African University and National Development, 11(1-2) p. 57-74.

Motilal Sharma (1972), Development of University Advisory Teaching Services, 3 p. 416.

Mukherjee, B.C. (1987-88), The Vidya Sagar University: Its Objectives and Character 1985-86, 13(1-3) p. 125-26.

Mukherji, S.K., (1980), Developing Colleges of Basic Sciences and Humanities in Agricultural Universities, 5(2) p. 195.

Nagarajan, S. (1977), Some Historical Notes on the Decline of English, 2 p. 341.

Nagla, Bhupendra K. (1983), Youth Unrest in Contemporary Indian University, 8(3) p. 289-98.

Nair, V. Sankaran (1985), The Student Community in Pre-war Indian Polities, 10(3) p. 225-34.

Nair, J. Rajasekharan (1980-81), Turning point in Sex Differentials in Higher Education, 6(1-3) p. 122-27.

Nanda, Harinder (1982), Question Bank in Indian Universities Potential Uses and some Psychometric Issues, 7(3) p. 310-14.

Narasimham, B. (1978), Post-graduate Courses in Horticulture, 3 p. 411.

Narayanan, R. (1982), Higher Education in an Authoritarian Society: A Case Study of Brazil, 7(3) p. 219-26.

Natrajan, R. (1985), Cybernetic Considerations and Engineering Education, 10(3) p. 169-78.

Natrajan, R. (1986-87), Management of Student Activities in Higher Education, 12(1-3) p. 57-68.

Natarajan, V. (1978), Question Choice in Examinations, 3 p. 247.

Natarajan, V. and Ved Prakash (1979), Moderation of Examination Results, 4 p. 407.

Natarajan, V. and Ved Prakash (1982), A Method of Equating Marks from Different Boards, 8(2) p.209.

Nayar, B.K., Rao, C.R.S. and Gupta, S.S. (1979), Indian Students and Trainees in Scientific and Technical Fields who Went Abroad during 1965-1975, 4 p. 171.

Neetu Sancheti (1984), The Ford Foundation and Indian Education: Some Issues of Motives and Power, 10(1-2) p. 9-22.

Neetu Sancheti (1987-88), Institutional Autonomy and Inter and International Networks in Indian Management Education, 13(1-3) p. 87-100.

Nigam, M.S. (1976), Study of the Finances of University of Rajasthan, 1 (3)

Nirmal Malhotra (1987-88), Dissenting Academics and Their Libraries, 13(1-3) p. 134-37.

Nirmal Singh (1980), A Perspective on Higher Education in India — The Case of Private Control, 5(1) p. 21.

Okedara, C.A. (1982), Correlation between Students Scores in a Drama Course and Their Assessment of their Teacher and Available Resources in Ibadan Nigeria, 8(1) p. 90-96.

Oza, D.K. (1979), A Career in Applied Scientific Research — A Case Study of Attitudes of the Young, 4 p. 111.

Oza, G.M. (1976), Need for Environmental Conservation Centres in Indian Universities, 1(3)

Ozah, D.K. (1976), Career Guidance for Mathematics Students — A Case Study, 1(3).

Padamanabhan, C.B. (1982), An Approach to Financial Management in Education with Special Reference to Colleges in India, 7(3) p. 293-96.

Padamanabhan, C.B. (1983), Financial Management of Universities in India, 9(2) p. 282-84.

Padamanabhan, C.B. (1985-86), Orientation Programmes in Management of University Financer, 11(1-2) p. 211-16.

Palsane, M.N. and Desai, H.G. (1977), Grading in the Examinations : An Illusory Reform, 2 p.59.

Palsane, M.N. and Khedekar, A.V. (1978), Internal Assessment — Objective Test and Final Examination, 3 p. 237.

Palsane, M.N. (1979), Continuing and Non-formal Education: Universities Introduction with and Contribution to Continuing Education, 4 p. 343.

Pande, I.C. (1979), Reorientation of Geological Education, 4 p. 327.

Pandey, Rajendra (1985-86), Student Activism in British India, 11(1-2) p. 145-56.

Partha Chatterjee, Shibani Kinkar Chaube and Sobhanlal Dutta Gupta (1977), Teaching Political Science: The Debate on New Orientations, 2 p. 5.

Parthasarathy, R. and Patel, R.J. (1987-88), Semester System in Gujarat Agricultural University, 13(1-3) p. 138-45.

Parveen Akhtar Hassan (1982), The Semester System 7(3) p. 306-09

Patel, Surendra J. (1985), The Swift Narrowing of the Educational Distance between the Developing Countries and the Third World 1950-1981, 10(3) p. 143-52.

Patnaik, B.N. (1986-87), Medium of Technical Education in India, 12(1-3) p. 51-56.

Patnaik, B.N. and Geeta, K. (1988), Against De-emphasising Grammar in Foreign Language Teaching, 14(1-3) p. 178-85.

Patricia Broadfoot (1982), International Trends in Educational Assessment, 7(3) p. 227-36.

Pattanayak, D.P. (1980-81), Crisis in Higher Education in India, 6(1-3) p. 51-54.

Patted, G.M. (1978), Professional Preparation of College Teachers in Modern Democracies, 3 p. 123.

Patted, G.M. (1984), College Teaching — Description and Analysis, 9(3) p. 381-88.

Peterson, Steven A. and Albert Somit (1978), Student Protest : A Biomedical Perspective, 3 p. 333.

Pillai, J.K. and Gabriel, P.J. (1983), Abilities and Subject Specialization, 9(1)

Pillay, G. Subramania (1979), Linkage of Higher Education with Environment, 4 p. 373.

Pillay, G. Subramania (1980), Refining the Questions, 5(3) p. 422.

Pitkhane, S.V. (1983), Education : An Input for Dairy Industry, 8(3) p. 385-89.

Prabhu, S.S. and Venkataramiah, H.V. (1977), Examination Reform: Letter Grading System Some Blind Spots, 2 p. 69.

Prasad, C. (1980), Agricultural Extension Curriculum and Change Agents — Some New Guidelines, 5(1) p. 75.

Prasad, Nageshwar (1977), Growth of Institutions, Scientific, Achievements and the Status of Indian Physicists, 2 p. 407.

Prasal, U.S. (1983), Vocational of Commerce Education, 9(2) p. 271-76.

Pratap, R. (1984), Performance Appraisal of University Academic Staff — An Approach, 10(1-2) p. 111-13.

Pratibha Deo, (1980-81), Revaluation at the University Examination: Its Effect on the Results of Candidates, 6(1-3) p. 83-104.

Premi, Kusum K. (1984), Educational Equality and Economic Opportunities: A Comparative Study of Scheduled Castes and Non-scheduled Castes, 9(3) p. 363-72.

Price, R.F. (1983), China's Immediate Future : Renewed Cultural Borrowing, 8(3) p. 299-310.

Punekar, Vijaya, B. (1981), Communication in Ragging, 7(1-2) p. 145.

Philip, G. Altbach (1977), Scholarly Publishing in the Third World, 2 p. 295.

Philip, G. Altbach (1979), The University as Centre and Periphery, 4 p. 157.

Philip, G. Altbach (1980), The Crisis of the Professoriate, 5(3) p. 317.

Quaraishi, Z.M. (1976), On Curriculum and Teaching in Higher Education, 1(3)

Rabindranathan, M.R. (1979), Regional Imbalance in the Growth of Higher Education in India, 4 p. 33.

Rabindranathan, M.R. (1988-89), Progress of Research in Indian Universities, 14(1-3) p. 101-25.

Radha Devi, D. (1985-86), Occupational Distribution of Engineering and Medical Graduates, 1971, 11(1-2) p. 169-74.

Raghaviah, Y. (1983), The Midget Bureaucratic Phenomenon Reflections on System Transformations in Universities, 9(2) p. 157-76.

Radhika Ramasubban (1982), Economic Dualism and Educational Policy — Reflections of an Amateur, 8(22) p. 179.

Raghaviah, Y. (1981), Deliberative and Decision-making Process in an Australian University, 7(1-2). p. 73.

Raghbir Singh and Surjit Singh Gill (1979), A Study of Time Utilization by Rural School and College Students During Summer Vacation, 4 p. 81.

Rais Ahmed (1980), Reorientation in Teaching, Learning and Evaluation, 5(3) p. 331.

Rais Ahmed (1982), Universities : Perspection and Problems, 7(3) p. 177-88.

Rais Ahmed (1984), INST-IB and Higher Education, 9(3) p. 301-304.

Raja Ganesan, D. (1978), Wanted Research Focus on Hostels, 3 p. 280.

Raja Ganesan, D. (1980), A Short Training Programme in Question Writing for College Teachers, 5(2) p. 255.

Rajaguru G., Satapathy, C. and Patra, B.P. (1978), Trimester System of Education: As Perceived by Students, 3 p. 386.

Rajyaguru, H.M. (1983), Social Work Practice: A Recent Definition, 9(2) p. 217-28

Rama, G.W. (1983), Education and Democracy, 9(1) p. 1.
Rama Murthy, M.S. (1983), Stress-Experience of Higher Education Students, 9(2) p. 245-48.
Ramana, V.V. and Prasad Rao, C.R. (1983), Variation in Economic Position of College Teachers by College Management, Sex and Caste, 9(2) p. 259-68
Ramakrishna, G. (1981), Higher Education: A Perspective from Periphery, 7(1-2) p. 51.
Ramasubban, T.A., Ravindra Singh, M.L. Bansal and Singla, S.K. (1979), Interconversion of Awards in Trimester Traditional Systems of Education for the P.G. Programme, 4 p. 273.
Ram Reddy, G. (1985-86), The Indira Gandhi Open National University: Its Role in Higher Education, 11 (1-2) p. 156-68.
Rami Reddy, A. Venkata and G. Prathapa Simha, G. (1979), Which Do They Want: IA or TS &A Comparative Study, 4 p. 400.
Rami Reddy, A. Venkata (1979), A Two-Year Follow Up Study on Internal Assessment, 4 p. 47.
Rami Reddy, A. Venkata (1980), Student's Reactions Towards Eng. and Regional Media : A Comparative Study, 5(1) p. 101.
Rana, R.P.S. (1980-81), Post Graduate Educational and Research Cost Analysis, 6(1-3) p. 155-60.
Rangaswami, G. (1977), Self Improvement of Agricultural Universities, 2 p. 387.
Ranu Varikar and others (1985), Teaching English and Learning English, 10(3) p. 243-46.
Rao, C.N.R. (1976), University Chemical Education : Retrospect and Prospect, 1(3).
Rao, C.N.R. (1981), Materials Science Education, 7 (1-2) p. 83.
Rao, V.K.R.V. (1980-81), Some Thoughts on Higher Education, 6(1-3) p. 1-8.
Rastogi, S.P. (1979), Attitudes and Beliefs of Harijan Students, 4 p. 251.
Rastogi, S.P. (1981), Constitutional Safeguards for Harijans: An Evaluation, 7(1-2) p. 133.
Ray, Anil Baran (1978), Parochialism vs. Cosmopolitanism in Indian Higher Education, 3 p. 55.
Ray, Anil Baran (1979), Revolt, Activism and Apathy: Reflections on Socio-Political Expectations of Students in India, 4 p. 301.
Rishi Anand and Shankaram, V. (1977), An Endeavour Towards Anatomy of Science Education, 2(1, 2&3) p. 197.

Rohatgi, P.K. (1979), Activities of the Technological Forecasting and Research Management Cell of Indian Institute of Science, Bangalore, 4 p. 109.

Roy, C. (1986-87), The Trainees Role in English Teaching, 12(1-3) p. 69-80.

Rudra, K.K. and Rastogi, S.P. (1979), Regional Distribution of Selected Technical Educational Facilities in India, 4 p. 23.

Rudra, A. (1981), Teaching of Statistics to Students of Economics, 7(1-2) p. 93.

Russel, King and Tony Macelli (1982), Geography, Multiple Process Analysis and the Gole Project: An Exercise in Interdisciplinary Multi-level Education, 8(1) p. 53-62.

S.S. (1978), Higher Education and the New Context, 3 p. 1.

S.S. (1982), Higher Education — A Comparative and Historical Perspective, 7(3) p. 1-V.

Sailabala Devi (1984), Cost Structure of Higher Education: A Case Study of Orissa, 10(1-2) p. 57-72.

Samant, Chitta R. (1985), Open Learning Systems and Educational Mass Media : An Analysis, 19(3) p. 283-85.

Samant, D.G. (1978), Implications of Grades for University Teachers, 3 p. 269.

Sanyal, Bikas C. (1982), Higher Education and the Labour Market in Asia, 8(2) p. 167.

Samant, D.G. (1979), Implications of Grades for University Teachers, 4 p. 271.

Samanta, R.K. (1983), Agricultural Research Service Scientists: Their Value Orientation, 9(1) p. 114.

Samuel Mathai (1980-81), UGC : A Personal View, 6(1-3) p. 55-62.

Sankara, Raddy G.H. and Lohi Das, T. (1979), Semester Pattern and Internal Assessment System in Agricultural Universities in India : A Critical Review, 4 p. 413.

Santhanam, M.R. (1977), Teaching Environments in Colleges, 2 p. 101.

Santanagopalan, S. (1977), Student Participation in University Government in Australia, 2 p. 120.

Saraswathi, L.S. (1976), Teacher Evaluation by the Taught, 1(1-3)

Sathiaraj, P.J. (1984), Student Perception of the Purposes of Higher Education, 9(3) p. 395-98.

Satish Chandra (1978), Farm Advisory Service — A Model, 3 409.

Satish Chandra (1984), The University Grants Commission and its Role, A review, 10(1-2) p. 3-8.

Satyanarayana (1982), Educational Problems of Scheduled Caste College Students in Karnataka, 7(3) p. 253-59.

Satya Raju, R. (1983), Commerce Curriculum in India: Need for Reforms, 9(2) p. 277-78.

Saxena, A.K. (1985), Training Programme for College Teachers, 10(3) p. 273-82.

Sayeed, Omer Bin and Verma, Ravi Kumar (1980), University System: Organisational Context, Structure and Performance, 5(3) p. 409.

Seddey, S.C. and Gupta, R.K. (1983), Determinants of Levels of Higher Education in States, 9(1) p. 133.

Selvasratnam, V. (1988-90), Universities in Malaysia, 11 (1-2) p. 89-96.

Seshadri, C., Education, Equality and Culture: An Analysis

Shah, G.B. (1978), University Goes to Masses, 3 p. 273.

Shah, K.J. (1927), Reorientation of Courses, 2 p. 1.

Shah, K.J. Randhir Singh and Barlingay, S.S. (1978), Reactions to the 'Objective' Testing Techniques, 3 p. 253.

Shah, K.R. (1980), Demand and Financing of Higher Education in Canada, 5(2) p. 251.

Shah, Madhuri R. (1985), Conference of Vice-Chancellors of the Asian and Pacific Region (March 18-21, 1985) Welcome address, 10(3) p. 137-42.

Shahare, M.L. and Ramasami, T. (1981), Examination of Union Public Service Commission vis-a-vis Higher Education, 7(1-2) p. 45.

Shakuntala Balaraman (1981), Psychology in Search of an Identity, 7(1-2) p. 117.

Shankaram, V. and C. Dorasami, K. (1982), Moderation of Question Papers in Mathematics Education, 8(2). p. 246.

Shankar Narayan, D. (1980), University Computer Centre: Structure, Functions and Management, 5(1) p. 109.

Shankar Narayan, D. (1982), Computer Science and Technology : Facility Requirements and Certification of Academic Programmes, 7(3) p. 324-26.

Sharma, Arvind (1979), Do All Students in Department of Studies in Religion Constitute a Single Population?, 4 p. 86.

Sharma, Purohit D.K. and Darji, D.R. (1980), Effective Management of Universities and Research, 5(1) p. 112.

Sharma, G.D. (1978), National Seminar on University and College Finances, 3 p. 413.

Sharma, G.R. (1979), Adjustment Problems of Non-professional College Students, 4 p. 262

Sharma, K.N. (1977), Intergenerational Gap or Culture Conflict?, 2 p. 411.

Sharma, Mohindera (1979), A Study of Conflict in a University, 4 p.1.

Sharma, N.L. and Surendra (1978), Job-oriented Training and Specialisation in Geology, 3 p. 173.

Sharma, P.C. (1980-81), Some Psycho-social Attributes of Student Leaders: A Differential Study, 6(1-3) p. 136-50

Sharma, Radha Rani (1982), Sessional Evaluation in College : A Research Study, 7(3) p. 280-85.

Sharma, R.R. (1985-86), Campuses of Higher Education Genesis of Unrest, 11(1-2) p. 187-90.

Sharma, S.L. (1978), The Modernizing Effects of University Education on the Value Orientations of Students

Sheddey, S.C. (1983), Trends in Professional Education among Women, 8(3) p. 327-33.

Sheilu, Sreenivasan (1979), Foreign-Aided I.I.T. Education, 4 p. 187

Shirur, Rajani R. (1982), Teaching Learning in Higher Education — MBO Style, 7(3) p. 302-05.

Shiva Reddy, B. (1982), Distribution of Higher Education Subsidies: A Case Study of Punjab University, 8(1) p. 79-84

Shukla, U. (1977), On University Mathematics, 2 p. 261.

Shukla, U. (1984), Student Unrest in India Causes and Remedies, 10(1-2) p. 122-24.

Singh, Amar and Prasad, C. (1978), A Study of Job Satisfaction of Personnel in Agricultural Universities, 3 p. 111.

Singh, Bir (1980), Admission to Universities—A Miscellany, 5(2) p. 260.

Singh, M. Raghuram (1981), Professional Teacher Attitude of B.Ed. and M.Ed. Student-teachers and its Correlates, 7(1-2).

Singh, R.K. (1984), Reading Development: Some Questions, 10(1-2) p. 117-19.

Singh, Raghavendra S. and Ramjee Lal (1984), Assessment of Teacher Effectiveness in Higher Education Procedure and Problem, 10(1-2) p. 106-10.

Singh, Y.P. and Hira Nand (1977), Felt Training Needs of Social Science Teachers in Higher Agricultural Education, 2 p.423.

Singh, Virendra (1982), The Student Bodies in the Universities, 8(2) p. 288.

Singla, H.S. (1984), Public Examination in 2001, 9(3) p. 315-22.

Singla, R.K. (1982), E.S.P. A Socio-linguistic Consideration, 8(1) p. 107-109.

Sisodia, M.L. and Agrawal, B.M. (1982), Making Undergraduate Education more Relevant — A Model Developed at the University of Rajasthan, 8(2) p. 241.

Sisodia, M.L., Natarajan, V. and Patni, G.C. (1979), Analysis of Question Bank in Mathematics, 4 p. 392

Somnath Chattopadhyay and Agrawal, K.G. (1979), Organisation Culture: Its Perception and the Medical Faculty, 4 p. 245.

Sood, Renu (1980-81), Role of Achievement Anxiety Alienation and Value Discrepancy in Academic Achievement of Scheduled Caste Students, 6(1-3) p. 117-21.

Soundara Rajan, M.V. (1983), Over-crowding in University and College Hostels, 9(1) p. 124.

Srinivasaraghavan, T. (1979), Evaluation of Performance of Candidates at Post-graduate Examinations, 4 p. 410.

Srivastava, Anand P. (1988-89), Characteristics of Modern Indian Scholarship and Learning, 14(1-3) p. 19-39.

Srivastava, Chitra (1980-81), Faculty Leadership Styles and Intellectual Commitment among College Students, 6(1-3) p. 131-35.

Srivastava, R.C. (1978), Teachers' and Students' Participation in College Administration, 3 p. 260.

Srivastava, R.C. (1979), Faculty and Student Status in Administration, 4 p. 225.

Srivastava, R.C. (1983), Participation, Faculty Satisfaction and Perceived Institutional Climate, 9(1) p. 94.

Shrivastava, S.K. (1983), Job Satisfaction and Organisational Climate among University Teachers, 9(2) p. 251-53.

Subramaniam, V. (1980), Rationalising Communication Strategy in College Classes, 5(3) p. 335.

Subbanaryan, Peri (1977), Does M.Phil Facilitate Teaching?, 2 p. 425.

Sushila Singhal (1987-88), Effective Teachers — How Good is the Student Consensus, 13(1-3) p. 101-108.

Sushila Singhal, Genesis of Student Unrest: Results of a Multimethod Analysis, 3 p. 27.

Swaminathan, M.S. (1981), Higher Education into the 21st Century, 7(1-2) p. 23.

Swapan K. Bhattacharya, Developing Unit Structure in University Organisation – A Study of Alternative Approach, 5(2) p. 243.

Swaraj and others (1983), Student Participation in the Management of Education Systems, 8(3) p. 342-48.

Swaran Pratap et al. (1983), A Comparative Study of Anxiety Level against Graduate, Post-graduate and Ph.D. Students, 9(2) p. 249-50.

Swaran Pratap and Gupta, N.K. (1985), Unemployment of Psychological Wellbeing in Professional Graduates, 10(3) p. 271-72.

Takwale, Ram G. (1985), Restructuring first Degree Courses and their Link with Community, 10(3) p. 153-68.

Thiagarajan, A. Ponnambala (1988-89), A Study of Degree Examination Results of SC Students, 14(1-3) p. 151-56.

Tiwari, N.P. (1982), Role of English Language in Technical Education System, 8(1) p. 102-106.

Tharu, J. (1977), Towards a Meaningful System of Grades, 2 p. 73.

Uday Desai (1983), University Vice-Chancellors: Profile of the Educational Elites, 8(3) p. 265-88.

Udgaonkar, B.M. (1977), New Directions for International Scientific Cooperation, 2 p.33, 167.

Ujagar Singh (1977), Determinants of Choice of Studies at University Level, 2 p. 253.

Ujagar Singh (1983), Professional Choice by University Students: A Sociological Perspective, 8(3) p. 334-41.

Ujagar Singh (1986-87), Relevance of University Education to National Aspirations, 12(1-3) p. 151-58.

Uplaonkar, Ambarao T. (1982), Social Background and Occupational Aspirations of College Students: A Case of Scheduled Castes vis-a-vis Non-scheduled Castes Students in Higher Education, 8(1) p. 63-73.

Uplaonkar, Ambarao T. (1985), Educational and Occupational Aspirations of College Students, 10(3) p. 185-200.

Uplaonkar, Ambarao T. (1985-86), Protective Discrimination and the Equality of Opportunity, 11(1-2) p. 117-26.

Vasantha Ramkumar (1978), Contradictions in Universities and the need for Managerial Skills, 3 p. 21.

Venkatapathy, R. (1984), Influence of Institution of Autonomy among Students, 9(3) p. 389-91.

Verghese, Alexander, V. (1984), Education, Earning and Occupation of Weaker Castes, 9(3) p. 373-80.

Verma, Amita and Saraswathi, T.S. (1983), The Child Development Curriculum and its Relevance to the Job Competencies Expected in the Field, 9(1) p. 119.

Verma, Lokesh K. (1980), Analysis of Re-evaluation Cases in Northern Universities, 5(2) p. 213.

Verma, Lokesh K. (1982), Attitude of University Examiners in Arts and Science Subject Towards Spot Evaluation, 7(3) p. 286-87.

Verma, Shivendra K. (1988-89), Language in Education in a Multilingual Society, 14(1-3) p. 41-51.

Vijai Govind (1987-88), University Level Books in India: An Appraisal, 13(1-3) p. 26-33.

Viney Kripal and others (1985-86), Wastage among Scheduled Caste and Scheduled Tribe I.I.T. Students, 11(1-2) p. 111-16.

Viney Kripal (1987-88), Teaching Language to Scheduled Caste Student: A Humanistic Approach, 13(1-3) p. 63-68.

Vipula Chaturvedi and Chaturvedi, M.C. (1977), Higher Technical Education – Patterns, Trends and Qualifications for Developing Countries, 2 p. 377.

Vishwanathan, R. and Rohatgi, P.K. (1978), Unemployed Engineers Scheme at the Indian Institute of Science, 3 p. 271.

William Madtha, S.S. (1977), Conscientization : The Aim of University Education, 2 p. 309

Yadav, M.S. and Mukhopadhyay, M. (1977), Multi-Media Approach to Collegiate Instruction, 2 p. 118.

Yadav, M.S. and Menon, M.B. (1978), Development of Question Bank for a Course on Educational Evaluation at B.Ed. Level, 3 p. 357.

Yadav, M.S., Menon S., B. Kumar, and P. Arun (1981), Educational Research as Scientific Inquiry, 7(1-2) p. 111.

Yadav, M.S. and others (1985), Research and Teaching, 10(3) p. 177-84.

Yadav, M.S. and others (1986-87), Research Policy in the Perspective of National Development, 12(1-3) p. 29-50.

Yadav, Siya Ram and Sharma, R.A. (1987-88), Cost and Academic Performance of Correspondence Education, 13(1-3) p. 111-14.

Yoram Neumann and Ephrain Ben Baruch (1982), Analysis of Factor Influencing Faculty Attitudes Towards Changes in the US Tenure System, 8(1) p. 29-40.

Zakia, A. Siddiqi and Khatoon, Z. (1978), Comparison of Students' Performance Under the Semester and Non-Semester System of Education in the Aligarh Muslim University, 3 p. 369.

Guidelines for Introduction of M.Phil 1978, Courses, 3 p. 283.

List of Selected Books on Education Published in India

Adaval, S.B. ed. (1968), *The Third Indian Year Book of Education: Educational Research*, NCERT.

Adiseshiah, W.T.V and Pavanasam, R. (1974), *Sociology in Theory and Practice.* New Delhi, Santhi Publishers.

Aggarwal, J.C. and Agrawal, S.P. (1982), *Role of UNESCO in Education*. New Delhi, Vikas Pub. House, Pvt. Ltd.

Altbach, P.G. ed. (1968), *Turmoil and Transition: Higher Education and Student Politics in India.* Bombay, Lalvani.

Anderson, W.A. and Parker, Frederik B. (1966), *Society: Its Organisation and Operation*. New Delhi, Affiliated East West Press (P. Ltd).

Bajwa, Ranjit S., and Smith, Wilfred, R. (1980), *Educational Sociology : A Modern Cultural Approach.* Ambala Cantt, India Pub.

Bayti, Jamnalal (1986), *Readings in Education*. New Delhi, Uppal Publishing House.

Belok, and Green, J.L. ed.), *Philosophy and Education.* Meerut, Any Prakashan.

Belok, Michael, V. and Haggerson Nelson ed. (1983), *Naturalistic Research Paradigms : Theory and Practice.* Meerut. Any Books.

Best, J.W. (1963), *Research in Education.* New Delhi, Prentice Hall of India.

Bhatia, H.R. (1977), *A Textbook of Educational Psychology*. Delhi, Macmillan.

Bhatt, S.R. (1986), *Knowledge, Value and Education: An Axoimetic Analysis*. Delhi, Gian.

Bigge, M.L. (1967), *Learning Theories for Teachers.* Delhi, Universal Book Stall.

Bogardus, Emoryn S. (1969), *The Development of Social Thought*. Bombay, Vakils, Feffer and Sunions.

Brainerd, Charler, J. (1978), *Piagets' Theory of Intelligence*. New Delhi, Prentice Hall Inc.

Bruner, J.S. (1964), *The Process of Education*. Delhi, Atmaram.

Buch, M.B. (1974), *A Survey of Research in Education.* Baroda, Centre of Advance Study in Education and Psychology, Baroda, M.S. University.

Buch, M.B. (1979), *Second Survey of Research in Education*. Baroda, Society for Educational Research and Development.

Buch, M.B., (ed) 1987, Third Survey of Research in Education 1978-1983, New Delhi, NCERT.

Burlock, E.B. (1974), *Personality Development*. New Delhi, Tata McGraw Hill.

Coleman, J.C. (1976), *Abnormal Psychology and Modern Life*. Bombay, D.B. Taraporevala Sons.

Cooper, R.A. and Weekes, A.J. (1983), *Data, Models and Statistical Analysis.* New Delhi, Heritage.

Corey, S.M. and Shukla (1962), *Practical Classroom Research by Teachers*. New Delhi, National Institute of Basic Education.

Daham, O.P. and Bhatnagar, O.P. (1980), *Education and Communication for Development*. New Delhi, Oxford and IBH.

Dececco, John P. and Crawford (1977), *Psychology of Learning and Instruction*. New Delhi, Prentice Hall.

Desai, Chitra (1976), *Girl's Education and Social Change*. Bombay, A.R. Sheth.

Desai, H.G. (1979), *Style Manual for Dissertations/Theses*. Rajkot, Saurashtra University.

Devadas, Rajammal P. and Kulandaivel, K. (1976), *A Handbook of Methodology of Research.* Sri R.K. Coimbatore, Mission Vidyalaya Teachers' College.

Dinkmeyer, Don C. (1967), *Child Development the Emerging Self.* New Delhi, Prentice-Hall.

Edwards, Allen L. (1969), *Techniques of Attitude Scale Construction*. Bombay, Vakils, Feffer & Simsons.

Ehsanual, Haq (1981), *Education and Political Culture in India: The Limits of Schooling System and Political Socialisation*. New Delhi, Sterling.

Freeman, F.S. (1965), *Theory and Practice of Psychological Testing.* New Delhi, Oxford & IBH.

Garrett, H.E. (1965), *General Psychology*. New Delhi, Eurasia.

Gore, M.S., et al. eds. (1967), *Papers in the Sociology of Education in India*. New Delhi, NCERT.

Grewal, J.S. and Gupta, B.S. (1980), *Working with Community and Teacher Education*. Agra, Ram Prasad.

Griffin and Pareek, U. Planned (1970), *Change in Education*. Bombay, Somaiya.

Groose, R.F. and Birney, R.C. (eds.) (1968), *Transfer of Learning*. New Delhi, Affiliated East West Press.

Hilgard, Earnest R. and Bower Gordon, H. (1975), *Theories of Learning*. New Delhi, Prentice Hall.

Hill, W.F. (1967), *Learning*. Bombay, B.I. Publication.

Hurlock, E.B. (1973), *Adolescent Development*. New Delhi, McGraw Hill.

Hurlock, E.B. (1982), *Developmental Psychology*. New Delhi, Tata McGraw Hill.

Hussain, Zakir (1975), *Educational and Cultural Foundation, Education and National Development*. New Delhi.

India, Ministry of Human Resource Development (1986), *Innovations in Education*. New Delhi, Ministry of H.R.D.

Inkeles, Alex (1966), *What is Sociology?* New Delhi, Prentice Hall.

Jha, Sahitya Nand (1985), *Education for Socialism, Secularism and Democracy*. Delhi, Amar Prakashan.

Jindal, B.L. (1984), *Schooling and Modernity*. New Delhi, Inter India Publications.

Joshi, K. (1975), *Education for Personality Development*. New Delhi, NCERT.

Joshi, R.N. (1979), *Education Elsewhere and Here: A Key to Prosperity*. Bombay, Bharatiya Vidya Bhavan.

John, V.V. (1969), *Education and Language Policy*. Bombay, Nachiketa.

Johnson, Harry M. (1970), *Sociology*. Madras, Allied.

Kalia, Narendra Nath (1979), *Sexism in Indian Education, the lies we tell our Children*. New Delhi, Vikas.

Kamat, A.R. (1985), *Education and Social Change in India*. Bombay, Samaiya.

Kamlesh, M.L. (1986), *Methodology of Research in Physical Education and Sports*. New Delhi, Metropolitan.

Kanhere, Usha, S. (1987), *Women and Socialisation*. New Delhi, Mittal.

Kapoor, Ravi (1985), *Education and Social Stratification in South East Asia*. Delhi, Idarah-i Adabiyat-i.

Kerlinger, Fred, N. (1978), *Foundations of Behavioural Research.* Delhi, Surjeet, Kohlo, V.K. (1987, Indian Education and its Problems. Haryana, Vivek.

Koul, Lokesh (1984), *Methodology of Educational Research*. New Delhi, Vikas.

Kuppuswamy, B. (1974), *A Textbook of Child Behaviour and Development.* Delhi, Vikas.

Kuppuswamy, B. (1964), *Advanced Educational Psychology.* Delhi, University Publishers.

Loomis, Charles P. and Lone K. Looms, *Modern Social Theories*. New Delhi, Affiliated East-West Press.

Mangal, S.K. (1986), *Educational Psychology*, Ludhiana, Prakash.

Mathew, Mohan (1972), *Child Psychology in Indian Perspective.* Trivandrum, M.P.T. Publishers.

Miller R.I. (1969), *Education in a Changing Society.* Ludhiana, Lyall Book Depot.

Mohanty, J. (1982), *Indian Education in the Emerging Society.* New Delhi, Sterling.

Mohanty, Jagannath (1982), *Indian Education in the Emerging Society*. New Delhi, Sterling.

Morre, Wilbert, E.E. (1965), *Social Change*. Delhi, Prentice Hall.

Morse, William C. and Winngo, G. Max (1962), *Psychology and Teaching.* Bombay, B. Taraporevale.

Munn, Norman L. et al (1975), *Introduction to Psychology* (3rd edn.) New Delhi, Oxford and IBH.

Mussen, Paul H. ed. (1970), *Handbook of Research Methods in Child Development*. New Delhi, Willey Eastern.

Nagpaul, Hans (1980), *Culture, Education and Social Welfare Need for Indigenous Foundations.* New Delhi, S. Chand.

Narashimha, Reddy Kanaknala (1984), *Students, Teachers and Parents: Academi Interactions in Education Setting.* Delhi, Ajanta.

Narvane, V.S. (1978), *Modern Indian Thought.* New Delhi, Orient Longmans.

Natarajan, V. and Kulshrestha, S.P. ed. (1983), *Evaluation Methodology and Examination Reform*. Dehra Dun, Jugal Kishore.

Nayana, Tara, S. (1985), *Education in Rural Environment*. New Delhi, Ashis.

Nazareth M. Pla (1984), *Education Goals, Aims and Objectives.* New Delhi, Vikas.

Nirmal Singh (1983), *Education Under Siege: A Sociological Study of Pvt. Colleges*. New Delhi, Concept.

Page, James D., (1976)), *Abnormal Psychology*. New Delhi, Tata McGraw Hill.

Pal, S.K. and Saxena, P.C. ed (1985), *Quality Control in Educational Research*. New Delhi, Metropolitan.

Paliwal, M.R. (1984), *Social Change and Education*. New Delhi, Uppal.

Pandey, R.S. (1982), *An Introduction to Major Philosophies of Education*. Agra Vinod.

Patel, M.S. (1953), *Educational Philosophy of Mahatma Gandhi*. Ahmedabad, Navajiwan,.

Patel, P. Surabhi (1983), *Equality of Educational Opportunity in India*. New Delhi, National.

Per, Dalin (1978), *Limits to Educational Change*. New Delhi, Macmillan.

Rao, K. Sudha (1986), *Influence of Continuous Evaluation on Learning*. New Delhi, NCERT.

Rao, M.S.A.), *Education, Social Stratification and Mobility*. New Delhi, NCERT.

Reddy, V., Narayan, Karan (1979), *Man, Education and Values*. Delhi, B.R. Publications.

Reyna, R. (1971), *Introduction to Indian Philosophy*. New Delhi, Tata McGraw-Hill.

Ruhela, S.P. and Vyas, K.C. (1970), *Sociological Foundations of Education in Contemporary India*. Delhi, Dhanpat Rai and Sons.

Ruhela, S.P. ed. (1970), *Towards a Sociology of Teaching Profession*. New Delhi, NCERT.

Ruhela, S.P. ed. (1969), *Social Determinants of Educability in India*. Delhi, Jain Brothers.

Ruhela, Satya Pal, ed., *Sociology of the Teaching Profession in India*. New Delhi, NCERT.

Sadhy, A.N. and Singh, Amarjit (1980), *Research Methodology in Social Sciences,* Bombay, Himalaya.

Saiydian, K.G. (1963), *Education Culture and Social Order*. Asia.

Seetharamu, A.S. (1978), *Philosophies of Education*. New Delhi, Ashish.

Seetharamu, A.S. (1980), *Education and Rural Development*. New Delhi, Ashish.

Shah, A.B. (1978), *Social Context of Education*. Allied.

Shah, Beena (1984), *Sociology of Educational Development*. Nainital, Gyanoday.

Shankar, Udai (1958), *Problem Children*. Delhi, Atma Ram and Sons.

Sharma, Jai Krishnan (1986), *Education for 3rd World Countries*. Delhi, B.R. Publishing.

Sharma, R.N. (1968), *Principles of Sociology*. Bombay, Asia.

Shekhar, M.S. (1968), *Social Change in India*. Deccan College Post-Graduate and Research Institute.

Shingi, Prakash M., Singh, N.P., and Jadhav Dilip (1980), *Rural Youth*. New Delhi, Abhinav.

Shrivastava, O.M. (1981), *Literacy Work Among Small Farmers and Tribals*. New Delhi, Marwan.

Shukla, Suresh Chandra and Krishna Kumar (1985), *Sociological Perspective in Education: A Reader*. Delhi, Chanakya.

Sidhu, K.S., *Statistics in Education and Psychology*. New Delhi, Sterling.

Sidhu, Kulbir Singh (1984), *Methodology of Research in Education*, New Delhi, Sterling.

Singha, H.S. (1984), *Public Examinations: A Critique*. New Delhi, Vikas.

Singh, Baljit ed. (1983), *Economics of Indian Education*. New Delhi, Meenakshi.

Singh, K.R.P. (1987), *Educating India's Masses: A study of Dr. Zakir Hussain's Educational Thought*. Delhi, Unique.

Singhi, Narendra K. (1979), *Education and Social Change*. Jaipur, Rawat.

Sivakumar, Chitra (1982), *Education, Social Inequality and Social Change in Karnataka*. Delhi, Hindustan.

Skinner, Charles E. ed. (1964), *Educational Psychology* (4th ed.). New Delhi, Prentice-Hall.

Srinivas, M.N. (1966), *Social Change in Modern India*. Bombay, Allied.

Tagore, R. (1922), *Creative Unity*. New Delhi, Macmillan.

Thorndike, R.L. & Hagen, E. (1970), *Measurement and Evaluation in Psychology and Education*. New Delhi, Wiley Eastern.

Thirtha, N.V., Babel, *Language Dilemma in Indian Schools*. Madras, M. Seshachalam.

Thirtha, N.V., and Lalitha Thirth, *Education and Social Change*. Bangalore University Centre for Educational Sociology.

Thirtha, N.V., *National Integration*. Jalunder, University Publishers.

Thirtha, N.V., and Lalitha Thirth, *Education and Society: A study of Status and Roles*. Bangalore University, Centre for Educational Sociology.

Tumin, M.M. (1978, Social Stratification: *The Forms and Functions of Inequality*. New Delhi, Prentice Hall.

Unnithan, T.K.N. (1965), *Towards a Sociology of Culture in India*. New Delhi, Prentice Hall.

Varshney, Uma (1983), *Education for Political Socialization*. Meerut, Meenakshi.

Veena, D.R. (1982), *Education and Economic Growth*. New Delhi, Ashish.

Verma, R.P.S. (1979), *Socio-Emotional Climate and Schools Learning*. Agra, National Psychological Corporation.

Vyas, Ram Narayan (1976), *Education and Human Society*. Delhi, Ajanta.

Young, Panlino, V. (1968), *Scientific Social Surveys and Research*. Bombay, Asia.

Selected Journals on Education Published in India

Communication Research, Sage Publications, New Delhi.

Educational Administration Quarterly, Sage Publications, New Delhi.

Education and Psychology Review, Editor, Faculty Education and Psychology, M.S. University of Baroda.

Education Quarterly, Indian Ministry of Human Resource Development, Department of Education, Shastri Bhavan, New Delhi 110054, India.

Educational Forum, Editor, Educational Forum, Central Institute of Education, 33, Chhatra Marg, Delhi-7.

Educational Media International, Media International, Post Box 2058, Gurukrupa Mansions, 44, Nagappa Swastik Circle, Bangalore-560 020.

Future, Regional Office for South Central Asia, UNICEF House, 73, Lodi Estate, New Delhi-110 003, India.

Human Resources Abstracts, Sage Publication (India) Pvt. Ltd., Post Box No. 4215. New Delhi-110 048.

ICSSR Journal of Abstracts and Reviews — Economics, ICSSR, New Delhi.

Indian Dissertation Abstracts ICSSR, New Delhi (Back Volume), Periodica India, 2509, Sector-16, Faridabad, 121002, India.

Indian Educational Review National Council of Educational Research and Training, Publication Department, Sri Aurobindo Marg, New Delhi 110016, India.

Indian Educational Review, General Editor, Journals Cell, NCERT, Sri Aurobindo Marg, New Delhi-16.

Indian Journal of Adult Education Indian Adult Education Association, 17-B Indraprastha Marg, New Delhi, India.

Indian Journal Chemical Education, The Chief Executive, National Council of Science Education, Sri Aurobindo Marg, New Delhi-16.

Indian Journal of Social Sciences, Sage Publication India Pvt. Ltd., Post Box. 4215, New Delhi-110 048.

International Educator, Kalaniketan Publishers, Nandavanam, Trivandrum.

Journal of Education and Psychology, Editor, Journal of Education &. Psychology, MB Patel College of Education, Sardar Patel Uty., Vallabh Vidyanagar, Best Katra — Gujarat.

Journal of Educational Equity and Leadership, Sage Publication (India) Pvt. Ltd., Post Box No. 4215, New Delhi-110 048.

Journal of Educational Research and Extension, Editor, Journal of Research and Extension, Sri Ramakrishna Mission Vidyalaya Teacher's College, Coimbatore.

Journal of Educational Research and Extension, Ramakrishna Mission Vidyalaya Teachers College, Sri Ramakrishna Vidyalaya P.O. Coimbatore Dt., Tamil Nadu, India.

Journal of Higher Education, Publication Officer, University Grants Commission, 35, Ferozeshah Road, New Delhi-110 001, India.

Journal of Higher Education (India), University Grants Commission, Bahadurshah Zafar Marg, New Delhi 110002, India.

Journal of India Education, General Editor, Journal Cell, NCERT, Sri Aurobindo Marg, New Delhi-16.

Journal of Indian Education National, Council of Educational Research and Training, Publication Department, Sri Aurobindo Marg, New Delhi 110016, India.

Journal of Psychological Research, Editor, Journal of Psychological Research, Dept. of Psychology, University of Madras, Madras-600 005.

Manas: A Journal of Scientific Psychology, Executive Editor, Manas, 32, Netaji Subhash Marg, New Delhi.

Manpower Journal, Chief Editor, Institute of Applied Manpower Research, Indraprastha Estate, Ring Road, New Delhi-110 002.

Mathematics Education, Editor, Mathematics Edn., Station Road, P.O. Siwan, Bihar-841 226.

Mathematics Journal, Department of Education, Bikaner, Rajasthan, India.

Mathematics Teacher, 3, Thiruvengadam Street, Raja Annamalapuram, Madras-28, Tamil Nadu, India.

NIE Journal, Business Manger, Publication Unit, NCERT, NIE Campus, Sri Aurobindo Marg, New Delhi-16.

New Frontiers in Education, Mari Jacob, C-6, Community Centre, Safdarjung Development Area, New Delhi 110016, India

Physics Education (India), Macmillan India Ltd, 21 Patullos Road, Madras 600 002, India.

Progress of Education, Pune Vidyarthi Griha Prakashan, 1786 Sadashiv Peth, Poona, 411 030, India.

Saxena, P.C. and Pal, S.K., ed., 1985, *Quality Control in Educational Research*, New Delhi, Metropolitan.

Turner, R., 1962, *Indian's Urban Future*. Bombay, Oxford University Press.

Wilks, S.S., 1964, *Elementary Statistical Analysis Calculation*. New Delhi, Oxford, I.B.H.

Workers Education (India), Central Board for Workers Education, 1400 West High Court Road, Gokulpeth, Nagpur-440 010, India.

List of Selected Books on Education Published in Abroad

Abramson, Paul R., 1980, *Personality*. New York, Holt Rinehart and Winston.

Adler, G., 1948, *Studies in Analytical Psychology*. New York, Norton.

Aiken, L.R., 1985, *Psychological Testing and Assessment*, Boston, Allyn and Bacon.

Allport, G.W., 1954, *Personality*. New York, Holt.

Allport, G.W., 1961, *Pattern and Growth in Personality*. New York, Rinehart, and Winston.

Allport, G.W., 1955, *Becoming*. New Haven, Yale University Press.

Amabile, Terese, M. and Stubbs, Margaret, L. ed., 1982, *Psychological Research in the Classroom Issues for Educators and Researchers*. New York, Pergamon Press.

Anastasi, 1965, *Psychological Testing*. New York, McGrillar.

Anastasi, Anne, 1982, *Psychological Testing*. Macmillan.

Anastasi, A., 1958, *Differential Psychology*. New York, Macmillan.

Anastasi, A., 1976, *Psychological Testing*. 4th ed., London, Collier MacMillan.

Anderson, John, E., 1955, *Psychology of Development and Personal Adjustment*. New York, Henry Holt.

Anderson, R.C. and Faust, G.W., 1973, *Educational Psychology*. New York, London, Harper and Row.

Anderson, S.B. and Bell, S., 1878, *The Profession and Practice of Programme Evaluation*. London, Jossey-Bass.

Andrews, T.G. ed., 1948, *Methods of Psychology*. New York, John Wiley and Sons.

Apple, M., 1979, *Ideology and Curriculum*. London, Routledge & Kegan Paul.

Apple, Michael W., 1982, *Cultural and Economic Reproduction in Education: Essay on Class, Ideology and the State*. London, Routledge and Kegan Paul.

Archer, Margaret S., ed., 1982, *Sociology of Educational Expansion, Take-off, Growth and Inflation in Educational System*. Beverely Hills, Sage.

Arkoff, Abe, 1968, *Adjustment and Mental Health*. New York, McGraw-Hill.

Arnstine, D., 1967, *Philosophy of Education: Learning and Schooling*. New York, Harper & Row.

Aron, Raymond, 1982, *Main Currents in Sociological Thought*. Harmondsworth, Penguin.

Arthur, Jersild T., 1968, *Child Psychology*. London, Prentice-Hall.

Ary, Donald, Jacobs, L.C. and Razavich Asghar, 1972, *Introduction to Research in Education*. New York, Holt Rinehart and Winston.

Ausubel, David, P., 1952, *Ego Development and Personality*. New York, Grune and Stratton.

Ausubel, D.P., Novak, J.D. and Hanesian, H., 1978, *Educational Psychology — A Cognitive View*. New York, Holt Rinehart and Winston.

Ausubel, David P. and Floyd, Robinson G., 1966, *Educational Psychology*. Holt, Rinehart and Winston.

Baller, Warren, R. and Charles, Don, C., 1961, *The Psychology of Human Growth and Development*. New York, Holt, Rinehart and Winston.

Bandura, A., 1977, *Social Learning Theory*. Englewood Cliff N.J., Prentice Hall.

Bantock, G.H., 1981, *The Parochialism of the Present, Contemporary Issues in Education*. London, Routledge & Kegan Paul.

Bany, H.A. and Johnson, L.V., 1964, *Classroom Group Behaviour: Group Dynamics in Education*. New York, John Wiley.

Bany, M.A., Johnson, L.V., 1964, *Classroom Group Behaviour*, New York, MacMillan.

Barrow, R., 1978, *Radical Education*. New York, John Wiley.

Barrow, Robin, 1981, *Philosophy of Schooling*, Brighton, Wheat Sheaf Books.

Barton, Len and Walker, 1984, *Social Crisis and Educational Research*. London, Croom Helm.

Basset, G.B., 1978, *Individual Differences: Guidelines for Educational Practice*. Sydney, George-Alien & Unwin.

Bayles, E.E., 1966, *Pragmatism in Education*. New York, Harper & Row.

Bell, Earl H., *Social Foundation of Human Behaviour*. New York & Evanston.

Bell, Robert R., ed., 1962, *The Sociology of Education: A Source Book*. Haramood, Illinois, Dorsey Press.

Bell, R.R. and Stub, H., 1968, *Sociology of Education*. Illinois, Dorsey Press.

Berlin, Harry, 1975, *Cognitive Basis of Language Development*, New York, Academic Press.

Bernard, Harold W., 1952, *Mental Hygiene for Classroom Teachers*. New York, McGraw Hill Book Co.

Bernard, Harold W., 1954, *Psychology of Learning and Teaching*. New York, McGraw Hill.

Bernard, Harold W., 1957, *Adolescent Development in Culture*. New York, World Book.

Bernard, W. and Leopold, J., 1975, *Test Yourself*. London, Corg. Books.

Bernbanum, Gerald, 1977, *Knowledge and Ideology in the Sociology of Education*. London, MacMillan.

Berne, E., 1963, *The Structure and Dynamics of Organisations and Groups*. Lippincott, Pennsylvania.

Bewer, G.H. and Sapce, J.T., 1960, *Psychology of Learning and Motivation Psychology*, New York, Academic Press.

Bhattacharya, Srinibas, 1963, *Guidance in Education*. New York, Asia.

Biehler, Robee, F., 1978, *Psychology Applied to Teaching*. Boston, Houghton Mifflin.

Bierstedt, Robert, *The Social Order*. New York Tata McGraw Hill.

Bigge, M.L. and Hunt, M.P., 1962, *Psychological Foundations of Education*. New York, Harper & Row, Tokyo, weather Hill.

Bijou, S.W. and Ruiz, R., 1981, *Behaviour Modification: Contributions to Education*. New Jersey, Erlbaum, Hillsdale.

Bischolf, Ledford, 1970, *Interpreting Personality Theories*. London, Harper and Row.

Blackledge, David and Hunt, Barry, 1985, *Sociological Interpretations of Education*, London, Croom Helm.

Blair, Myers, Glenn, Jones, Stewart R. and Simpson, Ray H., 1954, *Educational Psychology*. 2nd ed., New York, MacMillan.

Blaug Mark, et al., 1969, *The Causes of Graduate Unemployment in India*. London, Allen Lane.

Bloom, Benjamin S., 1964, *Stability and Change in Human Characteristics*. New York, Wiley.

Bloom, B.S. and Others, 1956, *Taxonomy of Educational Objectives: The Classification of Educational Goals*. New York, Longmans Green.

Bloom, B.S., 1976, *Human Characteristics and School Learning*. New York, McGraw Hill.

Bloom, B., Madaus, G. and Hastings, T., 1982, *Evaluation to Improve Learning*, New York, McGraw Hill.

Blos, P., 1941, *The Adolescent Personality*. New York, Appleton Century Crofts.

Blum, G.S., 1953, *Psychoanalytic Theories of Personality*. New York, McGraw Hill.

Bogardus, 1949, *Sociology*. New York, McMillan.

Bonny, Merl E., 1960, *Mental Health In Education*. Boston, Allyn and Bacon.

Borg, W.R. and Gall, M.D., 1979, *Educational Research — An Introduction*. (3rd edn.), New York, Longman.

Bourne, Lyle E. and Ekstrand, Bruce R., 1979, *Psychology: It's Principles and Meanings*. New York, Holt, Rinehart and Winston.

Bower, G. and Hilgard, E.A., 1981, *Theories of Learning* (5th edn.). New York, Prentice-Hall, Englewood Cliffs.

Bowen, J.A., 1971, *History of Western Education*. Vol. 2, London, Methuen & Co.

Boyd, W., 1964, *The History of Western Education*. London, Adam & Charles Black.

Boynton, P. and Boynton, J., 1938, *Psychology of Child Development*. Mineapolis, Educational Publishers.

Brameld, T., 1971, *Patterns of Educational Philosophy*. New York, Hold, Rinehart & Winston.

Brameld, T., 1956, *Towards a Reconstructed Philosophy of Education*. New York, Dryden Press.

Brameld, T., 1961, *Education for the Emerging Age*. New York, Harper & Row.

Brascamp, L.A. and Brown, R.D., 1980, *Utilization of Evaluative Information*. Jossey-Bass, San Francisco.

Brembeck, Coel, S., 1966, *Social Foundations of Education — A Cross Cultural Approach*. New York, John Wiley.

Brent Allen, 1983, *Philosophy and Educational Foundations*. London, George Allen and Unwin.

Broadfood, Particia and other, ed., 1981, *Politics and Educational Change : An International Survey*. London, Croom Helm.

Brock, Colin and Tulasiewicz, ed., 1985, *Cultural Identity — Educational Policy*. London, Croom Helm.

Brookover, W.B., et al., 1955, *A Sociology of Education*. New York, American Book.

Broudy, H.S., 1977, *Building a Philosophy of Education*. New York, Krieger.

Brown, C., Harper, E., and Strivens, J., 1986, *Social Education: Principles and Practices*. Falmar Press.

Brown, Francis, J., 1961, *Educational Sociology*. New York, Prentice Hall.

Brown, Geoffrey and Desforges, Charles, 1979, *Piaget's Theory*. London, Routledge and Kegan Paul.

Brown, L.M., 1970, *Aims of Education*. New York, Teacher's College Press.

Brownell, W.A., 1928, *Development of Child's Number Ideas in Primary Grades*. Chicago, University of Chicago Press.

Brownhill, R.J., 1983, *Education and the Nature of Knowledge*. London, Croom Helm Ltd.

Brubacher, J.S., 1947, *A History of Problems of Education*. London, McGraw Hill.

Brubacher, J.S., ed., 1955, *Modern Philosophies of Education: Fifty-Four Year Book NSSE*. Chicago, University of Chicago Press.

Brubacher, J.S., ed., 1955, *Philosophies of Education: Forty-First Year Book NSSE Part 1*. Chicago, University of Chicago Press.

Bruce, W., 1978, *Conducting Educational Research*. 2nd ed., New York, Harcourt Brace Jorenovich.

Bruner, J.S., 1960, *The Process of Education*. Cambridge, Harvard University Press.

Bruner, J.S., Oliver, R.R. and Greenfield, P.M., 1966, *Studies in Cognitive Growth*. New York, John Wiley.

Bulmer, Martin, 1982, *The Uses of Social Research*. London, George Allen and Unwin.

Bulta, R.F., 1941, *Cultural History of Education, Reassuming an Educational Tradition*. London, McGraw Hill.

Burgen, Robert G., ed., 1985, *Issues in Educational Research: Qualitative Methods*. London, Falmer Press.

Burroughs, G.E.R., 1975, *Design and Analysis in Educational Research*. 2nd ed., Oxford, Alden & Mowbray.

Burton, A., ed., 1956, *Case Studies in Counselling and Psychology*. Englewood Cliffs, N.J., Prentice Hall.

Butcher, James N., 1972, *Personality Assessment*. New York, Academic Press.

Butler, J.D., 1966, *Idealism in Education*. New York, Harper Row.

Butts, R.F., 1947, *A Cultural History of Education*. London, McGraw Hill.

Bybee, Rodger W. and Sund, Robert B., 1982, *Piaget for Education*. 2nd ed., Columbus, Charles Merrill.

Callahan, Joseph F. and Clard, Leonard H., 1977, *Foundations of Education: Planning for Competence*. New York, MacMillan.

Caplan, Gerald, 1955, *Emotional Problems of Early Childhood*. New York, Academic Press.

Caplan, Gerald, ed., 1961, *Prevention of Mental Disorders in Childhood*. New York, Basic Books.

Carroll, Herbert A., 1956, *Mental Hygiene: The Dynamics of Adjustment*. 3rd ed., Englewood Cliffs, N.J., Prentice Hall Inc.

Carr, Wilfred, 1986, *Becoming Critical: Education, Knowledge and Action Research*. London, Falmer Press.

Cartwright, Dorwin and Zander, Alvin, ed., 1962, *Group Dynamics: Research and Theory*. 2nd ed., New York, Row, Peterson and Co.

Castles, Stephen and Wustenberg, Wiebke, 1979, *The Education of the Future*. London, Plato Press Ltd.

Cattel, R.B., 1946, *Description and Measurement in Personality*. New York, World Book Co.

Cattel, R.B., 1971, *Abilities: Their Structure, Growth and Action*. Boston, Houghton-Mifflin.

Cearning, Frederick and Sangree, Lucinda, ed., 1979, *Towards a Cultural Theory of Education and Schooling*. The Hague, Mouton, Chandrasekar.

Clark, B.R., 1962, *Educating the Expert Society*. Sanfrancisco, Chandler.

Chamberlin, J.G., 1969, *Toward a Phenomenology of Education*. Philadelphia, Westminster.

Chesler, Mark A. and Cawe, William M., 1981, *Sociology of Education: Access to Power and Privilege*. New York, MacMillan Co.

Clemen, Johnson M., *A Review of Research Methods in Education*. Chicago, Rand McNally College.

Cohen, Brenda, 1983, *Means and Ends in Education*. London, George Allen & Unwin.

Cohen, Harold L. and Filipezak, James, 1971, *A New Learning Environment*. London, Jossey-Boss.

Cohen, R. and Dirk, Schoeffer, L., 1973, *Patterns of Personality Judgement*. New York, Academic Press.

Colardarsi, Arthur P., 1955, *Educational Psychology*, U.S.A., Henry Holt and Co.

Cole, Luella, 1959, *Psychology of Adolescence*. 5th ed., New York, Holt, Rinehart and Winston.

Cole, S. Brembeck, 1971, *Social Foundations of Education: Environment Influences in Teaching Learning*. New York, John Wiley.

Cook, L.A. and Cook, E.E.A., 1960, *Sociological Approach to Education*. New York, McGraw Hill.

Cooley, William W. and Lohnes, Paul R., 1976, *Evaluation Research in Education*. New York, Irvington.

Coombs, A.W. and Snygg, D., 1959, *Individual Behaviour*. 2nd ed., New York, Harper and Row.

Cooper, David E., 1983, *Authenticity and Learning Nietzsche Educational Philosophy*. London, Routledge and Kegan Paul.

Corrigan, Paul, *Schooling: The Smesh Street Kidgs*. London, MacMillan.

Cowburn, Will, 1986, *Clan, Ideology and Community Education*. London, Groom Helm.

Cox, R. Peter, ed., 1975, *Equalities and Inequalities in Education*. London, Academic Press.

Craft, Maurice, 1981, *Teaching in a Multicultural Society*. London, Falmer Press.

Cronbach, L.J., 1973, *Educational Psychology*. New York, Harcourt Bruce.

Crow, L.D. and Crow, A., 1965, *Adolescents Development and Adjustment*. 3rd ed., Kohapur, Mogha Prakashan.

Crow, Lester D. and Crow, Alice, 1956, *Human Development and Learning*. New York, American.

Crow, L.D. and Crow, A., 1965, *Adolescent Development and Adjustment*, New York, McGraw Hill.

Crow, Lester D. and Crow, Alice, 1951, *Mental Hygience*. New York, McGraw Hill.

Crow, Lester D. and Crow Alice, 1965, *Reading in Educational Psychology*. U.S.A., Adams and Co.

Cuber, John F., 1968, *Sociology: A Synopsis of Principles*. New Jersey, Prentice Hall.

Curtis, S.J. and Boultwood, M.E.A., 1953, *A Short History of Educational Idea*. London, University Tutorial Press.

Dearden, R.F., 1983, *Theory and Practice in Education*. London, Routledge and Kegan Paul.

Dearden, R.F., Hirst, P.H. and Petres, R.S., ed., 1972, *A Critique of Current Educational Aims*. Boston, Routledge & Kegan Paul.

Dale, Roger and others, ed., 1981, *Schooling and the National Interest*. Lewas, (U.K.), Falmer Press.

Dandekar, W.N., 1970, *Fundamentals of Experimental Psychology*. 3rd ed., Kohapur, Mogha Prakashan.

David, E. Cooper, 1980, *Illusions of Equality: International Library of the Philosophy of Education*. London, Routledge & Kegan Paul.

Day, H.I., and Berlyne, D.D., 1971, 'Intrinsic Motivation in Lesser, G. ed., *Psychology and Educational Practice*. Chicago, Scott, Foresman.

Deb, A.K., 1968, *Subnormal Mind*. Calcutta, Chakrawarthy Chatterjee.

Dececco, John P., 1963, *Human Learning in the School: Reading in Educational Psychology*. New York, Holt, Rinehart and Winston.

DeCastells, S., Luke, A. and Egan, K., ed., 1986, *Literacy, Society and Schooling*. Cambridge University Press.

Deese, J. and Hulse, S.H., 1967, *The Psychology of Learning*. New York, McGraw Hill.

Deese, James, 1958, *Psychology of Learning*. New York, McGraw Hill.

Demaine, Jack, 1981, *Contemporary Theories in the Sociology of Education*. London, MacMillan Press Ltd.

Dentler, R.A. and Shapire, B.J., 1976, *Readings in Educational Psychology*, New York, Harper.

Denton, D.E., ed., 1974, *Existentialism and Phenomenology in Education*. New York, Teachers College Press.

Derek, Blackman, 1974, *Operant Conditioning*. London, Methuen.

D Vesta, F.J. and Thompson, G.G., 1970, *Educational Psychology*. New York, Appleton Century Crofts.

D'evelyn, Katherine E., 1957, *Meeting Children's Emotional Needs*. New Jersey, Prentice Hall Inc.

Dewey, J., 1916, *Democracy and Education*. New York, MacMillan.

Dicapro, N.S., 1974, *Personality Theories*. New York, Harper.

Dobson, C.B. et al., 1981, *Understanding Psychology*. London, George Weindenfeld and Nicolson.

Dollard, J. and Miller, N.E., 1950, *Personality and Psychotherapy*. New York, McGraw Hill.

Donald, Ary et al., 1972, *Introduction to Research in Education*. New York, Holt, Rinehart & Winston.

Donetson, E., 1973, *Personality: A Scientific Approach*. California, Goodyear.

Douglas, O.B. and Holland, B.P., 1948, *Foundations of Educational Psychology*. New York, MacMillan Co.

Downey, Merdel and Kelley, A.V., 1979, *Theory and Practice of Education: An Introduction*. 2nd ed., London, Harper and Row.

Doyle, J.F., 1973, *Educational Judgements*. London, Routledge & Kegan Paul.

Drew, Chifford J., 1980, *Introduction to Designing and Conducting Research*. 2nd ed., London, C.V. Mosby Company.

Duport, Beatrice, 1981, *Unequal Education: A Study of Sex Differences in Secondary School Curricula*. Paris, UNESCO.

Durkhiem, E., 1966, *Education and Sociology*. New York, The Free Press.

Dyer, Jean Roger, 1979, *Understanding and Evaluating Educational Research*. London, Addison-Wesley.

East, Hope G., 1975, *Community Hierarchy and Open Education*. London, Routledge and Kegan Paul.

Ebel, R.L. and Frisbei, D.A., 1986, *Essentials of Educational Measurement*. Prentice Hill.

Ebel, R.L., 1972, *Essentials of Educational Measurement*, Englewood Cliffs, N.J., Prentice Hall.

Eby, F., 1952, *The Development of Modern Education*. New York, Prentice Hall.

Ellis, Arthur et al., 1986, *Introduction to the Foundations of Education*. Englewood Cliffs, Prentice Hall.

Elvin, L., 1977, *The Place of Commonsense in Educational Thought*. London, George Allen & Unwin.

Elven, Robert B., 1980, *An Introduction to Theories of Personality*. New York, Academic Press.

Englehart, Max D., 1972, *Methods of Educational Research*. Chicago, Rand McNally.

Erikson, 1950, *Childhood and Society*. New York, W.W. Norton.

Eson, Marris, 1972, *Psychological Foundations of Education*. New York, Holt, Rinehart and Winston.

Etizioni, A. and Etizioni, E., eds., 1964, *Social Change*. New York, Basic Books.

Entwistle, N.J. and Nishet, J.D., 1972, *Educational Research in Action*. London, University of London Press.

Eysenck, H.J., 1972, *Psychology is about People*, London, Penguin Press.

Eysenck, H.J., 1960, *Handbook of Abnormal Psychology*. London, Pitman Medican.

Eysenck, K.J., 1970, *The Structure of Human Personality*. London, Methuen.

Fagerlind, Ingemar and Saha, Lawrence, J., 1983, *Education and National Development: A Comparative Perspective*. Oxford Pergamon Press.

Fedner, W.T., 1953, *Experimental Design, Theory and Application*. New Delhi, Oxford and IBH.

Feldman, Robert S., ed., 1986, *The Social Psychology of Education: Current Research and Theory*. Cambridge University Press.

Ferguson, George F., 1981, *Statistical Analysis in Psychology and Education*. New York, McGraw Hill.

Festinger, U. and Katz., *Research Methods in Behavioural Sciences*. N.Y., Bold Dryden.

Finch, Janet, 1986, *Research and Policy — The Uses of Qualitative Methods in Social and Educational Research*. London, Falmer Press.

Fitzerald, Hiram E., 1977, *Developmental Psychology*. Illinois, The Dorsey Press.

Fitzgibbons, Robert E., 1981, *Making Educational Decisions: An Introduction to Philosophy of Education*. New York, Harcourt Brace Joranovich.

Flanders, Ned A., 1970, *Analysing Teacher Behaviour*. California, Addison Wesley.

Flavell, J.H., 1963, *The Developmental Psychology of Jean Piaget*. New Jersey, D'Van Nostrand Co.

Flescher, Irwin, 1972, *Children in the Learning Factory: The Search for a Humanizing Teacher*. Philadephia, Chilton Book.

Fletcher, C. and Thomson, N., ed., 1980, *Issues in Community Education*. Falmer, Barcombe.

Flew, Antony, 1976, *Sociology, Equality and Education*. London, MacMillan Press.

Fox, David J., 1969, *The Research Process in Education*. New York, Holt, Rinehart and Winston.

Fowler, Floyd J., Jr., 1984, *Survey Research Methods*. London, Sage.

Franze, Fredenburgh A., 1971, *The Psychology of Personality and Adjustment*. Philippines, Cunnings.

Friere, P., 1970, *Pedagogy of the Oppressed*. New York, Harder & Herder.

Friere, P., 1974, *Education for Cultural Consciousness*. New York, Seabury Press.

Friere, P., 1976, *Education: The Practice of Freedom*. London, Writers and Readers.

Frendam, P., 1958, *Principles of Scientific Research*. London, Macdonald.

Freud, Sigmund, 1943, *A General Introduction to Psychoanalysis*. New York, Garden City.

Frost, S.E., 1966, *Historical and Philosophical Foundations of Western Education*. Ohio, Charles E. Merrill.

Fyans, Leslic J., ed., 1980, *Achievement Motivation: Recent Trends in Theory and Research*. New York, Pleneum Press.

Gabel, S., Oster, G.D. and Butnik, S.M., 1986, *Understanding Psychological Testing in Children*. New York, Pleneum.

Gabriel, John, 1968, *Children Growing Up The Development of Children's Personalities*. London, Hodder and Stoughton.

Gage, N.L. and Borliner, D.C., 1975, *Educational Psychology*. Chicago, Rand McNally.

Gagne, R.M., 1977, *The Conditions of Learning*. N.Y., Holt, Rinehart and Winston.

Gagne, Robert M. and Briggs, Leslie J., 1984, *Principles of Instructional Design*. New York, Holt, Rinehart and Winston.

Gagne, William J., et al., 1972, *Learning Environments: Readings in Educational Psychology*. New York, Holt, Rinehart and Winston Inc.

Galfo, Armand, J., 1975, *Interpreting Educational Research*. Dubuque, Lowa, Wm.C. Brown.

Gallagher, J.R. and Harris, H.I., 1974, *Emotional Problems of Adolescents*. Rev. edn., New York, Oxford University Press.

Galtung, 1967, *Theory and Methods of Social Research*. London, Allen Unwin.

Garforth, F.W., 1980, *Educative Democracy*. Oxford University Press.

Garrison, K.C., 1965, *Psychology of Adolescence*. New Jersey, Prentice Hall.

Garrison, Karl C., 1952, *Growth and Development*. Rev. ed., New York, Longman.

Gates, Arthur I., et al., 1963, *Educational Psychology*. 3rd edn., New York, MacMillan.

Gay, L.R., 1987, *Educational Research: Competencies for Analysis and Application*. London, Merrill.

Gephart, W.J. and Ingle, R.B., 1969, *Educational Research (Selected Readings)*. Ohio, C.E. Merrill.

Getzels, J. and Jackson, P.W., 1962, *Creativity and Intelligence: Explorations with Gifted Students*. New York, John Wiley.

Gibson, J.T., 1968, *Educational Psychology : A Programmed Text*. New York, Appleton Century.

Gibson, Janice T., 1976, *Psychology for the Classroom*. New Jersey, Prentice Hall Inc.

Giddens, Anthony, 1987, *Social Theory and Modern Sociology*. Oxford, Polity Press.

Gilbert, S., 1979, *Foundations of Educational Research*. Englewood, Clifts, New Jersey, Prentice-Hall.

Gilmer, H.B., 1970, *Psychology*. New York, Harper and Row Publishers.

Giroux, H.A., 1983, *Critical Theory and Educational Practice*. Victoria, Deakin University Press.

Giroux, Henry A., 1983, *Theory and Resistance in Education*. London, Heinemann Educational Books.

Glaser, R., ed., 1965, *Teaching Machines and Programmed Learning: A Source Book, Vol. 2: Data and Directions*. Washington D.C., Department of Audiovisual Instruction, National Education Association.

Gleeson, Denis, ed., 1977, *Identity and Structure: Issues in the Sociology of Education*. Nafferton, Nafferton Books.

Glock, M.D., 1971, *Guiding Learning: Readings in Educational Psychology*. New York, John Wiley.

Glueck, S. and Glueck, E., 1962, *Family Environment and Delinquency*. Boston, Houghton Mifflin.

Gold Milteon, 1965, *Education of the Intellectually Gifted*. Columbus Ohio, Charles E. Merrill.

Goldstein, H.D. and Lanyon, R., 1971, *Readings in Personality Assessment*. New York, Wiley.

Golloway, C, 1976, *Psychology for Learning and Teaching*. New York, McGraw Hill.

Good, Barran and Scates, *Methodology of Educational Research*.

Good, C.V., 1941, *Essential of Educational Research Methodology and Design*. New York, Appleton Century Crofts.

Goodman, P., 1964, *Compulsory Miseducation*. New York, Horizon Press.

Goodenough, Florence L. and Tyler, Leona E., 1959, *Developmental Psychology*. New York, Appleton Century Crofts.

Good, T.L. and Brophy, J.E., 1977, *Educational Psychology: A Realistic Approach*. N.Y., Holt, Rinehart and Winston.

Goslin, A.H. and Steward, W.A.C., 1965, *The School in Contemporary Society*. Scott, Freeman.

Gowan, John Curtis, Demos, George D. and Torrance, Paul E., 1967, *Creativity: Its Educational Implications*. New York, John Wiley.

Graig, R.C., 1975, *Contemporary Educational Psychology*. N.Y., Nehrens W.H. Clarizo, H.F. John Wiley.

Graves, F.P., 1937, *A History of Education Before the Middle Ages*. New York, MacMillan.

Green, Edward J., 1962, *The Learning Process and Programmed Instruction*. New York, Holt, Rinehart and Winston.

Gronlund, Norman E., 1981, *Measurement and Evaluation in Teaching*. ed. 4, New York, MacMillan.

Gronx, Henry A., 1981, *Ideology Culture and the Process of Schooling*. London, Falmer Press.

Guilford, J.P., 1967, *Nature of Human Intelligence*. New York, McGraw Hill.

Guilford, J.P., 1971, *Analysis of Intelligence*. New York, McGraw Hill.

Guilford, J.P., 1950, *Fields of Psychology*. New York, D'Van Nostrand.

Hadfield, J.A., 1952, *Psychology and Mental Health*. London, George Allen and Unwin.

Hadin, Catherine, 1987, *Research Design: Strategies and Choices in the Design of Social Research*. London, Allen and Unwin.

Hahn, Milton E. and Maclan, Malcolm S., 1955, *Counselling Psychology*. 2nd ed., New York, McGraw Hill.

Hall, C.S. and Lindzey, G., 1970, *Theories of Personality*. New York, John Wiley.

Hall, C.S. and Lindzey, G., 1978, *Theories of Personality*. New York, Wiley.

Halsey, A.H. et al., eds., 1965, *Education, Economy and Society*. London.

Hamm, Russel L., 1981, *Philosophy and Education: Alternatives in Theory and Practice*. Danvill, The Interstate Printers & Publishers.

Haptrop, Richard P., ed., 1973, *Foundations of Futurology in Education*. ETC Publication, Illiner's.

Hart, J.K., 1935, *Education for an Age of Power*. New York, Harper & Brothers.

Harris, Duncan and Bell, Chris, *Evaluating and Assessing for Learning*. Kogan Page.

Harris, Chester, W., 1960, *Encyclopaedia of Educational Research*, New York, MacMillan.

Hawkins, John N., 1983, *Education and Social Change in the People's Republic of China*. New York, Praeger.

Henerson, Marlene E., et al., 1978, *How to Measure Attitudes*. Beverly Hills, Sage.

Hocking, W.E., 1939, *Types of Philosophy*. New York, Charles Scribness Sons.

Helson, Henry, 1959, *Theoretical Foundations of Psychology*. New York, D'Van Nostrand.

Helson, Henry and Bevan, William, ed., 1964, *Contemporary Approaches to Psychology*. New York, D'Van Nostrand Reinhold.

Henson, D.A. et al., 1967, *On Education: Sociological Perspectives*. New York, Wiley and Sons.

Hetherington, E.M. and Parke, R.D., 1979, *Child Psychology: A Contemporary View Point*. New York, McGraw Hill.

Heyns, Roger W., 1958, *The Psychology of Personal Adjustment*. New York, Henry Holt.

Hilgard, Ernest R., 1962, *Introduction to Psychology*. New York, Harcourt, Brace & World.

Hilgard, E.R. and Bower, G.H., 1974, *Theories of Learning*. 4th ed., New York, Appleton.

Hilgard, Earnest R., 1956, *Theories of Learning*. New York, Appleton-Century Crofts.

Hilgard, E.R. and Bower, G.H., 1960, *Theories of Learning*. 3rd ed., New York, Appleton.

Hill, John P. and Sheltron, ed., 1971, *Readings in Adolescent Development and Behaviour*. New Jersey, Prentice Hall.

Hill, Windfred F., 1963, *Learning: A Survey of Psychological Interpretation*. Rev. ed., London, Methuen.

Hirst, P.H., 1974, *Knowledge and the Curriculum: A Collection of Philosophical Papers*. London, Routledge & Kegan Paul.

Holmes, Brian, ed., 1985, *Equality and Freedom: A Comparative Study*. London, George Allen and Unwin.

Holt, Maurice, 1981, *Evaluating the Evaluators*. London, Hodder and Stoughton.

Honigmann, John J., *Personality in Culture*. New York, Holt, Rinehart and Winston.

Horton, Paul B. and Leslie, Gerald R., 1970, *The Sociology of Social Problems*. New Jersey, Prentice Hall.

Howard, Keith and Sharp, John A., 1983, *Management of a Student Research in Research Project*. Hants, Gower.

Hull, C.L.A., 1952, *A Behaviour System: An Introduction to Behaviour Theory Concerning the Individual Organisation*. New Haven, Yale University Press.

Hummel, Charles, 1977, *Education Today for the World of Tomorrow*. Paris, UNESCO.

Hunt, Maurice P., 1975, *Foundations of Education, Social and Cultural Perspectives*. New York, Holt, Rinehart and Winston.

Hunt, Morton, 1985, *Profiles of Social Research: The Scientific Study of Human Interactions*. New York, Russel Sage Foundation.

Hurlock, E.B., 1956, *Child Development*. 3rd ed., New York, McGraw Hill.

Hussen, Paul H., ed., 1960, *Handbook of Research Methods in Child Development*. New York, John Wiley.

Husen, Torsten and Kegan, Maurice, 1984, *Educational Research and Policy: How do they Relate*. Oxford, Pergamon Press.

Hustler, David, Cassidy, Tony and Cuffted, *Action Research in Classroom and Schools*. London, George Allyn and Unwin.

Hyman, H.H., 1955, Survey, *Design and Analysis — Principles, Cases, Procedures*. New York, The Free Press.

Illich, I., 1971, *Deschooling Society*. New York: Harper & Row.

Ingram, Christine P., 1935, *Education of the Slow Learning Child*. Yonkers, World Book Co.

Inhelder, Barbel, et al., 1974, *Learning and the Development of Cognition*. London, Routledge & Kegan Paul.

International Bureau of Education, 1980, *Educational Goals*. Paris, UNESCO.

James, Lawrence R. et al., 1982, *Casual Analysis: Assumptions, Models and Data*. Sage.

Jeffreys, M.V.C., 1976, *Education: Its Nature and Purpose*. London, George Allen & Unwin.

Jensen, Clayne R. and Hirst, Cyntha, C., 1980, *Measurement in Physical Education and Athletics*. New York, MacMillan.

Jenks, Chris, ed., 1977, *Rationality, Education and the Social Organization of Knowledge*. London, Routledge and Kegan Paul.

Jerolimek, John, 1981, *Schools in Contemporary Society: An Analysis of Social Currents, Issues and Forces*. New York, MacMillan.

Jerome, Ragan and Cynthia, 1978, *Psychology and Education*. New York, Long Harcourt Brace, Jovanovich.

Jersild, A.T., 1964, *The Psychology of Adolescence*. New York, MacMillan.

Johnson, Clemens M., 1977, *A Review of Research Methods in Education*. Chicago, Rand McNally.

Johnson, G. Orville and Blake, Kathryn, 1960, *Learning Performance of Retarded and Normal Children*. Syracuse, New York, Syrascuse University.

Jones, Charles J., 1967, *Learning*. New York, Harcourt, Brace and World.

Jones, F.L. and Devis Peter, 1986, *Models of Society*. London, Croom Helm.

Jung, C.G., 1933, *Psychological Type*. New York, Harcourt.

Kallam, S.G., et al., 1975, *Mental Health and Going to School*, Chicago, University of Chicago Press.

Kaplan, Bernard and Wapner, Seymour, ed., 1960, *Perspectives in Psychological Theory*. U.S.A., International.

Kaplan, Louis and Baron, Denis, 1952, *Mental Hygiene and Life*. New York, Harper and Brothers.

Kaplan, Martin, 1980, *What is an Educated Person? The Decades Ahead*. New York, Praeger.

Karmel, Louis J. and Karmel, Marylin C., 1978, *Measurement and Evaluation in the Schools*. (2nd ed.), New York, MacMillan.

Kennedy, J.J., 1982, *Analysing Qualitative Data*. Pergamon.

Kerckhoff, Alan, 1980, *Research in Sociology of Education and Socialization*. Vol. 1, Greenwich, Jai Press.

Kerlinger, F.N., 1964, *Foundations Behavioural Research: Educational and Psychological Inquiry*. New York, Holt, Rinehart and Winston.

Kimbel, Gregory A., ed., 1967, *Foundations of Conditioning and Learning*. New York, Appleton-Century Crofts.

King, J. Edmund, 1977, *Reorganising Education*. Vol. 1, London, Sage.

Kingsley, Howard L., 1962, *The Nature and Conditions of Learning*. 2nd ed., Englewood Cliffs, N.J., Prentice-Hall.

Kirchoff, Alan C., ed., 1981, *Research in Sociology of Education and Socialization*, Greenwich, Jai Press.

Klausmeier, Harbert J., 1961, *Learning and Human Abilities — Educational Psychology*. New York, Harper and Bros.

Kloskowska, Antonia and Martinotti, Guido, ed., 1977, *Education in a Changing Society*. London, Sage.

Kneller, George F., 1978, *Foundations of Education*. 3rd ed., New York, John Wiley & Sons.

Kneller, G.F., 1971, *Introduction to the Philosophy of Education*. New York, John Willy & Sons.

Kosecoff, Jacqueline and Fink, Arlin, 1981, *Evaluation Basis: A Practitioner's Manuel*. London, Sage.

Lacey, Colin, 1977, *The Socialisation of Teacher*. London, Mathuen.

Langford, Glenn, 1985, *Education, Persons and Society: A Philosophical Enquiry*. Hampshire, MacMillan.

Langford, G. and O'Connor, D.J., 1973, *New Essays in the Philosophy of Education*. London, Routledge & Kegan Paul.

Lassers, L. and Low, G.A., 1960, *A Study of the Relative Effectiveness of Different Approaches of Speech Training for Mentally Retarded Children*. Washington, U.S. Office of Education, Co-operative Research Bureau.

Lawrence, E., 1970, *The Origin and Growth of Modern Education*. Baltimore, Penguin.

Lazarus, Richard S., 1963, *Personality and Adjustments*. New Jersey, Prentice-Hall.

Leaba, Clarence J., 1961, *Man: A General Psychology*. U.S.A., Holt, Rinehart and Winston.

Lecky, Prescott, 1945, *Self Consistency: A Theory of Personality*. New York, Island Press.

Leeper, Ward R. and Maddson, Peter, 1959, *Towards Understanding Human Personalities*. New York, Appleton- Century Crofts.

Lehman, Irvin J., et al., 1978, *Educational Research: Readings in Focus*. Holt, Rinehart and Winston.

Lerner, Daniel, 1962, *The Passing of a Traditional Society: The Role of Mass Media in Modernizing the Middle-East*. New York, Free Press of Glencoe.

Levin, J., 1977, *Elementary Statistics in Social Research*. 2nd ed., New York, Harper & Row.

Lindgren, Henry C., 1956, *Educational Psychology in the Classroom*. London, John Wiley.

Loukes, Harold, et al., 1983, *Education: An Introduction*. Oxford, Martin Robertson.

Lowell, K. and Venon, P.E., 1973, *Educational Psychology and Children*. London, University of London Press.

Lowenthal, F. and Vandamme, F., ed., 1986, *Pragmatics and Education*. New York, Planeum.

Lucas, J.C., 1972, *Our Western Educational Heritage*. New York, MacMillan.

Lyon, Harold, C. Jr., 1971, *Learning to Feel and Feeling to Learn*. Ohio, Charles E. Merill.

Lynch, M.D. and Hunstberger, D.V., 1975, *Elements of Statistical Inference for Education and Psychology*. Allyn & Bacon.

Madan, Sarup, 1982, *Education, State and Crisis: A Marxist Perspective*. London, Routledge & Kegan Paul.

Madge, John, 1976, *The Tools of Social Science*. London, Longman.

Mahrer, A.R., 1978, *Experiencing: A Humanistic Theory of Psychology and Psychiatry*. New York, Bruner/Mazel.

Maier, H.W., 1965, *Three Theories of Child Development*. New York, Harper.

Malik, Rab Nawaz, 1983, *Development of Muslim Educational Thought, 700-1900*. Michigen, University Microfilm International.

Mann, John, 1972, *Learning To Be: The Education of Human Potential*. New York, Free Press.

Mannheim, K. and Steward, W.A.C., 1962, *An Introduction to Sociology of Education*. London, Routledge and Kegan Paul.

Mannheim, K. and Freedom, 1951, *Power and Democratic Planning*. London, Routledge and Kegan Paul.

Martin, W.O., 1969, *Realism in Education*. New York, Harper & Row.

Maslow, A.H., ed., 1959, *New Knowledge in Human Values*. London, Harper & Row.

Mason, E.J. and Bramble, W.J., 1978, *Understanding Educational Research*. New York, McGraw Hill Book Co.

Maslow, Abraham H. and Mittleman, B., 1951, *Principles of Abnormal Psychology*, New York, Harper and Bros.

Maslow, Abraham H., 1954, *Motivation and Personality*. New York, Harper and Row.

Mathews, Michael R., 1980, *Marxist Theory of Schooling: A Study of Epistemology and Education*. Sussex, Harvester Press.

Mayee, J.B., 1971, *Philosophical Analysis in Education*. New York, Harper & Row.

Mayer, F., 1964, *A History of Educational Thought*. Columbas, Charles E. Marrill.

McAshan, H.H., *Elements of Educational Research*. New York, McGraw Hill.

McCandless, Boyal R. and Richard R., 1979, *Adolescents: Behaviour and Development*. 2nd ed., New York, Holt, Rinehart and Winston.

McCandless, B.R., 1977, *Children*. New York, Holt Rinehart and Winston.

McClellan, J.E., 1976, *Philosophy of Education*. New Jersey, Prentice Hall.

McDermott, J.J., ed., 1973, *The Philosophy of John Dewey*. Vol. 2, New York, Putnam.

McGuigan, F.G., ed., 1973, *Contemporary Approaches to Conditioning and Learning*. D.C. Washington.

McKinney, Fred, 1949, *Psychology of Personal Adjustment*. New York, Chapman and Hall.

Mehrens, W.A. and Lehmann, I.J., 1984, *Measurement and Evaluation, Evaluation in Education and Psychology*. New York, Holt, Rinehart.

Meschaheryakov, A., 1979, *Awakening to Life*. Moscow, Progress.

Miles, M. and Huberman, A., 1984, *Qualitative Data Analysis: A Source Book of New Methods*. Sage, Beverly Hills.

Mitchell, 1959, *Sociology*. London, University Tutorial Press.

Mitchell, J. and Oakley A., ed., 1976, *The Rights and Wrong of Women*. England, Penguin.

Mitzel, H.E., 1982, *Encyclopaedia of Educational Research*. (Vol. 1-4), New York, Free Press.

Mohammad, Wasiallah Khan, ed., 1981, *Education and Society in the Muslim World*. Jeddah, King Abdulaziz University.

Mook, Douglas, G., 1982, *Psychological Research, Strategy and Tactics*. New York, Harper & Row Publishers.

Moore, T.W., 1974, *Educational Theory: An Introduction*. Boston Routledge & Kegan Paul.

Moore, Nick, 1987, *How to do Research*. 2nd ed., London, Library Association.

Moore, T.W., 1982, *Philosophy of Education: An Introduction: International Library of the Philosophy of Education*. Routledge Education Books.

Moorish, Ivor, 1972, *The Sociology of Education — An Introduction*. London, George Allen and Unwin.

Morgan, Clifford T., 1962, *Introduction to Psychology*. 2nd ed., New York, McGraw Hill.

Moroney, M.J., 1953, *Facts From Figures*. Penguin.

Morris, Eson E., 1972, *Psychological Foundation of Education*. New York, Holt, Rinehart and Winston.

Morris, V., 1966, *Existentialism in Education*. New York, Harper & Row.

Morrish, I., 1967, *Disciplines of Education: Philosophy-Plato, Rousseau, Dewey Psychology-Freud, Piaget, Skinner, Sociològy. Derkheim, Mannheim, Mead*, London, George Allen & Unwin.

Mouly, George, J., 1960, *Psychology in Effective Learning*. New York, Holt, Rinehart and Winston.

Mouly, George J., 1962, *Psychology for Effective Teaching*. New York, Holt, Rinehart and Winston.

Mouly, G.F., 1971, *Reading in Educational Psychology*. New York, Holt, Rinehart and Winston.

Mourer, Hobart O., 1960, *Learning Theory and Behaviour*. New York, John Wiley and Sons.

Munn, Norman L., 1962, *Introduction to Psychology*. Boston, Houghton Mifflin Co.

Musgrove, Frank, 1982, *Education and Anthropology: Other Cultures and the Teacher*. Chichester, John Wiley.

Musgrane, P.W., 1975, *Sociology of Education*. London, Methuen.

Mussen, Paul H. and Conger, Janeway J., 1956, *Child Development and Personality*. New York, Harper and Brothers.

Myrdal, G., 1944, *An American Dilemma*, New York, Harper.

Nakosteen, M., 1968, *History of Islamic Origins of Western Education*. Boulder, University of Colorado Press.

Nicole, J.W. and Richard, W., 1960, *Handbook of Abnormal Psychology*. London, Vision.

Niessen, Mannfred and Peschar, Jules, ed., 1982, *Comparative Research on Education: Overview, Strategy and Applications in Eastern and Western Europe*. Oxford, Pergamon Press.

Nisbet, ed., 1985, *Research, Policy and Perspective*. London, Kogan Page.

Nisbet, J. and Hendry, I.B. et al., 1980, *Towards Community Education*. Oxford, Pergamon.

Nunnally, J.C., 1972, *Educational Measurement and Evaluation*. New York, McGraw Hill.

Oakes, Jeanmie, 1985, *Keeping Track: How Schools Structure Inequality*. New Haven, Yale University.

Oates, John, ed., 1979, *Early Cognitive Development*. London, Croom Helm.

O'Connor, D.J., 1957, *An Introduction to the Philosophy of Education*. London, Routledge-Kegan Paul.

OECD, 1983, *Education, Urban Development and Local Inequalities*. Paris, Centre for Educational Research and Innovation.

O'day, Rosemary, 1982, *Education and Society 1500-1800: The Sociological Foundations of Education in Early Modern Britain*. New York, Longman.

Ogburn, W.F., 1922, *Social Change*. New York, Viking Press.

O'Hear, Antony, 1981, *Education, Society and Human Nature: An Introduction to Philosophy of Education*. Routledge and Kegan Paul.

Olson, David R., 1970, *Cognitive Development*. New York, Academic Press.

Olson, W.C. and Hughes, B.O., 1943, *Child Behaviour and Development*. New York, McGraw Hill.

Open University, 1981, *(Educational Studies, Society, Education and the State Series 10-11). Class, Gender and Education*. Milton Keynes.

Open University, 1981, *Observing Classroom Processes (Educational Studies, Curriculum Evaluation and Measurement in Educational Institutions Series 3)*, Milton Keynes.

Open University, 1981, *Measuring Learning Outcomes. Series 4*, Milton Keynes.

Open University, 1982, *Organization and Use of Evaluation*, Milton Keynes (Series, 6).

Ottaway, A.K.C., 1955, *Education and Society*. London, Routledge and Kegan Paul.

Ozman, A. Howard and Creven, M. Samuel, 1986, *Philosophical Foundations of Education*. London, Merrill.

Painter, F.V.N., ed., 1905, *Great Pedagogical Essays: Plato to Spencer*, New York, American.

Palton, Michael Quin, 1980, *Qualitative Evaluation Methods*. London, Sage.

Parsons, Talcott, 1951, *The Social System*. New York, Free Press.

Patty and Johnson, 1953, *Personality and Adjustment*. London, McGraw Hill.

Paul, Torrance E., 1965, *Rewarding Creative Behaviour*. Engle-wood Cliffs, N.J., Prentice Hall.

Pelrosyan, M., 1972, *Humanism*. Moscow, Progress.

Penman, Kenneth A. and Adams, Samuel H. 1980, *Assessing Athletic and Physical Education Programmes: A Manual with Reproducible Forms*. Boston, Allyn and Bacon.

Perry, L.R., 1967, *Four Progressive Educators: B. Russell, A.S. Neil, H. Lour, W.H. Kilpatrik*. New York, MacMillan.

Pervin, L.A., 1970, *Personality: Theory, Assessment and Research*. New York, Wiley.

Peters, R.S. 1963, *Authority, Responsibility and Education*. London, George Allen & Unwin.

Philip, A.E., Cullock, Mc. J.W. and N.J. Smith, 1975, *Social Work Research and the Analysis of Social Data*. New York, Pergamon Press.

Piaget, Jean, 1959, *The Language and Thought of the Child*. London, Routledge and Kegan Paul.

Piaget, Jean, 1962, *Play, Dreams and Imitation in Childhood*. London, Routledge and Kegan Paul.

Plake, B.S. & Writt, J.C., 1986, *The Future of Testing*. Erlbanum, Hillisdale.

Popham, James W., 1967, *Educational Statistics — Use and Interpretation*. New York, Harper & Row.

Popper, K.R., 1959, *The Logic of Scientific Discovery*. London, Routledge and Kegan Paul.

Power, E.J., 1969, *Evolution of Educational Doctrine: Major Educational Theorists of the Western World*. New York, Appleton-Century-Grofts.

Pratte, R., 1977, *Ideology and Education*. New York, McDay.

Pressisen, Barbara Z., 1985, *Unlearned Lessons*. London, Falmer Press.

Pressy, Sidney L., et al., 1959, *Psychology in Education*. New York, Harper and Brothers.

Pringle, M.R. and Varma, V.P., 1974, *Advance in Educational Psychology*. London, University of London.

Pumfrey, Peter, D., 1985, *Reading: Tests and Assessment Techniques*, 2nd ed., Kent, Hodder and Stoughton P.

Purvis, Jons and Hales, Margaret, ed., 1983, *Achievement and Equality in Education*, London, Routledge and Kegan Paul.

Radhakrishnan, S. and Moore, *Source Book of Indian Philosophy*. London, George Allen & Unwin.

Ray, William, 1970, *Moral Development*. London, George Allen & Unwin.

Reid, Ivan, 1978, *Sociological Perspectives on School and Education*. London, Open Books.

Reid, L.A., 1962, *Philosophy and Education*. London, Heineman.

Remmers, H.H. and others, 1957, *Growth, Teaching and Learning: A Book of Reading*. New York.

Richardson, John G., ed., 1986, *Handbook of Theory and Research for Sociology of Education*. London, Greenwood.

Rich, John Martin, 1971, *Humanistic Foundations of Education*. Ohio, Charles A. Johns.

Rivlin, Harry N., 1936, *Educating for Adjustment*. New York, Appleton-Century-Crofts.

Roberts, Thomas, B., 1975, *Four Psychologies Applied to Education, Freudian, Behavioural, Humanistic and Transpersonal*. New York, Schenmukan.

Robinson, Paul W., 1981, *Fundamentals of Experimental Psychology*. 2nd ed., New Jersey, Prentice-Hall.

Robinson, G., 1969, *Educational Psychology*. New York, Holt, Rinehart and Winston.

Robinson. Philip, 1976, *Education and Poverty*. London, Mathuen.

Robinson, Philip, 1981, *Perspective in the Sociology of Education*. London, Routledge and Kegan Paul.

Roe, Keith, 1983, *Mass Media and Adolescent Schooling: Conflict or Co-existence?* Sweden, Almquist and Wiksell International.

Rogers, Colin, 1982, *Social Psychology of Schooling: The Expectancy Process*. London, Routledge and Kegan Paul.

Rogers, C.R., 1980, *A Way of Being*. Houghton Mifflin, Boston.

Rogers, Everett, M., *Modernization Among Peasants: The Impact of Communication*. New York, Holt, Rinehart and Winston.

Rogers, Everett M. and Shoemaker, Floyd F., 1971, *Communication of Innovations — A Cross Cultural Approach*. New York, Free Press.

Roman, F.W., 1930, *The New Education in Europe*. London, Routledge.

Rosenbaum, Max and Snadowsky, Alvin, 1976, *The Intensive Group Experience: A Guide*. New York, Free Press.

Rose, A.M., ed., 1955, *Mental Health and Mental Disorder*, New York, Norton.

Ross, J.S., 1960, *Ground-work of Education Theory*. London, George G. Harrap.

Rowntree, Derek, ed., 1987, *Assessing Students: How Shall we Know Them?* London, Kogan Page.

Ruddy, Savah and Woodhead, Martin, 1980, *Family, Work and Education*. Open University Press.

Rudy, W., 1965, *Schools in An Age of Mass Culture*. New York, Prentice-Hill.

Rummel, J.F., 1964, *An Introduction to Research Procedure in Education*. 2nd ed., New York, Harper & Row.

Russell, B., *Wisdom of the West*. London, Allen & Unwin.

Russell, B., 1947, *History of Western Philosophy*. London, George Allan & Unwin.

Russel, Bertrand, 1956, *Education and the Social Order*. London, George Allen and Unwin.

Russell, B., 1972, *Education and the Good Life*. New York, Leveright.

Sarup, M., 1978, *Marxism and Education*, Boston, Routledge & Kegan Paul.

Schofield, H., 1972, *The Philosophy of Education*. London, George Allen & Unwin.

Scimecca, Joseph A., 1980, *Education and Society*. London, Holt, Rinehart and Winston.

Severin, Frank T., 1973, *Discovering Man in Psychology: A Humanistic Approach*. New York, McGraw Hill.

Sherman, Howard J., 1979, *Sociology, Traditional and Radical Perspectives*. New York, Harper and Row.

Shils, E.A., 1961, *The Intellectual Between Tradition and Modernity: The Indian Situation*. Hauge, Mountnon.

Shore Maurice J., et al., ed., 1950, *Twentieth Century Mental Hygiene*. New York, Social Science.

Simmons, Roberto G., 1981, *Research in Community and Mental Health*. Vol. 2, Greenwich, Jai Press.

Sinclser, 1967, *Sociology — An Introduction*. New York, Willey Eastern.

Sinclair, M.E., 1980, *School and Community in the Third World*. London, Croom Helm.

Singer, Robert, N., 1975, *Motor Learning/and Human Performance*. New York, Macmillan.

Smith, Henry P., 1954, *Psychology in Teaching*. New York, Prentice Hall.

Soltis, J.F., ed., 1981, *Philosophy and Education*. *Eightieth Year Book of N.S.S.E.*, Chicago, University of Chicago Press.

Soltis, J.F., 1968, *An Introduction to the Analysis of Educational Concepts*. London, Addison Wesley.

Soltis, J.F., ed., 1981, *Philosophy of Education Since Mid-century*. New York, Teachers' College Press.

Sorenson, Herbert, 1954, *Psychology in Education*. London, McGraw Hill.

Sowell, Thomas, 1986, *Education: Assumptions Versus History*. Stanford University, Hoover Institution Press.

Spence, K.W. and Spence, J.T., ed., 1968, *The Psychology of Learning and Motivation*. Vol. I and II.

Splindler, G.D., *Education and Culture*. New York, Holt, Rinehart and Winston.

Stemmer, Nathan, 1983, *Roots of Knowledge*. Oxford, Basil Blackwell.

Stephens, J.M., 1956, *Educational Psychology*. New York, Henry Holt and Co.

Sternberge, Robert J., 1985, *Beyond I.Q.: A Trianchic Theory of Human Intelligence*. Cambridge, Cambridge University Press.

Stevenson, George S., 1956, *Mental Health Planning for Social Action*. New York, McGraw Hill.

Stoddard, G.B. and Wellman, B.L., 1934, *Child Psychology*. New York, Macmillan.

Storm, R.D., (1969), *Psychology for the Classroom*. New York, Prentice Hall.

Stones, E., 1970, *Readings in Educational Psychology*. London, Methuen.

Storange, Jack Ray, 1965, *Abnormal Psychology Understanding Behaviour Disorder*. London, McGraw Hill.

Straker-Welds, Martin, ed., 1984, *Education for a Multi-cultural Society*. London, Bell and Hyman.

Straughan, Roger and Wilson John, ed., 1987, *Philosophers on Education*, London, Methnen.

Swartz, Paul, 1963, *Psychology: The Study of Behaviour*. New York, D. Vann Nostrand Company.

Swoft, D.F., 1969, *The Sociology of Education*. London, Routledge and Kegan Paul.

Symonds, P.M., 1943, *The Dynamics of Human Adjustment*. New York, Appleton Century.

Tanner, J.M. and Inhelder, Barbel, ed., 1958, *Discussions in Child Development — Readings*. London, Tavistock.

Taylor, William, 1973, *Research Perspectives in Education*. London, Routledge and Kegan Paul.

Teevan, Richard and Birncy, Robert C., ed., 1964, *Theories of Motivation in Learning*. New Jersey.

Tescond, C.A. and Morris, V., 1972, *The Antimen Culture: Bureau-Technocracy and the Schools*. Urban, University of Illinois Press.

Thompson, Gardner and Di Vesta, 1959, *Educational Psychology*. New York, Appleton-Century-Crofts.

Thompson, George G., 1952, *Child Psychology*. Boston, Houghton Mifflin.

Thorndike, B.L., 1982, *Applied Psychometrics*, Boston, Houghton Mifflin.

Thorndike, R.L., 1950, *How Children Learn the Principles and Techniques of Problem-solving*. Chicago, University of Chicago Press.

Thrope, L.B. and Schumuller, Allen M., 1954, *Contemporary Theories of Learning with Applications of Educational Psychology*. New York, Ronnald Press.

Thut, I.N., 1967, *The Study of Education*. New York, McGraw Hill.

Torrance, Paul E., 1965, *Rewarding Creative Behaviour*. New Jersey, Englewood Cliffs, Prentice Hall.

Travers, Robert M., 1963, *Essentials of Learning: An Overview for Students of Education*. New York, MacMillan.

Travers, Robert M.W., 1978, *An Introduction to Educational Research*. New York, Macmillan.

Tuckman, B.W., 1978, *Conducting Educational Research*. 2nd ed., New York, Harcourt Brace, Javanovich.

Tuckman Bruce, W., 1979, *Analysing and Designing Educational Research*. New York, Harcourt Brace, Javanovich.

Turner, John C. and Giles, Howard, ed., 1981, *Intergroup Behaviour*. Oxford, Basil Blackwell.

Turney, L. Billey and P. Robb, George, 1971, *Research in Education : An Introduction*. Hindle, Illinois, Dryden Press.

Tye, Kenneth A. and Novotney Jerold M., 1975, *Schools in Transition: The Practitioner as Change Agent*, New York, McGraw Hill.

Tyler, William, 1977, *The Sociology of Educational Inequality*. London, Mathuen.

Ulich, R., 1964, *Education and The Idea of Mankind*. New York, Harcourt Brace & World Inc.

Ulich, R., 1947, *Three Thousand Years of Educational Wisdom*. Cambridge, Harward University Press.

UNESCO, 1982, *Inequalities in Educational Development: An IIEP Seminar*. Paris, Unesco.

Vaidya, Narendra, 1982, *Researches on Adolescent Thought: A Framework*. Regional College of Education.

Van, Dalen, Debonald, B. and Meyer, William, J., 1979, *Understanding Educational Research: An Introduction*. New York, MacGraw Hill.

Van, Dalen Debonald, Band Meyer William, J., 1968, *Understanding Education Research*, London, McGraw Hill.

Vandenberg, D., 1971, *Being and Education: An Essay in Existential Phenomenology*. Englewood Cliffs, N.J. Prentice-Hall.

Van, Scotter; Richard, D. and others, 1979, *Foundations of Education: Social Perspectives*. Englewood Cliffs, Prentice Hall.

Vernon, P.E., 1964, *Personality Assessment*. London, McThuon.

Vidler, D.C., 1977, Achievement Motivation in Ball, S. ed., *Motivation in Education*. New York, Academic Press.

Wain, Kennath, 1987, *Philosophy of Lifelong Education*. London, Croom Helm.

Walizen, Michael H. and Wienir Paul L., 1978, *Research Methods and Analysis*. New York, Harper & Row.

Walker, Stephen and Barton, Len, ed., 1983, *Gender, Class and Education*. Lewes, Falmer Press.

Waller, S., 1975, *Learning and Reinforcement*. London, Methuen.

Wallin, J.C., 1935, *Personality Maladjustments and Mental Hygiene*. New York, McGraw-Hill.

Waller, Willard, 1965, *The Sociology of Teaching*, New York, John Wiley.

Walsh, Herber M., 1980, *Introducing the Young Child to the Social World*. New York, Macmillan.

Walters, Marian Van, 1925, *Youth in Conflict*. New York, New Republic.

Warnock, M., 1987, *Schools of Thought*. London, Faber & Faber.

Watson, Keith, ed., 1982, *Education in the Third World*. London, Croom Helm.

Watson, Keith, ed., 1984, *Dependence and Interdependence in Education: International Perspectives*. London, Croom Helm.

Wedge, B.M., ed., 1958, *Psycho-Social Problems of College Men*. New Haven, Yale University Press.

Weiss, D.J., 1983, *New Horizons in Testing: Latent Trait Test Theory and Computerized Adaptive Testing*. New York, Academic Press.

West, Philip T., 1985, *Educational Public Relations*. London, Sage.

Westman, J.C., 1973, *Individual Difference in Children*. New York, Wiley.

Wilberman, L., 1979, *The Psychology of Individual and Group Differences*. California, Freeman.

Williamson, Bill, 1979, *Education, Social Structure and Development*. London, Macmillan.

Wilson, A.R., Roebeck, M.C. and Michael, W.B., 1979, *Psychological Foundations of Learning and Teaching*. New York, McGraw Hill.

Wilson, M.J., ed., 1979, *Social and Educational Research in Action*. New York, Longmans.

White, Jennings, 1939, *Guide to Mental Health*. Great Britain, C.W. Daniel.

White, John, 1982, *Aims of Education*. London, Routledge and Kegan Paul.

White, William F., 1969, *Psychological Principles Applied to Classroom Teaching*. New York, McGraw Hill.

Wolman, B.B., 1965, *Contemporary Theories and Systems in Psychology*. New York, Harper and Row.

Wolman, B. Benjamin, 1965, *Handbook of Clinical Psychology*. New York, McGraw Hill.

Woodworth, R.S., 1967, *Contemporary Schools of Psychology*. London, Methuen.

Woodworth, Robert S. and Marquis, Donald G., 1949, *Psychology*. 20th ed., London, Methuen.

Woods, Peter, 1983, *Sociology and the School: An Internationist Viewpoint*. London, Routledge and Kegan Paul.

Woody, R.H., 1969, *Behavioural Problem Children in the Schools*. New York, Appleton Century Crofts.

Wordsworth, B.J., 1978, *Piaget for the Classroom Teachers*. New York, Longman.

Wringe, Colin, 1984, *Democracy, Schooling and Political Education*. London, George Allen & Unwin.

Yelon, S. and Weinstein, G.W., 1977, *A Teacher's World: Psychology in the Classroom*. New York, McGraw Hill.

Yin, Robert, K., 1984, *Case Study Research*. London, Sage.

Ysseldyke, J.E. Algozzine, B., 1982, *Critical Issues in Special and Remedial Education*. Boston, Houghton Mifflin.

Zwerling, L. Steven, ed., 1986, *Community College and Its Critics*. London, Jossey-bass.

List of Selected Journals on Education Published in Abroad

Aboriginal Child at School, University of Queensland, Department of Education, St Lucia, Queensland 4067, Australia.

Academe, American Association of University Professors, Suite 500, 1012 14th Street, N.W., Washington, D.C. 20005, U.S.A.

Academic Medicine, Hanley and Belfus, Inc., 210 South 13th Street, Philadelphia, PA 19107, U.S.A.

Academic Therapy, PRO-ED, Inc., 5341 Industrial Oaks Blvd, Austin, TX 78735, U.S.A.

ACHPER National Journal, Australian Council for Health, Physical Education and Recreation, P.O. Box 294 Eastwood, S.A. 5063, Australia.

ACT Papers in Adult Education and Training, Canberra College of Advanced Education, School of Education, P.O. Box 1, Belconnen 2616, Australia.

Action in Teacher Education, Association of Teacher Educators, 1900 Association Drive, Reston, VA 22091, U.S.A.

Adult Education, American Association for Adult and Continuing Education.

Adult Education, National Institute of Adult Continuing Education, 19B De Montfort Street, Leicester LEI 7GE, England.

Adult Education and Development, German Adult Educational Association, Deutscher Volkshochschul Verlag, Rheinallee 1, 5300 Bonn 2, West Germany.

Adult Education in Finland, Society for Popular Culture, Museokatu 18 A 2,00100 Helsinki 10, Finland.

Adult Education Quarterly, American Association for Adult and Continuing Education, 1201 16th Street, N.W., Suite 301, Washington, D.C. 20036, U.S.A.

Adults Learning, National Institute of Adult Continuing Education, 19B De Montfort Street, Leicester LEI 7GE, England.

Advances in Mathematics, Executive Editor, Academic Press Inc. III Fifth Avenue, New York, 10003 U.S.A.

Adventure Education, Studies in Education Ltd., Nafferton, Driffield, N. Humberside YO25 0JL, England.

Alberta Journal of Educational Research, University of Alberta, Faculty of Education, 845 Education South, Edmonton, Alberta T6G 2G5, Canada.

All-in Success, Centre for the Study of Comprehensive Schools, Wentworth College, University of York, York YOI 5DD, England.

American Biology Teacher, National Association of Biology Teachers, 11250 Roger Bacon Drive, #19, Reston, VA 22090, U.S.A.

American Educational Research Journal, American Educational Research Association, 1230 17th Street, N.W., Washington, D.C. 20036, U.S.A.

American Journal of Distance Education, Pennsylvania State University, Rackley Building, University Park, PA 16802, U.S.A.

American Journal of Education, University of Chicago Press, 5801 South Ellis Avenue, Chicago, IL 60637, U.S.A.

American School Board Journal, National School Boards Association, 1680 Duke Street, Alexandria, VA 22314, U.S.A.

American Secondary Education, Bowling Green State University, Room 319, Education Building, Bowling Green, OH 43403, U.S.A.

Anthropology and Education Quarterly, American Anthropological Association, 1703 New Hampshire Av. N.W., Washington, D.C. 20009, U.S.A.

Applied Cognitive Psychology, John Wiley & Sons Ltd, Baffins Lane, Chichester, Sussex PO19 1UD, England.

Applied Linguistics, Oxford University Press, Walton Street, Oxford OX2 6DP, England.

Applied Measurement in Education, Lawrence Erlbaum Associates, Inc., 365 Broadway, Hillsdale, NJ 07642, U.S.A.

Applied Psycholinguistics, Cambridge University Press, The Pitt Building, Trumpington Street, Cambridge CB2 IRP, England.

AREE: The Annual Review of Environmental Education, Council for Environmental Education, School of Education, University of Reading, London Road, Reading RG1 5AQ, England.

Arithmetic Teacher, National Council of Teachers of Mathematics, Inc., 1906 Association Drive, Reston, VA 22091, U.S.A.

Art Education, National Art Education Association, 1916 Association Drive, Reston, VA 22091, U.S.A.

Artificial Intelligence Review, Blackwell Scientific Publications Ltd, Osney Mead, Oxford OX2 OEL, England.

Asian Education and Training, Broadgate Press Ltd, 7 Plough Yard, London EC2A 3LP, England.

Aspects of Education, University of Hull, Institute of Education, 173 Cottingham Road, Hull HU5 2EH, England.

Assessment and Evaluation in Higher Education, University of Bath, School of Education, Claverton Down, Bath BA2 7AY, England.

ATEA Journal, American Technical Education Association, Inc., North Dakota State School of Science, Wahpeton, ND 58075, U.S.A.

Australian Educational and Developmental Psychologist, Board of Educational and Developmental Psychologists, Nedlands Campus, Western Australia College of Advanced Education, Stirling Highwav, Nedlands, Western Australia 6009.

Australian Educational Researcher, Australian Association for Research in Education, Inc., University of New England, Mossman Street, Armidale, N.S.W. 2351, Australia.

Australian Journal of Adult Education, Australian Association of Adult Education, Inc., P.O. Box 1346, Canberra City, A.C.T. 2601, Australia.

Australian Journal of Early Childhood, Australian Early Childhood Association, Inc., Knox Street, P.O. Box 105, Watson, A.C.T. 2602, Australia.

Australian Journal of Education, Australian Council for Educational Research Ltd. P.O. Box 210, Hawthorn, Victoria 3122, Australia.

Australian Journal of Educational Technology, Australian Society for Educational Technology, P.O. Box 772, Belconnen, A.C.T. 2616, Australia.

Australian Journal of Remedial Education, Australian Special Books Services, 319 High Street, Kew, Victoria 3101, Australia.

Australian Journal of TAFE Research and Development, TAFE National Centre for Research and Development Ltd, 252 Kensington Road, Leabrook, S.A. 5068, Australia.

Australian Mathematics Teacher, Australian Association of Mathematics Teachers Inc., 20 Kookaburra Street, Kenmore Hills, Queensland 4069, Australia.

Australian Science Teachers Journal, Australian Science Teachers Association, P.B. Box 383, Dickson, A.C.T. 2602, Australia.

Australian TAFE Teacher, Technical and Further Education Teachers' Association, P.O. Box 415, Carlton South 3053, Australia.

Australian Teacher, Australian Teachers Federation, P.O. Box 410, Carlton, Australia 3050.

Australian Teacher of the Deaf, Australian Association of Teachers of the Deaf, P.O. Box 100, Croydon Park, N.S.W. 2133, Australia.

Australian Technical Teacher, Technical Teachers Association of Australia, 101 Gap Greek Road, Brookfield, Queensland 4069, Australia.

Australian Universities' Review, Federation of Australian University Staff Associations, 25 Palmerston Court, South Melbourne, Victoria 3205, Australia.

Banking and Financial Training, Philip Thorn Associates Ltd, 53 Ridgemount, Guildford, Surrey GU2 5TH, England.

Basic Education, Council for Basic Education, 725 15th Street, N.W., Washington, D.C. 20005, U.S.A.

Behavioural Approaches with Children, Association for Behavioural Approaches with Children, Centre for Child Study, Department of Educational Psychology, University of Birmingham, P.O Box 363, Birmingham B15 2TT, England.

Bildung und Wissenschaft, Inter Nationes, Kennedyallee 91-103, D-5300 Bonn 2, West Germany.

Biochemical Education, Pergamon Journals Ltd, Headington Hill Hall, Oxford OX3 0BW, England.

BPS Education Section Review, British Psychological Society, St. Andrew's House, 48 Princess Road East, Leicester LET 7DR, England.

British Educational Research Journal, Carfax Publishing Company, P.O. Box 25, Abingdon, Oxfordshire OX14 3UE, England.

The British Journal of Disorders of Communication, The College of Speech Therapists, 47 St. Johns Wood High Street, London, N.W.8.

British Journal of Education and Work, Trentham Books Ltd, 151 Etruria Road, Hanley, Stock-on-Trent, Staffordshire STI 5NS, England.

British Journal of Educational Psychology, Scottish Academic Press Ltd, 33 Montgomery Street, Edinburgh EH7 5JX, Scotland.

British Journal of Educational Studies, Basti Blackwell Ltd, 108 Cowley Road, Oxford OX4 IJF, England.

British Journal of Educational Technology, National Council for Educational Technology, 3 Devonshire Street, London WIN 2BA, England.

British Journal of Guidance and Counselling, Hobsons Publishing plc, Bateman Street, Cambridge CB2 1LZ, England.

British Journal of In-Service Education, Studies in Education Ltd, Nafferton, Driffield, N. Humberside YO25 0JL, England.

British Journal of Language Teaching, British Association for Language Teaching, 21 The Green, The Paddocks, Charlbury, Oxfordshire OX7 3QA, England.

British Journal of Music Education, Cambridge University Press, Edinburgh Building, Shaftesbury Road, Cambridge CB2 2RU, England.

British Journal of Physical Education, Physical Education Association of Great Britain and Northern Ireland, Ling House, 162 King's Cross Road, London WC1X 9DH, England.

British Journal of Psychiatric Social Work, The Association for Special Workers, 71, Albany St., Regent's Park, London, NWl.

British Journal of Religious Education, Christian Education Movement, 2 Chester House, Pages Lane, London N10 1PR, England.

British Journal of Sociology of Education, Carfax Publishing Company, P.O. Box 25, Abingdon, Oxfordshire OX14 3UE, England.

British Journal of Special Education, National Council for Special Education, *Subscriptions:* Carfax Publishing Company, P.O. Box 25, Abingdon, Oxfordshire OX14 3UE, England.

British Journal of Visual Impairment, Association for the Education and Welfare of the Visually Handicapped, the South Regional Office of the Blind, 55 Eton Avenue, London NW3 3ET, England.

Bulletin of Environmental Education, Streetwork Ltd, c/o Nottingdale Studies Centre, 189 Freston Road, London W1O 6TH, England.

Bulletin of Physical Education, British Association of Advisers and Lecturers in Physical Education, 6 Ladywood Mead, Leeds LS8 2LZ, England.

Bulletin of Teaching and Learning, Newcastle-upon-Tyne Polytechnic, Ellison Building, Ellison Place, Newcastle-upon- Tyne NEI 8ST, England.

Bulletin of the International Bureau of Education, UNESCO, 7 Place de Fontenoy, 75700 Paris, France.

Business Education Forum, National Business Education Association, 1914 Association Drive, Reston, VA 2209, U.S.A.

Business Education World, McGraw-Hill Book Co., Gregg Division, 1221 Avenue of the Americans, New York, N.Y. 10020, U.S.A.

Cambridge Journal of Education, Carfax Publishing Company, P.O. Box 25, Abingdon, Oxfordshire OX1 3UE, England.

Canadian Administrator, University of Alberta, Department of Educational Administration, Edmonton, Alberta T6G, 2G5, Canada.

Canadian and International Education, Comparative and International Education Society of Canada, Faculty of Education, University of Calgary, Calgary, Alberta T2N 1N4, Canada.

Canadian Journal of Counselling, Canadian Guidance and Counselling Association, P.O. Box 13059, Kanata, Ontario K2K 1X3, Canada.

Canadian Journal of Education, Canadian Society for the Study of Education, 14 Henderson Avenue, Ottawa, Ontario K1N 7P1, Canada.

Canadian Journal of Educational Communication, Association for Media and Technology in Education in Canada, Wellington Board of Education, 500 Victoria Road, North Guelph, Ontario N1E 6K2, Canada.

Canadian Journal of English Language Arts, Canadian Council of Teachers of English, Box 3382, Station B, Calgary, Alberta T2K 4M1, Canada.

Canadian Journal of Higher Education, Canadian Society for the Study of Higher Education, Bureau de Recherche Institutionelle, Universite de Montreal. C.P. 6128, Succursale 'A', Montreal, Quebec H3C 3J7, Canada.

Canadian Journal of University Continuing Education, Canadian Association of University Continuing Education, University of Guelph, Room 154, Johnston Hall, Guelph, Ontario N1G 2W1, Canada.

Canadian Modern Language Review, Ontario Modern Language Teachers' Association, 4 Oakmount Road, Welland, Ontario L3C 4X8, Canada.

Canadian Review of Art Education Research, Canadian Society for Education Through Art, 3186 Newbound Court, Malton, Ontario L4T 1R9, Canada.

Canadian Vocational Journal, Canadian Vocational Association, P.O. Box 3435, Station D, Ottawa, Ontario K1P 6L4, Canada.

Capstone Journal of Education, University of Alabama, P.O. Box Q. Tuscaloosa, AL 35487, U.S.A.

Career Development Quarterly, National Career Development Association, American Association for Counseling and Development, 5999 Stevenson Avenue, Alexandria, VA 22304, U.S.A.

Caribbean Journal of Education, University of the West Indies, Faculty of Education, Mona, St Andrew, Jamaica.

Change, Heldref Publications, Inc., 4000 Albemarle Street, N.W., Washington, D.C. 20016, U.S.A.

Chemical Engineering Education, American Society for Engineering Education, Chemical Engineering Division, University of Florida, Chemical Engineering Department Gainesville, FL 32611, U.S.A.

Child and Man, Steiner School Fellowship, The Sprig, Ashdown Road, Forest Row, East Sussex RH18 5BN, England.

Child Development, University of Chicago Press, P.O. 37005, Chicago, IL 60637, U.S.A.

Child Education, Scholastic Publications Ltd, Westfield Road, Southam, Nr Leamington Spa, Warwickshire CV33 OJH, England.

Child Language Teaching and Therapy, Edward Arnold (Publishers) Ltd, 41 Bedford Square, London WC1B 3DQ, England.

Child Study Journal, State University of New York College at Buffalo, Faculty of Applied and Professional Studies, Bacon Hall 312J, 1300 Elmwood Avenue, Buffalo, N.Y. 14222, U.S.A.

Childhood Education, Association for Childhood Education International, 3615 Wisconsin Avenue, N.W., Washington, D.C. 20016, U.S.A.

Children and Society, Whiting and Birch Ltd, 90 Dartmouth Road, Forest Hill, London SE23 3HZ, England.

Children's Environments Quarterly, City University of New York, Center for Human Environments, 33 West 42 Street, New York, N.Y. 10036, U.S.A.

Children's Literature in Education, Agathon Press, Inc., 15 East 26th Street, New York, N.Y. 10010, U.S.A.

Chinese Education, M.E. Sharpe, Inc., 80 Business Park Drive, Armonk, N.Y. 10504, U.S.A.

Classroom Computer Learning, Peter Li, Inc., 2451 East River Road, Dayton, OH 45439, U.S.A.

Clearing House, Heldref Publications, Inc., 4000 Albemarle Street, N.W., Washington, D.C. 20016, U.S.A.

Cognition, Elsevier Science Publishers B.V. North Holland, P.O. Box 211,1000 AE Amsterdam, The Netherlands.

Cognition and Instruction, Lawrence, Erlbaum Associates, Inc., 365 Broadway, Suite 102, Hillsdale, N.J. 07642, U.S.A.

College and Research Libraries, Association of College and Research Libraries, American Library Association, 50 East Huron Street, Chicago, IL 60611, U.S.A.

College and Research Libraries News, Association of College and Research Libraries, American Library Association, 50 East Huron Street, Chicago, IL 60611, U.S.A.

College Board Review, College Board, 45 Columbus Avenue, New York, N.Y. 10023, U.S.A.

College Mathematics Journal, Mathematical Association of America, 1529 18th Street, N.W., Washington, D.C. 20036, U.S.A.

College Student Journal, Project Innovation, 1362 Santa Cruz Court, Chula Vista, CA 92010, U.S.A.

College Teaching, Heldref Publications, Inc., 4000 Albemarle Street, N.W., Washington, D.C. 20016, U.S.A.

Collegiate Microcomputer, Rose-Hulman Institute of Technology, Terre Haute, IN 47803 U.S.A.

Comenius, SUN Postbus 1609, 6501 BP Nijmegen, The Netherlands.

Comlon, London Chamber of Commerce and Industry, Commercial Education Scheme, Marlowe House, Station Road, Sidcup, Kent DA15 7BJ, England.

Communication Quarterly, Eastern Communication Association, Department of Speech, Temple University, Philadelphia, PA 19122, U.S.A.

Community College Review, Department of Adult and Community College Education, North Carolina State University, Raleigh, N.C. 27607, U.S.A.

Comparative Education, Carfax Publishing Company, P.O. Box 25, Abingdon, Oxfordshire OX14 3UE, England.

Comparative Education Review, University of Chicago Press, 5801 South Ellis Avenue, Chicago, IL 60637, U.S.A.

Compare, Carfax Publishing Company, P.O. Box 25, Abingdon, Oxfordshire, OX14 3UE, England.

Computer Education, Computer Education Group, North Staffordshire Polytechnic, Computer Centre, Blackheath Lane, Stafford, England.

Computers and Education, Pergamon Journals Ltd, Headington Hill Hall, Oxford OX3 0BW, England.

Computers in Adult Education and Training, Penros Publications, Department of Education, University of Keele, Staffordshire ST5 5BG, England.

Computers in Life Science Education, National Resource for Computers in Life Science Education, Mail Stop RC-70, University of Washington, Seattle, WA 98185, U.S.A.

Computers in the Schools, Haworth Press, Inc., 28 East 22nd Street, New York, N.Y. 10010, U.S.A.

Computing Teacher, International Council for Computers in Education, University of Oregon, 1787 Agate Street, Eugene, OR 97403, U.S.A.

Contemporary Education, Indiana State University, School of Education, Statesman Towers, Room 1005, Terre Haute, IN 47809, U.S.A.

Contemporary Educational Psychology, Academic Press, Inc., 111 Fifth Avenue, New York, N.Y. 10003, U.S.A.

Continuing Higher Education Review, National University Continuing Education Association, Ohio State University, 244 Mt. Hall, 1050 Carmack Road, Columbus, OH 43210, U.S.A.

Convergence, International Council for Adult Education, 29 Prince Arthur Avenue, Toronto, Ontario M5R 1B2, Canada.

Coombe Lodge Report, Further Education Staff College, Blagdon, Bristol BS18 6RG, England.

CORE (Collected Original Resources in Education), Carfax Publishing Company, P.O. Box 25, Abingdon, Oxfordshire OX14 3UE, England.

Council for Research in Music Education Bulletin, University of Illinois, School of Music, Urbana, IL 61801, U.S.A.

Curriculum, Studies in Education Ltd, Nafferton, Driffield, N. Humberside YO25 0JL, England.

Curriculum and Teaching, James Nicholas Publishers, P.O. Box 244, Albert Park, Australia 3206.

Curriculum, Inquiry, John Wiley & Sons, Inc., 605 Third Avenue, New York, N.Y. 10016, U.S.A.

Curriculum Perspectives, Australian Curriculum Studies Association, West Australian College of Advanced Education, Goldsworthy Road, Claremont, WA 6010, Australia.

Curriculum Review, Curriculum Advisory Service, 517 South Jefferson Street, Chicago, IL 60607, U.S.A.

Day Care and Early Education, Human Sciences Press, Inc., 72 Fifth Avenue, New York, N.Y. 10011, U.S.A.

Death Studies, Hemisphere Publishing Corporation, 1010 Vermont Avenue, N.W., Washington, D.C. 20005, U.S.A.

Delta, Massey University, Department of Education, Palmerston North, New Zealand.

Didatica, Universidade Estadual Paulista, Biblioteca Central da UNESP, Av. Vincente Ferreira, 1278-CP 420, 17500 Marilia, SP, Brazil.

Directions, University of the South Pacific, Institute of Education, P.O. Box 1168, Suva, Fiji.

Discourse, University of Queensland, Department of Education, St Lucia, Queensland 4067, Australia.

Discourse Processes, Ablex Publishing Corporation, 355 Chestnut Street, Norwood, NJ 07648, U.S.A.

Dissertation Abstract International, Section A (The Humanities), University Microfilms International, Ann Arbor, Michigan, 48106 USA.

Distance Education, Darling Downs Institute Press, Toowoomba, Queensland 4350, Australia.

Durham and Newcastle Research Review, School of Education, University of Durham, Leazes Road, Durham DH1 1TA, England.

EAF Journal: Journal of Educational Administration and Foundations, Faculty of Professional Studies, Lakehead University, Thunder Bay, Ontario, Canada P7B 5E1.

Early Child Development and Care, Gordon and Breach Science Publishers, 42 William IV Street, London WC2N 4DE, England.

Early Years, Trentham Books Ltd, 151 Etruria Road, Stoke-on-Trent, Staffordshire ST1 5NS, England.

Economics of Education Review, Pergamon Journals, Inc., Maxwell House, Fairview Park, Elmsford, N.Y. 10523, U.S.A.

edtech, National Council for Advisers in Educational Technology, Education Department, Shirehall, Abbey Foregate, Shrewshbury SY2 6ND, England.

Educafrica, UNESCO Regional Office for Education in Africa, Publication Service, BREDA, B.P. 3311, Dakar, Senegal.

Educare, National Bureau for Students with Disabilities, 336 Brixton Road, London SW9 5AA, England.

Education (Germany), Institute fur Wissenschaftliche Zusammenarbeit, Tubingen, Landhausstr. 18, West Germany.

Education (Malta), Faculty of Education, University of Malta, Tal-Qroqq, Malta.

Education (UK), Longman Group (UK) Ltd, Journals Division, Fourth Avenue, Harlow, Essex CM19 5AA, England.

Education (USA), Innovation, 13622 Santa Cruz Court, Chula Vista, CA 92010, U.S.A.

Education and Computing, Elsevier Science Publishers B.V. (North Holland), P.O. Box 211, 11000 AE Amsterdam, The Netherlands.

Education and Health, HEA Schools Health Education Unit, Exeter University, Heavitree Road, Exeter EX1 2LU, England.

Education and Society, James, Nicholas Publishers, P.O. Box 329, Mount Eliza, Australia, 3930.

Education and the Law, Longman Group (UK) Ltd, Fourth Avenue, Harlow, Essex CM19 5AA, England.

Education and Training, MCB University Press Ltd, 62 Toller Lane, Bradford BD8 9BY, England.

Education and Urban Society, Sage Publications, Inc., 275 South Beverly Drive, Beverly Hills, CA 90212, U.S.A.

Education Bulletin, Transvaal Education Department, Publication and Editing Service, Private Bag X76, Pretoria 0001, South Africa.

Education Canada, Canadian Education Association, 252 Bloor Street West, Toronto, Ontario M5S IV5, Canada.

Education Digest, 416, Longshore Drive, Ann Arbour, Mich, 48107.

Education for Information, Elsevier Science Publishers B.V. (North Holland), P.O. Box 211, 1000 AE Amsterdam, The Netherlands.

Education in Asia and the Pacific, UNESCO Regional Office for Education in Asia and the Pacific, P.O. Box 1425, General Post Office, Bangkok 10500, Thailand.

Education in Chemistry, Royal Society of Chemistry, Burlington House, London W1V OBN, England.

Education in Science, Association for Science Education, College Lane, Hatfield, Hertfordshire AL10 9AA, England.

Education Libraries Journal, University of London Institute of Education Library, 11-13 Ridgmount Street, London WC1E 7AH, England.

Education North, Queen's University of Belfast and the University of Ulster, Room 15 E07, University of Ulster, Newtonabbey BT27 0QB, Northern Ireland.

Education Now, Education Now Publishing Cooperative Ltd, P.O. Box 186, Ticknall, Derbyshire DE7 WF, England.

Education Permanente, Universite de Paris-Dauphine, Ple Ml. de Laittre de Tassigny, 75776 Paris Cedex 16, France.

Education Research and Perspectives, University of Western Australia, Department of Education, Nedlands, WA 6009, Australia.

Education, Longman Group (UK) Ltd., Journals Division, Fourth Avenue, Harlow, Essex CM19 5AA, England.

Education Today, Salisbury Publishing, 109 Kingsway, London WC2, England.

Education with Production, Foundation for Education with Production, P.O. Box 20906, Gaborone, Botswana.

Educational Administration Quarterly, Sage Publications, Inc., 275 South Beverly Drive, Beverly Hills, CA 90212, U.S.A.

Educational and Child Psychology, British Psychological Society, St Andrews House, Leicester LE1 7DR, England.

Educational and Psychological Interactions, Malmo School of Education, P.O. Box 23501, S-200 45 Malmo, Sweden.

Educational and Psychological Measurement, Education and Psychological Measurement, Inc., P.O. 6907, College Station, Durham, NC 27708, U.S.A.

Educational and Training Technology International, Kogan Page Ltd, 120 Pentonville Road, London N19 9JN, England.

Educational Change and Development, Deanhouse Ltd, 41 Park Lane, Congleton, Cheshire CW12 3DG, England.

Educational Communication and Technology Journal, Association of Educational Communications and Technology, Inc., 1126 16th Street, N.W. Washington, D.C. 20036, U.S.A.

Educational Evaluation and Policy Analysis, American Educational Research Association, 1230 17th Street, N.W. Washington, D.C. 20036, U.S.A.

Educational Forum, Kappa Delta Pi Honor Society in Education, 116 Ramseyer Hall, 29 West Woodruff Avenue, Columbus, OH 43210, U.S.A.

Educational Gerontology, Hemisphere Publishing Corporation, 76 Madison Avenue, New York, N.Y. 10016, U.S.A.

Educational Horizons, Pi Lambda Theta, Inc., 4101 E. Third Street, Bloomington, IN 47401, U.S.A.

Educational Leadership, Association for Supervision and Curriculum Development, 125 North West Street, Alexandria, VA 22314-2798 U.S.A.

Educational Management and Administration, Longman Group (UK) Ltd, Journals Division, Fourth Avenue, Harlow, Essex CM19 5AA, England.

Educational Media International, Kogan Page Ltd, 120 Pentonville Road, London N1 9JN, England.

Educational Perspectives, University of Hawaii at Manoa, College of Education, 1776 University Avenue, Honolulu, HI 96822, U.S.A.

Educational Philosophy and Theory, Philosophy of Education Society of Australia, Centre for Social and Cultural Studies, University of New England, Armidale, N.S.W. 2350, Australia.

Educational Planning, International Society of Educational Planning, University of Alabama, P.O. Box 870302, 312 Wilson Hall, Tucsaloosa, AL 354878, U.S.A.

Educational Policy, Butterworth Publishers, 80 Montvale Avenue, Stoneham, MA 02180, U.S.A.

Educational Psychologist, Lawrence Erlbaum Associates, Inc., 365 Broadway, Hillsdale, NJ 07642, U.S.A.

Educational Psychology, Carfax Publishing Company, P.O. Box 25, Abingdon, Oxfordshire OX14 3UE, England.

Educational Psychology in Practice, Longman Group (UK) Ltd, Journal Division, Fourth Avenue, Harlow, Essex CM19 5AA, England.

Educational Psychology Review, Plenum Publishing Corporation, 233, Spring Street, New York, NY 10013-1578, U.S.A.

Educational Record, American Council on Education, One Dupont Circle, Washington, D.C. 20036, U.S.A.

Educational Research, NFER-NELSON Publishing Company, Ltd. *Subscriptions*: Carfax Publishing Company, P.O. Box 25, Abingdon, Oxfordshire OX14 3UE, England.

Educational Research Quarterly, University of South California, School of Education, University Park WPH-703, Los Angeles, CA 90089, U.S.A.

Educational Researcher, American Educational Research Association, 1230, 17th Street, N.W., Washington, D.C. 20036, U.S.A.

Educational Review, Carfax Publishing Company, P.O. Box 25, Abingdon, Oxfordshire OX14 3UE, England.

Educational Studies, Carfax Publishing Company, P.O. Box 25, Abingdon, Oxfordshire OX14 3UE, England.

Educational Studies in Mathematics, D. Reidel Publishing Company, Box 17, 3300 AA Dordrecht, The Netherlands.

Educational Technology, Educational Technology Publications, Inc., 720 Palisade Avenue, Englewood Cliffs, NJ 07632, U.S.A.

Educational Technology Research and Development, Association for Educational Communications and Technology Inc., 1126 16th Street, N.W., Washington, D.C. 20036, U.S.A.

Educational Theory, University of Illinois, Education Building, 1310 South 6th Street, Champaign, IL 61820, U.S.A.

Electronic Learning, Scholastic, Inc., 730 Broadway, New York, N.Y. 10003, U.S.A.

Elementary School Guidance and Counseling, American School Counselor Association, American Association for Counseling and Development, 5999 Stevenson Avenue, Alexandria, VA 22304, U.S.A.

Elementary School Journal, University of Chicago Press, 5801 South Ellis Avenue, Chicago, IL 60637, U.S.A.

ELT Journal Oxford University Press, Walton Street, Oxford OX2 6DP, England.

Engineering Design Education and Training, Design Council, 28 Haymarket, London SW1Y 4SY, England.

Engineering Education, American Society for Engineering Education, One Dupont Circle, Washington, D.C. 20036, U.S.A.

English for Specific Purposes, Pergamon Journals Ltd, Headington Hill Hall, Oxford OX3 OBW, England.

English in Education, National Association for the Teaching of English, 49 Broomgrove Road, Sheffield S10 2NA, England.

English Journal, National Council of Teachers of English, 1111 Kenyon Road, Urbana, IL 61801, U.S.A.

English Language Teaching, Subscription Department, Oxford University Press, Press Road, Neasden London-NW 10.

English Quarterly, Canadian Council of Teachers of English, P.O. Box 3382, Station B, Calgary, Alberta T2M 4M1, Canada.

English Teaching Forum, Superintendent of Documents, US Government Printing Office, Washington, D.C., 20402, U.S.A.

Environmental Education, National Association for Environmental Education, Westbourne Teachers Centre, Westbourne Road, Sheffield S1O 2QQ, England.

Environmental Education and Information, Environmental Institute, Greaves School, Bolton Road, Swinton, Manchester M27 2UX, England.

Equity and Excellence, University of Massachusetts, School of Education, 130 Furcolo, Amherst, MA 01003, U.S.A.

European Journal of Education, Carfax Publishing Company, P.O. Box 25, Abingdon, Oxfordshire OX14, 3UE, England.

European Journal of Engineering Education, Carfax Publishing Company, P.O. Box 25, Abingdon, Oxfordshire OX14 3UE, England.

European Journal of Psychology of Education, Instituto Superior de Psicologia Aplicada, Rua Jardim do Tobaco 44, 1100 Lisboa, Portugal.

European Journal of Special Needs Education, NFER-NELSON Publishing Company Ltd, Darville House, 2 Oxford Road East, Windsor, Berks SL4 1DF, England.

European Journal of Teacher Education, Carfax Publishing Company, P.O. Box 25, Abingdon, Oxfordshire OX14 3UE, England.

Evaluation and Research in Education, Multilingual Matters Ltd, Bank House, 8a Clevedon Road, Avon BS21 7HH England.

Exceptional Child, University of Queensland Press, P.O. Box 42, St Lucia, Queensland 4067, Australia.

Exceptional Children, Council for Exceptional Children, 1920 Association Drive, Reston, VA 22091, U.S.A.

Executive Educator, National Schools Boards Association, 1680 Duke Street, Alexandria, VA 22314, U.S.A.

Feminist Teacher, Feminist Teacher Collective, Ballantine Hall 442, Indiana University, Bloomington, IN 47401, U.S.A.

Florida Vocational Journal, Centre for Instructional Development and Services, Florida State University, Tallahassee, FL 32306, U.S.A.

For the Learning of Mathematics, FLM Publishing Association, 4346 Marcil Avenue, Montreal, Quebec H4A 2Z8, Canada.

Forum, Educating for Economic Awareness, National Curriculum Council, Newcombe House, 45 Notting Hill Gate, London W11 3B, England.

Forum for the Discussion of New Trends in Education, PSW (Education) Publications, 11 Beacon Street, Lichfield WS13 7AA, England.

Forum of Education, Sydney College of Advanced Education, P.O. Box 63, Camperdown, NSW 2050, Australia.

Gender and Education, Carfax Publishing Company, P.O. Box 25, Abingdon, Oxfordshire OX14 3UE, England.

Gifted Education International, AB Academic Publishers, Box 97, Berkhamstead, Hertfordshire HP4 2PX, England.

Green Teacher, Heol Pentrerhedyn, Machynlleth, Powys SY20 8DN, Wales.

Guidelines, SEAMEO, RELC Building, 30 Orange Grove Road, Singapore 1025.

Harvard Educational Review, President and Fellows of Harvard College, Longfellow Hall, 13 Appian Way, Cambridge, MA 02138, U.S.A.

Head Teachers Review, National Association of Head Teachers, Holly House, 6 Paddockhall Road, Haywards Heath, West Sussex RH16 1RG, England.

Health at School, Health Education Publishing and Communications Ltd, 5 River Park Industrial Area, Billett Lane, Berkhamstead, Herts HP4 1HL, England.

Health Education, American Alliance for Health, Physical Education, Recreation & Dance, 1900 Association Drive, Reston, VA 22091, U.S.A.

Health Education Journal, Health Education Council, 78 New Oxford Street, London WC1A 1AH, England.

Health Education Quarterly, John Wiley & Sons, Inc., 605 Third Avenue, New York, N.Y. 10158, U.S.A.

Health Education Research, IRL Press Ltd, P.O. Box 1, Eynsham, Oxfordshire OX8 1JJ, England.

High School Journal, University of North Carolina Press, P.O. Box 2288, Chapel Hill, NC 27514, U.S.A.

Higher Education, Kluwer Academic Publishers, P.O. Box 322, 3300 AH Dordrecht, The Netherlands.

Higher Education in Europe, European Centre for Higher Education, 39 Stirbei Voda, R-70732 Bucharest, Romania.

Higher Education Management, OECD, 2 rue Andre-Pascal, 75775 Paris Cedex 16, France.

Higher Education Policy, Kogan Page Ltd, 120 Pentonville Road, London N1 9BR, England.

Higher Education Quarterly, Basil Blackwell Ltd, 108 Cowley Road, Oxford OX4 1JF, England.

Higher Education Research and Development, HERDSA, c/o TERC, P.O. Box 1, Kensington, N.S.W. 2033, Australia.

Higher Education Review, Tyrrell Burgess Associates Ltd, 34 Sandilands, Croydon CRO 5DB, England.

History and Social Science Teacher, Grolier Ltd, 1137 Western Road, London, Ontario N6G 1G7, Canada.

History of Education, Taylor & Francis Ltd, Rankine Road, Basingstoke RG24 OPR, England.

History of Education Quarterly, History of Education Society, New York University, 737 East Bldg, 239 Greene Street, New York, N.Y. 10003, U.S.A.

History of Education Review, Australian and New Zealand History of Education Society, Flinders University, Bedford Park, S.A. 5072, Australia.

History of Education Society Bulletin, History of Education Society, 4 Marydene Drive, Evington, Leicester LE5 6HD, England.

History Teacher, Queensland History Teachers' Association, P.O. Box 84, Spring Hill, Queensland 4000, Australia.

Human Rights Teaching, UNESCO 7 place de Fontenoy, 75700 Paris, France.

IEEE Transactions on Education, Institute of Electrical and Electronic Engineers Education Society, 345 East 47th Street, New York, N.Y. 10017, U.S.A.

Industrial and Commercial Training, University Press Ltd, 62 Toller Lane, Bradford BD8 9BY, England.

Industry and Higher Education, Butterworth Scientific Ltd, P.O. Box 63, Westbury House, Bury Street, Guildford, Surrey GU2 5BH, England.

Infant Behavior and Development, Ablex Publishing Corporation, 355 Chestnut Street, Norwood, NJ 07648, U.S.A.

Information Technology and Learning, MUSE, P.O. Box 43, Houghton-on-the-Hill, Leicester LE7 9GX, England.

Initiatives, National Association for Women Deans, Administrators & Counselors, Suite 210, 1325 18th Street, N.W. Washington, DC 20036-6511, U.S.A.

Innovative Higher Education, Human Sciences Press, Inc., 72 Fifth Avenue, New York, N.Y. 10011, U.S.A.

Insight, Training Agency, 236 Grays Inn Road, London WCIX 8HL, England.

Instructional Science, Kluwer Academic Publishers, P.O. Box 322, 3300 AH Dordrecht, The Netherlands.

Intelligence, Ablex Publishing Corporation, 355 Chestnut Avenue, Norwood, NJ 07648, U.S.A.

Interactive Learning International, John Wiley & Sons Ltd, Baffins Lane, Chichester, West Sussex PO19 1UD, England.

Interchange, Ontario Institute for Studies in Education, 252 Bloor Street West, Toronto 5, Ontario M5S 1V6, Canada.

International Council for Distance Education Bulletin, Open University, Regional Academic Services, Walton Hall, Milton Keynes MK7 6AA, England.

International Education, College of Education, University of Tennessee, Knoxville, TN 37996, U.S.A.

International Journal of Adolescence and Youth, AB Academic Publishers, P.O. Box 97, Berkhamsted, Herts HP4 2PX, England.

International Journal of Applied Engineering Education, Pergamon Journals Ltd, Headington Hill Hall, Oxford OX3 0BW, England.

International Journal of Early Childhood, University of Toronto Press, Toronto, Ontario M5S 1A6, Canada.

International Journal of Educational Development, Pergamon Journals Ltd, Headington Hill Hall, Oxford OX3 0BW, England.

International Journal of Educational Management, MCB University Press Ltd, 62 Toller Road, Bradford BD8 9BY, England.

International Journal of Educational Research, Pergamon Journals Ltd, Headington Hill Hall, Oxford OX3 0BW, England.

International Journal of Electrical Engineering Education, Manchester University Press, Oxford Road, Manchester M13 9PL, England.

International Journal of Institutional Management in Higher Education, OECD, 2 rue Andre-Pascal, 75775 Paris Cedex 16, France.

International Journal of Instructional Media, Westwood Press, Inc., 251 Park Avenue South, New York, N.Y. 10010, U.S.A.

International Journal of Lifelong Education, Taylor & Francis Ltd, Rankine Road, Basingstoke RG24 OPR, England.

International Journal of Mathematical Education in Science and Technology, Taylor & Francis Ltd, Rankine Road, Basingstoke RG24 OPR, England.

International Journal of Mechanical Engineering Education, Ellis Horwood (Publishers) Ltd, Market Cross House, Cooper Street, Chichester, West Sussex PO19 1EB, England.

International Journal of Music Education, International Society of Music Education, University of Reading, School of Education, Music Education Centre, London Road, Reading RG1 5AQ, England.

International Journal of Physical Education, Verlag Kari Hofmann, Steinwasenstr. 6-8, Postfach 1360, 7060 Schorndorf, West Germany.

International Journal of Qualitative Studies in Education, Taylor & Francis Ltd, Rankine Road, Basingstoke RG24 OPR, England.

International Journal of Science Education, Taylor & Francis Ltd, Rankine Road, Basingstoke RG24 OPR, England.

International Journal of University Adult Education, International Congress of University Adult Education, University of New Brunswick, Box 4400, Frederiction, New Brunswick, E3B 5A3 Canada.

International Quarterly of Community Health Education, Baywood Publishing Company, Inc., 120 Marine Street, Farmingdale, N.Y. 11735, U.S.A.

International Research in Reading, International Reading Association, School of Education, South Pacific University, Seattle, WA 98119, U.S.A.

International Review of Education, Kluwer Academic Publishers, P.O. Box 566, 2510 CN The Hague, Te Netherlands.

International Schools Journal, European Council of International Schools, 18 Lavant Street, Petersfield, Hampshire GU32 3EW, England.

International Understanding at School, UNESCO, 7 Place de Fontenoy, 75770 Paris, France.

Investigations in Mathematics Education, Centre for Science and Maths. Edn., The Ohio State Uty. 1945 North High Street, Columbus, Ohio 43210 USA.

IRAL—International Review of Applied Linguistics in Language Teaching, Julius Groos Verlag, Postfach 102423, Hertzstr. 6, 6900 Heidelberg 1, West Germany.

Irish Journal of Education, St Patrick's College, Educational Research Centre, Dublin 9, Eire.

Issues in Race and Education, Carleton Gardens, Brecknock Road, London N19 5AQ, England.

Jewish Education, Council for Jewish Education, 426 West 58th Street, New York, N.Y. 10019, U.S.A.

Job Training News, Manpower Services Commission. Distribution Unit, Room E825, Moorfoot, Sheffield S1 4PQ, England.

Journal for Further and Higher Education in Scotland, Jordanhill College of Further Education, 76 Southbrae Drive, Glasgow G13 1PP, Scotland.

Journal for Higher Education Management, American Association of University Administrators, University of Alabama, P.O. Box 6221, University, AL 35468, U.S.A.

Journal for Research in Mathematics Education, National Council of Teachers of Mathematics, 1906 Association Drive, Reston, VA 22091, U.S.A.

Journal for the Education of the Gifted, University of North Carolina Press, 116 South Boundary Street, P.O. Box 2288, Chapel Hill, NC 27515-2288, U.S.A.

Journal for Vocational Special Needs Education, National Association of Vocational Education Special Needs Personnel, P.O. Box 13857, North Texas State University, Denton, TX 76203, U.S.A.

Journal für Mathematik-Didaktik, Ferdinand Schoningh, Postfach 2540, 4790 Paderborn, West Germany.

Journal of Access Studies, Forum for Access Studies, South Bank Polytechnic, 58 Clapham Common North Side, London SW4 9RZ, England.

Journal of Accounting Education, Maxwell Pergamon Macmillan plc, Headington Hill Hall, Oxford OX3 0BW, England.

Journal of Aesthetic Education, University of Illinois Press, 54 East Gregory, Champaign, IL 61820, U.S.A.

Journal of Alcohol and Drug Education, Alcohol and Drug Problems Association of North America, 1120 East Oakland, P.O. Box 10212, Lansing, MI 48901, U.S.A.

Journal of Applied Educational Studies, Oxford Society for Applied Studies in Education, Mill End House, Patch Elm Lane, Rangeworthy, Bristol BS17 5LU, England.

Journal of Architectural Education, Association of Collegiate Schools of Architecture, Inc., 1735 New York Avenue, N.W., Washington, D.C. 20036, U.S.A.

Journal of Art and Design Education, Carfax Publishing Company, P.O. Box 25, Abingdon, Oxfordshire OX14 3UE, England.

Journal of Biological Education, Institute of Biology, 20 Queensberry Place, London SW7 2DZ, England.

Journal of Cancer Education, Pergamon Journals Ltd. Headington Hill Hall, Oxford OX3 0BW, England..

Journal of Career Development, Human Sciences Press, Inc., Noyes Building, Columbia, MO 65211, U.S.A.

Journal of Chemical Education, Division of Chemical Education of the American Chemical Society, 20th and Northampton Streets, Easton, P.A. 18042, U.S.A.

Journal of Child Language, Cambridge University Press, The Edinburgh Building, Shaftesbury Road, Cambridge CB2 2RU, England.

Journal of Christian Education, Australian Teachers' Christian Fellowship, 120 Chalmers Street Surry Hills, N.S.W. 2010, Australia.

Journal of Classroom Interaction, University of Houston, College of Education, Farish Hall, Room 451, Houston, TX 77044, U.S.A.

Journal of College and University Law, National Association of College and University Attorneys, One Dupont Circle, Suite 650, Washington, D.C. 20036, U.S.A.

Journal of College and University Student Housing, Association of College and University Housing Officers, 101 Curl Drive, Suite 140, Columbus, OH 43210, U.S.A.

Journal of College Science Teaching, National Science Teachers Association, 1742 Connecticut Avenue, N.W., Washington, D.C. 20009, U.S.A.

Journal of College Student Development, American Association for Counseling and Development, 5999 Stevenson Avenue, VA 22304, U.S.A.

Journal of College Student Psychotherapy, Haworth Press, Inc., 12 West 32 Street, N.Y. 10001, U.S.A.

Journal of Community Education, Community Education Development Centre, Briton Road, Coventry CV2 4LF, England.

Journal of Computer Assisted Learning, Blackwell Scientific Publications Ltd, Osney Mead, Oxford OX2 0EL, England.

Journal of Computer-Based Instruction, Association for the Development of Computer-Based Instructional Systems, Western Washington University, Bellingham, WA 98225, U.S.A.

Journal of Computers in Mathematics and Science Teaching, Association for Computers in Mathematics and Science Teaching, P.O. Box 60730, Phoenix, AZ 85082, U.S.A.

Journal of Cooperative Education, Cooperative Education Association, 221 N. LaSalle Street, Chicago, IL 60601, U.S.A.

Journal of Creative Behavior, Creative Education Foundation, Inc., 1300 Elmwood Avenue, Buffalo, N.Y. 14222, U.S.A.

Journal of Curriculum and Supervision, Association for Supervision and Curriculum Development, 225 N. Washington Street, Alexandria, VA 22314, U.S.A.

Journal of Curriculum Studies, Taylor & Francis Ltd, Rankine Road, Basingstoke RG24 0PR, England.

Journal of Curriculum Theorizing, Corporation for Curriculum Research, 53 Falstaff Road, Rochester, N.Y. 14609, U.S.A.

Journal of Dental Education, American Association of Dental Schools, 1625 Massachusetts Avenue, N.W., Washington, D.C. 20036, U.S.A.

Journal of Developmental Education, Appalachian State University, Centre for Development Education, Boone, NC 28608, U.S.A.

Journal of Distance Education, Canadian Association for Distance Education, 151 Slater Street, Ottawa, Ontario, Canada K1P 5N2.

Journal of Drug Education, Baywood Publishing Company, Inc., 120 Marine Street, Farmingdale, N.Y. 11735, U.S.A.

Journal of Early Intervention, Council for Exceptional Children, Division for Early Childhood, 1920 Association Drive, Reston, VA 22901, U.S.A.

Journal of Economic Education, Heldref Publications, Inc., 4000 Albemarle Street, N.W., Washington, D.C. 20016, U.S.A.

Journal of Education, Boston University, School of Education, 605 Commonwealth Avenue, Boston, MA 02215, U.S.A.

Journal of Education Finance, West Kentucky University, Box U-502, Bowling Green, KY 42101, U.S.A.

Journal of Education for Business, Heldref Publications, Inc., 4000 Albemarle Street, N.W., Washington, D.C. 20016, U.S.A.

Journal of Education for Teaching, Carfax Publishing Company, P.O. Box 25, Abingdon, Oxfordshire OX14 3UE, England.

Journal of Education in Museums, GEM-Group for Education in Museums, Merseyside Country Museum, William Brown Street, Liverpool L3 8EN, England.

Journal of Education Policy, Taylor & Francis Ltd, Rankine Road, Basingstoke RG24 0PR, England.

Journal of Educational Administration, MCB University Press Ltd, 62 Toller Lane, Bradford BD8 9BY, England.

Journal of Educational Administration and History, University of Leeds, Museum of the History of Education, Parkinson, Leeds LS2 9JT, England.

Journal of Educational Computing Research, Baywood Publishing Company, Inc., 120 Marine Street, Farmingdale, N.Y. 11735, U.S.A.

Journal of Educational Gerontology, Association for Educational Gerontology, University of Keele, Staffordshire ST5 5BG, England.

Journal of Educational Measurement, National Council on Measurement in Education, 1230 17th Street, N.W., Washington, D.C. 20036, U.S.A.

Journal of Educational Psychology, American Psychological Association, Inc., 1200 17th Street, N.W., Washington, D.C. 20036, U.S.A.

Journal of Educational Public Relations, Educational Communication Centre, P.O. Box 657, 1830 Walnut Street, Camp Hill, PA 17011, U.S.A.

Journal of Educational Research, Heldref Publications, Inc., 4000 Albemarle Street, N.W., Washington, D.C. 20016, U.S.A.

Journal of Educational Statistics, American Educational Research Association, 1230 17th Street, N.W., Washington, D.C. 20036, U.S.A.

Journal of Educational Technology Systems, Baywood Publishing Company, Inc., 120 Marine Street, Box D, Farmingdale, N.Y. 11735, U.S.A.

Journal of Educational Television, Carfax Publishing Company, P.O. Box 25, Abingdon, Oxfordshire OX14 3UE, England.

Journal of Educational Therapy, Forum for the Advancement of Educational Therapy, 226 Chesterford Gardens, London NW3 7DE, England.

Journal of Educational Thought, University of Calgary, Faculty of Education, Room 502, Education Tower, Calgary, Alberta T2N 1N4, Canada.

Journal of Environmental Education, Heldref Publications, Inc., 4000 Albemarle St., N.W., Washington D.C. 20016, U.S.A.

Journal of European Industrial Training, MCB University Press Ltd., 62 Toller Lane, Bradford BD8 9BY, England.

Journal of Experimental Education, Heldref Publications, Inc., 4000 Albemarle Street, N.W., Washington, D.C. 20016, U.S.A.

Journal of Extension, Extension Journal, Inc., 805 Extension Building, 432 North Lake Street, Madison, WI 53706, U.S.A.

Journal of Further and Higher Education, National Association of Teachers in Further and Higher Education, Hamilton House, Mabledon Place, London WC1H 9BH, England.

Journal of General Education, Pennsylvania State University Press, 215 Wagner Building, University Park, PA 16802, U.S.A.

Journal of Geography, National Council for Geographic Education, Western Illinois University, Macomb, IL 61455, U.S.A.

Journal of Geography in Higher Education, Carfax Publishing Company, P.O. Box 25, Abingdon, Oxfordshire OX14 3UE, England.

Journal of Geological Education, National Association of Geology Teachers, Inc., P.O. Box 368, Lawrence, KS 66044, U.S.A.

Journal of Higher Education (USA), Ohio State University Press, 175 Mount Hall, 1050 Carmack Avenue, Columbus, OH 432210, U.S.A.

The Journal of Human Resources, Journals Dept., University of Wisconsin Press, P.O. Box 1379, Madison, Wisconsin-53701

Journal of Humanistic Education and Development, Association for Humanistic Education and Development, American Association for Counseling and Development, 5999 Stevenson Avenue, Alexandria, VA 22304, U.S.A.

Journal of Industrial Teacher Education, National Association of Industrial and Technical Teacher Educators, Purdue University, School of Technology, Lafayett, IN 47907, U.S.A.

Journal of Interactive Instruction Development, Communicative Technology Corporation, 50 Culpeper Street, Warrenton, VA 221826, U.S.A.

Journal of International and Comparative Education, Micropublicaciones, Aragon 123, 08015 Barcelona, Spain.

Journal of Law and Education, Jefferson Law Book Co., Colorado Building, 1341 G Street, N.W., Suite 408, Washington, D.C. 20005, U.S.A.

Journal of Learning Disabilities, 10 PRO-ED, Inc., 4341 Industrial Oakes Boulevard, Austin, TX 78735, U.S.A.

Journal of Legal Education, Association American Law Schools, Cornell Law School, Myron Taylor Hall, Ithaca, N.Y. 14853, U.S.A.

Journal of Materials Education, Materials Education Council, Materials Research Laboratories, Pennsylvania State University, University Park, PA 16802, U.S.A.

Journal of Medical Education, Association of American Medical Colleges, One Dupont Circle, Washington, D.C. 20036, U.S.A.

Journal of Memory and Language, Academic Press, Inc., 1250 Sixth Avenue, San Diego, CA 92100, U.S.A

Journal of Mental Deficiency Research, The National Society for Mentally Handicapped Children 5, Bulstrode St., London, W.I.

Journal of Mental Subnormality, The Midland Society for the Study of Mental Subnormality, Monyhull Hospital, Birmingham 14.

Journal of Moral Education, NFER-NELSON Publishing Company Ltd., *Subscriptions*: Carfax Publishing Company, P.O. Box 25, Abingdon, Oxfordshire OX14 3UE, England.

Journal of Multicultural and Cross-cultural Research in Art Education, United States Society for Education Through Art, Department of Art Education, University of Oregon, Eugene, OR 97403, U.S.A.

Journal of Multilingual and Multicultural Development, Multilingual Matters Ltd., Bank House, 8a Hill Road Clevedon, Avon BS21 7HH, England.

Journal of Negro Education, Howard University Press, 2400 6th Street, N.W., Washington, D.C. 20059, U.S.A.

Journal of Nutrition Education, Williams & Wilkins, 428 East Preston Street, Baltimore, MD 21202, U.S.A.

Journal of Personnel Evaluation in Education, Kluwer Academic Publishers, P.O. Box 322, 3300 AZ Dordrecht, The Netherlands.

Journal of Philosophy of Education, Carfax Publishing Company, P.O. Box 25, Abingdon, Oxfordshire OX14 3UE, England.

Journal of Physical Education, Recreation and Dance, American Alliance for Health, Physical Education, Recreation & Dance, 1900 Association Drive, Reston, VA 22091, U.S.A.

Journal of Psychiatric Education, Human Sciences Press, Inc., 72 Fifth Avenue, New York, N.Y. 10011, U.S.A.

Journal of Reading, International Reading Association Inc., P.O. Box 8139, Newark, DE 19714, U.S.A.

Journal of Reading Behavior, National Reading Conference, Inc., 107 Sibley Tower, Rochester, N.Y. 14604, U.S.A.

Journal of Reading Education, OTER, College of Education, University of Central Florida, P.O. Box 25000, Orlando, FL 32816, U.S.A.

Journal of Recreational Mathematics, Education on Science and Technology, John Wiley and Sons Ltd., Baffins Lane, Chichester Sussex, England.

Journal of Research and Development in Education, College of Education, University of Georgia, Athens, GA 30602, U.S.A.

Journal of Research in Childhood Education, Association for Childhood Education International, 11141 Georgia Avenue, Suite 200, Wheaton, MD 20902, U.S.A.

Journal for Research in Maths Education, National Council of Teachers of Mathematics 1201, Sixteenth St., N.W., Washington, DC 20036, U.S.A.

Journal of Research in Music Education, Music Educators National Conference, 1902 Association Drive, Reston, VA 22091, U.S.A.

Journal of Research in Reading, Basil Blackwell Ltd, 108 Cowley Road, Oxford OX4 1JF, England.

Journal of Research in Science Teaching, John Wiley & Sons, Inc., 605 Third Avenue, New York, N.Y. 10016, U.S.A

Journal of Research on Computing in Education, International Association for Computing in Education, 1230 17th Street, N.W. Washington, D.C. 20036, U.S.A.

Journal of Russian Studies, Association of Teachers of Russian, Department of Modern Languages, University of Strathclyde, 26 Richmond Street, Glasgow G1 1XH, Scotland.

Journal of School Health, American School Health Association, Box 708, Kent, OH 44240, U.S.A

Journal of School Psychology, Pergamon Journals, Inc., Maxwell House, Fairview Park, Elmsford, N.Y. 10523, U.S.A.

Journal of Science and Mathematics Education in Southeast Asia, Southeast Asian Ministers of Education Organisation, Regional Centre for Education in Science and Mathematics, 11700 Glugor, Penang, West Malaysia.

Journal of Sex Education and Therapy, American Association of Sex Educators, 11 Dupont Circle, N.W., Washington, D.C. 20036, U.S.A.

Journal of Social Work Education, Council of Social Work Education, Box 43469, Columbia Heights Station, Washington, D.C. 20009, U.S.A.

Journal of Special Education, 5341 Industrial Oaks Boulevard, Austin, TX 78735-8809, U.S.A.

Journal of Special Education Technology, Association for Special Education Technology, Exceptional Child Center, Utah State University, Logan, UT 84322, U.S.A.

Journal of Structural Learning, Gordon and Breach Science Publishers Ltd, 42 William IV Street, London WC2N 4DE, England.

Journal of Studies in Technical Careers, School of Technical Careers, Southern Illinois University at Carbondale, 908 South Wall Street, Carbondale, IL 62901, U.S.A.

Journal of Teacher Education, American Association of Colleges for Teacher Education, One Dupont Circle, Suite 610, Washington, D.C. 20036, U.S.A.

Journal of Teaching in Physical Education, Human Kinetics Publications, Inc., 1607 N. Market Street, Campaign, IL 61820, U.S.A.

Journal of Teaching in Social Work, Haworth Press, Inc., 12 West 32nd Street, New York, N.Y. 10001, U.S.A.

Journal of Technical Writing and Communication, Baywood Publishing Company, Inc., 120 Marine Street, Farmingdale, N.Y. 11735, U.S.A.

Journal of the British Association of Teachers of the Deaf, British Association of Teachers of the Deaf, The Rycroft Centre, Royal Schools of the Deaf, Stanley Road, Cheadle Hulme, Cheshire SK8 6RF, England.

Journal of Veterinary Medical Education, Association of American Veterinary Medical Colleges, Suite 828, 1522 K Street, N.W., Washington, D.C. 20005, U.S.A.

Journal of Vocational Education Research, American Vocational Education Research Association, Ohio State University, 1960 Kenny Road, Columbus, OH 43210, U.S.A.

Journalism Educator, Association for Education in Journalism and Mass Communication, University of South Carolina, Columbia, SC 29208, U.S.A.

Journalism Quarterly, Association for Education in Journalism and Mass Communication, University of South Carolina, Columbus, SC 29208, U.S.A.

Junior Education, Scholastic Publications Ltd, Westfield Road, Southam, Nr Leamington, Spa, Warwickshire, CV 33 0JH, England.

Jyväskylä Studies in Education, Psychology and Social Research, University of Jyväskylä Department of Psychology, Jyväskylä, Finland.

Kwartalnik Pedagogiczny, 5983 Panstwowe Wydawnictwo Naukowe, Miodowa 10, Warsaw, Poland.

Labour Education, Publications, International Labour Office, CH-1211 Geneva 22, Switzerland.

Language and Communication, Pergamon Journals Ltd, Headington Hill Hall, Oxford OX3 0BW, England.

Language and Education, Multilingual Matters Ltd, Bank House, 8a Hill Road, Clevedon, Avon BS21 7HH, England.

Language and Learning, Oldschool Ltd, 6/7 Hockley Hill, Birmingham B18 5AA, England.

Language and Speech, Kingston Press Services Ltd, 28 High Street, Teddington, Middlesex TW11 8EW, England.

Language Arts, National Council of Teachers of English, 1111 Kenyon Road, Urbana, IL 61801, U.S.A.

Language Culture and Curriculum, Multilingual Matters Ltd, Bank House, 8a Hill Road, Clevedon, Avon BS21 7HH, England.

Learning and Motivation, Academic Press, Inc., 111 Fifth Avenue, New York, N.Y. 10003, U.S.A.

Learning Disabilities Focus, Council for Exceptional Children, Division for Learning Disabilities, 1920 Association Drive, Reston, VA 22091, U.S.A.

Learning Disabilities Research, Council for Exceptional Children, Division for Learning Disabilities, 1920 Association Drive, Reston, VA 22091, U.S.A.

Learning Disability Quarterly, Council for Learning Disabilities, Department of Special Education, University of Kansas, Kansas City, KS 66103, U.S.A.

Learning Resources, Chesswood House Publishing Ltd, 542 Mount Pleasant Road, Ste 103, Toronto, Ontario M4S 2M7, Canada.

Learning Resources Journal, Learning Resources Development Group, 3 Laverock Hill, Mealbank, Kendal LA8 9EP, England.

Liberal Education (UK), Wigston College of FE, Station Road, Wigston Magna, Leicester LE8 2DW, England.

Liberal Education (USA), Association of American Colleges, 1818 R Street, N.W., Washington, D.C. 20009, U.S.A.

Lifelong Learning, American Association for Adult and Continuing Education, 1201 16th Street, N.W., Washington, D.C. 20036, U.S.A.

Machine-Mediated Learning, Taylor & Francis, Inc. 3 East 44th Street, New York, N.Y. 10017, U.S.A.

Magyar Pedagogia, Hungarian Academy of Sciences, Education Committee, Eotvos University, H-1052 Budapest, Hungary.

Maladjustment and Therapeutic Education, Association of Workers for Maladjusted Children, 95 Lawrence Avenue, New Malden, Surrey KT3 5LZ, England.

Management Education and Development, Association for Management Education and Development, Management Teacher Development Unit, University of Lancaster, Bailrigg, Lancaster LA1 4YW, England.

Management in Education, Harcourt Brace Jovanovich Ltd, 24-28 Oval Road, London NW1 7DX, England.

Mathematical Spectrum, Applied Probability Trust, Hicks Building, University of Sheffield, Sheffield S3 7RH, England.

Mathematics and Computer Education, MATYC Journal, Inc., P.O. Box 158, Old Bethpage, N.Y. 11804, U.S.A.

Mathematics in School, Longman Group (UK) Ltd, Journals Divisions, Fourth Avenue, Harlow, Essex CM19 5AA, England.

The Mathematics Student Journal, National Council of Teachers of Mathematics, 1201 16th St., N.W. Washington, DC 20036, USA.

Mathematics Teacher, National Council of Teachers of Mathematics, 1906 Association Drive, Reston, VA 22091, U.S.A.

Mathematics Teaching, Association of Teachers of Mathematics, Kings Chambers, Queen Street, Derby DE1 3DA, England.

McGill Journal of Education, Faculty of Education, McGill University, 3700 McTavish Street, Montreal, Quebec H3A, 1Y2, Canada.

Media and Methods, American Society of Educators, 1511 Walnut Street, Philadelphia, PA 19102, U.S.A.

Media Education, Media Centre, South Hill Park, Bracknell, Berkshire, England.

Media Education Journal, Comedia, 9 Poland Street, London W1V 3DG, England.

Medical Education, Blackwell Scientific Publications Ltd, Osney Mead, Oxford OX2 0EL, England.

Medical Teacher, Carfax Publishing Company, P.O. Box 25, Abingdon, Oxfordshire OX14 3UE, England.

Mental Health, The National Association for Mental Health, 39, Queen Anne St., London, W.1.

Micromath, Basil Blackwell Ltd, 108 Cowley Road, Oxford OX4 1JF, England.

Middle School Journal, National Middle School Association, 4807 Evanswood Drive, Columbus, OH 43229, U.S.A.

Minerva, International Council on the Future of the University, 59 St Martin's Lane, London WC2N 4JS, England.

Modern English Teacher, Modern English Publications Ltd, P.O. Box 129, Oxford, England.

Modern Language Journal, University of Wisconsin Press, Journals Division, 114 North Murray Street, Madison, WI 53715, U.S.A.

Modern Languages, Modern Language Association, Regent's College, Inner Circle, Regent's Park, London NW1 4WS, England.

Monitor, Association for Educational Data Systems, 1201 16th Street, N.W., Washington, D.C. 20036, U.S.A.

Montessori Courier, London Montessori Centre, 18 Balderton Street, London W1Y 1TG.

Moral Education Forum, City University of New York, Hunter College, 200 East 64th Street, New York, N.Y. 10021, U.S.A.

Multicultural Education Journal, Alberta Teachers' Association, Multicultural Education Council, 11010 142nd Street, Edmonton, Alberta T5N 2R1, Canada.

Multicultural Education Review, City of Birmingham Education Department, Multicultural Support Service, Bordesley Centre, Stratford Road, Birmingham B11 1AR, England.

Multicultural Teaching, Trentham Books Ltd, 151 Etruria Road, Stoke-on-Trent ST1 5NS, England.

Multiculturalism, Canadian Council for Multicultural and Intercultural Education, Guidance Centre, 10 Alcorn Avenue, Toronto, Ontario M4V 2Z8, Canada.

Multiracial Education, National Association for Multicultural Education, Tolpits Lane, Watford, Hertfordshire, England.

Music Educators Journal, Music Educators National Conference, 1902 Association Drive, Reston, VA 22091, U.S.A.

Music Teacher, Rhinegold Publishing Ltd, 239-241, Shaftesbury Avenue, London WC2H 8EH, England.

Muslim Education Quarterly, Islamic Academy, 23 Metcalfe Road, Cambridge CB4 2DB, England.

NACADA Journal, National Academic Advising Association, 212 Grange Building, University Park, PA, 16802, U.S.A.

NASD Journal, National Association for Staff Development 30 St Helena Street, Colchester, Essex CO3 3BA, England.

NASSP Bulletin, National Association of Secondary School Principals, 1904 Association Drive, Reston, VA 22091, U.S.A.

NASUWT Career Teacher Journal, NASUWT, Hillcourt Education Centre, Rose Hill, Rednal, Birmingham B45 8RS, England.

NATFHE Journal, National Association of Teachers in Further and Higher Education, Hamilton House, Mabledon Place, London WC1H 9BH, England.

National Education, New Zealand Educational Institute, P.O. Box 466, Wellington 1, New Zealand.

Negro Educational Review, Negro Educational Review, Inc., P.O. 2895, General Mail Center, Jacksonville, FL 32203, U.S.A.

New Directions for Community Colleges, Jossey-Bass Publishers, Inc., 350 Sansome Street, San Francisco, CA 94104, U.S.A.

New Directions for Continuing Education, Jossey-Bass Publishers, Inc., 350 Sansome Street, San Francisco, CA 94104, U.S.A.

New Directions for Experiential Learning, Jossey-Bass Publishers, Inc., 350 Sansome Street, San Francisco, CA 94104, U.S.A.

New Directions for Higher Education, Jossey-Bass Publishers, Inc., 350 Sansome Street, San Francisco, CA 94104, U.S.A.

New Directions for Institutional Research, Jossey-Bass Publishers, Inc., 350 Sansome Street, San Francisco, CA 94104, U.S.A.

New Directions for Program Evaluation, Jossey-Bass Publishers, Inc., 350 Sansome Street, San Francisco, CA 94104, U.S.A.

New Directions for Student Services, Jossey-Bass Publishers, Inc., 350 Sansome Street, San Francisco, CA 94104, U.S.A.

New Directions for Teaching and Learning, Jossey-Bass Publishers, Inc., 350 Sansome Street, San Francisco, CA 94104, U.S.A.

New Education, James Nicholas Publishers, P.O. Box 329, Mount Eliza, Australia 3930.

New Era in Education (formerly called New Era), World Education Fellowship, 54 Fonatarabia Road, London SW11 5PF, England.

New Horizons in Education, Australian World Education Fellowship, 21 Lynwood Crescent, Ashgrove, Queensland 4060, Australia.

New Zealand Journal of Educational Studies, Carfax Publishing Company, P.O. Box 25, Abingdon, Oxfordshire, OX14 3UE, England.

New Zealand Journal of Health, Physical Education and Recreation, New Zealand Association of Health, Physical Education & Recreation, Inc., Box 17-127, Wellington, New Zealand.

New Zealand Language Teacher, New Zealand Association of Language Teachers, Rosehill College, P.O. Box 106, Papakura, New Zealand.

NICEC Training and Development Bulletin, NICEC, Balls Park, Hertford SG13 8QF, England.

Nigeria Educational Forum, Ahmadu Bello University, Institute of Education, Zaria, Nigeria.

Nigerian Journal of Technical Education, National Board for Technical Education, P.M.B. 2239, Kaduna, Nigeria.

NOISE, National Organisation for Initiatives in Social Education, 14 Frederick Place, Clifton, Briston, England.

Nurse Education Today, Longman Group (UK) Ltd, Journals Division, Fourth Ave, Harlow, Essex CM19 5AA, England.

NUT Education Review, National Union of Teachers, Hamilton House, Mabledon Place, London WD1H 9BD, England.

Open Learning, Longman Group (UK) Ltd, Fourth Avenue, Harlow, Essex CM19 5AA, England.

Orbit, Ontario Institute for Studies in Education, 252 Bloor Street West, Toronto, Ontario M5S, IV6, Canada.

Oxford Review of Education, Carfax Publishing Company, P.O. Box 25, Abingom, Oxfordshire OX14 3UE, England.

Papua New Guinea Journal of Education, Papua New Guinea Council of Educational Administration, Education Department Library, Port Moresby Inservice College, P.O. Box 1791, Boroko, Papua New Guinea.

Pastoral Care in Education, Basil Blackwell Ltd, 108 Cowley Road, Oxford OX4 1JF, England.

Patient Education and Counselling, Elsevier Scientific Publishers (Ireland) Ltd, P.O. Box 85, Limerick, Ireland.

Peabody Journal of Education, Vanderbilt University, George Peabody College, Box 41, Nashville TN 37203, U.S.A.

Pedagogika, Filosoficka Fakulta, University Karlovyu Praze, Celetna 20, Praha 1, Czechoslovakia.

Performance and Instruction, National Society for Performance and Instruction, 1126 16th Street, N.W., Suite 315, Washington, D.C. 20036, U.S.A.

Performance Improvement Quarterly, Learning Systems Institute, 406 Dodd, Florida State University, Tallahassee, FL 32306, U.S.A.

Perspectives in Education, Department of Education, University of Witwatersrand, PO Wits, Johannesburg 2050, South Africa.

Perspectives Universitaires, Association des Universites Partiellement Ou Entierement de Langue Francaise, Universite de Montreal, B.P. 6128, Montreal, Quebec H3C 3J7, Canada.

The Personal and Guidance Journal, American Personnel and Guidance Association 1126, 6th St., NW, Washington D.C.

Phi Delta Kappan, Phi Delta Kappa, Inc., Eighth Street & Union Avenue, Box 789, Bloomington, IN 47401, U.S.A.

Philippine Education Quarterly, Arellano University, 2600 Legarde Street, Manila 2806, The Philippines.

Physical Education Review, Studies in Education Ltd, Nafferton, Driffield, N. Humberside, YO25 0JL, England.

Physics Education (UK), IOP Publishing Ltd, Techno House, Redcliffe Way, Bristol BS1 6NX, England.

Physics Teacher, American Association of Physics Teachers, Graduate Physics Building, State University of New York, Stony Brook, N.Y. 11794, U.S.A.

Planning and Changing, Illinois State University, Department of Educational Administration and Foundations, Normal, IL, 61761, U.S.A.

Planning for Higher Education, Society for College and University Planning, 2001 School of Education Building, University of Michigan, Ann Arbor, MI 48109, U.S.A.

Practical English Teaching, Mary Glasgow Publications Ltd, 131-133 Holland Park Ave, London W11 4UT, England.

Practising Administrator, Harcourt Brace Jovanovich Group (Australia) Pty Ltd, P.O. Box 300, North Ryde, N.S.W., 2113, Australia.

Prep School, Belgrave Educational Publishing, P.O. Box 140, Ipswich IP1 3TG, England.

Primary Education in Botswana, Primary Education in Botswana, P.O. Box 463, Gabororone, Botswana.

Primary Science Review, Association for Science Education, College Lane, Hatfield, Hertfordshire, AL10 9AA, England.

Primary Teaching Studies, Polytechnic of North London Press, Department of Teaching Studies, Prince of Wales Road, London, NW5, 3LB, England.

Principal, National Association of Elementary School Principals, 1801, North Moore Street, Arlington, VA 22209, U.S.A.

Problems and Experiences in the Teaching of English, La Nuova Italia, Via Ernesto Codignola, 50018 Scandicci (Firenze), Italy.

Prospects, UNESCO, 7, Place de Fontenoy, 75700 Paris, France.

Psychologie in Erziehung und Unterricht, Ernst Reinhardt Verlag, D-8000 Munchen 19, Kemnatenstrasse 46, West Germany.

Psychology in the Schools, Clinical Psychology Publishing Company, Inc., 4 Conant Square, Brandon, Vermont 05733, U.S.A.

Quarterly Journal of Speech, Speech Communication Association, 5105 Backlick Road, N.E., Anandale, VA 22003, U.S.A.

Quest, Human Kinetics Publications, Inc., P.O. Box 5076, Champaign, IL 61820, U.S.A.

Reading, Basil Blackwell Ltd, 108 Cowley Road, Oxford OX4 1JF, England.

Reading and Writing, Kluwer Academic Publishers, P.O. Box 322, 3300 AH Dordrecht, The Netherlands.

Reading-Canada-Lecture, University of Calgary, Faculty of Education, 608 Education Tower, 2500 University Drive, N.W., Calgary, Alberta T2N 1N4, Canada.

Reading Psychology, Hemisphere Publishing Corporation, 79 Madison Avenue, #1110, New York, N.Y. 10016, U.S.A.

Reading Research and Instruction, College Reading Association, 3340 S. Danbury Avenue, Springfield, MO 65807, U.S.A.

Reading Research Quarterly, International Reading Association, P.O. Box 8139, Newark, DE 19714, U.S.A.

Reading Teacher, International Reading Association, P.O. Box 8139, Newark, DE 19714, U.S.A.

Reflections on Higher Education, Higher Education Foundation, The Malthouse, 60 East Saint Helen Street, Abingdon OX14, 5EB, Oxfordshire, England.

Rehabilitation, The British Council for the Rehabilitation of the Disabled, Tavistock House South, Tavistock Square, London W.C.1.

Rehabilitation Education, Pergamon Journals Ltd, Headington Hill Hall, Oxford OX3 OBW, England.

RELC Journal, Regional Language Centre, RELC Building, 30 Orange Grove Road, Singapore 1025.

Religious Education, Religious Education Association, 409 Prospect Street, New Haven, CT 06510, U.S.A.

Remedial and Special Education, PRO-ED, Inc., 5341 Industrial Oaks Boulevard, Austin, TX 78735, U.S.A.

Research and Teaching in Developmental Education, New York College Learning Skills Association University Learning Center, Niagara University, N.Y. 14109, U.S.A.

Research Bulletin of the National Institute of Education Research (Tokyo), National Japanese Institute of Educational Research, 6-5-22, Shimomeguro, Meguro-ku, Tokyo 153, Japan.

Research in Education, Manchester University Press, 316-324 Oxford Road, Manchester M13 9PL, England.

Research in Higher Education, Human Sciences Press, Inc., Noyes Building, Columbia, MO 65211, U.S.A.

Research in Science and Technological Education, Carfax Publishing Company, P.O. Box 25, Abingdon, Oxfordshire OX14 3UE, England.

Research in the Teaching of English, National Council of Teachers of English, 1111 Kenyon Road, Urbana, IL 61801, U.S.A.

Research Papers in Education, NFER-NELSON Publishing Company Ltd, *Subscriptions*: Carfax Publishing Company, P.O. Box 25, Abingdon, Oxfordshire OX14 3UE, England.

Review of Educational Research, American Educational Research Association, 1230 17th Street, N.W., Washington, D.C. 20036, U.S.A.

Review of Higher Education, Association for the Study of Higher Education, One Dupont Circle, Suite 630, Washington, D.C. 20036, U.S.A.

Revue Francaise de Pédagogie, Institut National de Recherche Pédagogique, 29 rue d'Ulm, 75230 Paris Cedex 05, France.

Royal Air Force Education Bulletin, Services Publishing Services (SPS), Chapel Lane, Corby, Northants NN17 1AX England.

Scandinavian Journal of Educational Research, Carfax Publishing Company, P.O. Box 25, Abingdon, Oxfordshire OX14 3UE, England.

School Business Affairs, Association of School Business Officials International, 11401 North Shore Drive, Reston, VA 22090, U.S.A.

School Counselor, American Association for Counseling and Development, 5999 Stevenson Avenue, Alexandria, VA 22304, U.S.A.

School Governor, Ream Ltd, Top Floor, 6/7 Hockley Hill, Hockley, Birmingham B18 5AA, England.

School Librarian, School Library Association, Victoria House, 29-31 George Street, Oxford 2AY, England.

School Libraries in Canada, Canadian School Library Association, Canadian Library Association, 602-2000 Elgin Street, Ottawa, Ontario K2P 115, Canada.

School Organisation, Carfax Publishing Company, P.O. Box 25, Abingdon, Oxfordshire OX14 3UE, England.

School Psychology International, Sage Publications Ltd, 28 Banner Street, London EC1Y 8QE, England.

School Science and Mathematics, School Science and Mathematics Association, Inc., 126 Life Science Building, Bowling Green State University, Bowling Green, OH 43403, U.S.A.

School Science Review, Association for Science Education, College Lane, Hatfield, Hertfordshire AL10 9AA, England.

School Technology, Trent Polytechnic, National Centre for School Technology, Burton Street, Nottingham NG1 4BU, England.

Science and Children, National Science Teachers Association, 1742 Connecticut Avenue, N.W., Washington, D.C. 20009, U.S.A.

Science Education, John Wiley & Sons, Inc., 605 Third Avenue, New York, N.Y. 10016, U.S.A.

Science Teacher, National Science Teachers' Association, U.S.A.

Scottish Educational Review, Scottish Academic Press, 33 Montgomery Street, Edinburgh EH7 5JX, Scotland.

Scottish Journal of Adult Education, Scottish Institute of Adult and Continuing Education, 30 Rutland Square, Edinburgh EH1 2BW, Scotland.

Second Language Research, Edward Arnold (Publishers) Ltd, 41 Bedford Square, London WC1B 3DQ, England.

Secondary Heads Association Review, Hobsons Publishing Plc, Bateman Street, Cambridge CB2 1LZ, England.

Signal, Thimble Press, Lockwood Station Road, South Woodchester, Stroud, Gloucestershire GL5 5EQ, England.

Simulation/Games for Learning, Society for the Advancement of Games and Simulations in Education and Training, Centre for Extension Studies, University of Technology, Loughborough, Leicestershire LE11 3TU, England.

Singapore Journal of Education, Heinemann Publishers, Asia Pte Ltd, 41 Jalan Pemimpin, #03-05, Singapore 2057.

Slow Learning Child, Schonell Educational Research Centre, University of Queensland, 19, Park Avenue, Lower Hutt, Queensland.

Social Education, National Council for the Social Studies, 1201 16th Street, N.W., Washington, D.C. 20036, U.S.A.

Social Science Teacher, Association for the Teaching of the Social Sciences, 145, Upper Lewes Road, Brighton BN2 3FD, England.

Social Studies, Heldref Publications, Inc., 4000 Albemarle Street, N.W., Washington, D.C. 20016, U.S.A.

Social Work Education, Joint University Council, Royal Institute of Public Administration, Hamilton House, Mabledon Place, London WC1H 9BD, England.

Social Work in Education, National Association of Social Workers, Inc., 7981 Eastern Avenue, Silver Spring, MD 20910, U.S.A.

Sociology of Education, American Sociological Association, 1722 North Street, N.W., Washington, D.C. 20036, U.S.A.

South African Journal of Education, Bureau for Scientific Publications, P.O. Box 1758, Pretoria 0001, South Africa.

South Pacific Journal of Teacher Education, Carfax Publishing Company, P.O. Box 25, Abingdon, Oxfordshire OX14 3UE, England.

Southeast Asian Journal of Educational Studies, South Seas Society, P.O. Box 709, Singapore, 9014.

Soviet Education, M.E. Sharpe, Inc., 80 Business Park Drive, Armonk, N.Y. 10504, U.S.A.

Special Children, Special Children Ltd, 6/7 Hockley Hill, Hockley, Birmingham B18 5AA, England.

Special Services in the Schools, Haworth Press, Inc., 228, East 22nd Street, New York, N.Y. 10010, U.S.A.

Spectrum, Paternoster Press Ltd, Paternoster House, 3 Mount Radford Crescent, Exeter, Devon EX2 4JW, England.

Studies in Art Education, National Art Education Association, 1916 Association Drive, Reston, VA 22091, U.S.A.

Studies in Continuing Education, Studies in Continuing Education, Inc., ITATE, P.O. Box K12, Haymarket, N.S.W., 2000, Australia.

Studies in Educational Evaluation, Pergamon Journals Ltd, Headington Hill Hall, Oxford OX3 0BW, England.

Studies in Higher Education, Carfax Publishing Company, P.O. Box 25, Abingdon, Oxfordshire OX14 3UE, England.

Studies in Philosophy and Education, Kluwer Academic Publishers, P.O. Box 322, 3300 AH Dordrecht, The Netherlands.

Studies in Science Education, Studies in Education Ltd, Nafferton, Driffield, N. Humberside YO25 0JL, England.

Studies in Second Language Acquisition, Cambridge University Press, Edinburgh Building, Shaftesbury Road, Cambridge CB2 2RU, England.

Studies in the Education of Adults, National Institute of Adult Continuing Education, 19B De Montfort Street, Leicester LE1 7GE, England.

Support for Learning, Longman Group (UK) Ltd, Fourth Avenue, Harlow, Essex CM19 5AA, England.

System, Pergamon Journals Ltd, Headington Hill Hall, Oxford OX3 0BW, England.

Teacher Education Quarterly, Prakken Publication, Inc., P.O. Box 8623, Ann Arbor, MI 48107, U.S.A.

Teachers College Record, Teachers College Record Office, Columbia University, 525 West 120th Street, New York, N.Y. 10027, U.S.A.

Teachers' Forum, College Press (Pvt) Ltd, P.O. Box 3041, Harare, Zimbabwe.

The Teacher of the Blind, The College of Teachers of the Blind, Royal School of Industry for the Blind, Westbury on Trym, Bristol.

The Teacher of the Deaf, National College of Teachers of the Deaf, Longwill School for the Deaf, Bell Hill, Northfield, Birmingham.

Teachers of the World, World Federation of Teachers' Unions, Willhelm-Wollf-Str. 21, GDR-1110 Berlin, East Germany.

Teaching Arithmetic, Pergamon Press, Oxford, England.

Teaching and Learning in Medicine, Lawrence Erlbaum Associates, Inc., 365 Broadway, Hillsdale, NJ 07642-9969, U.S.A.

Teaching and Teacher Education, Pergamon Journals Ltd, Headington Hill Hall, Oxford OX3, 0BW, England.

Teaching Earth Sciences, (formerly Geology Teaching) Earth Science Teachers Association, University of Keele, Department of Education, Keele ST5 5BG, England.

Teaching English, Macdonald Publishers, Edgefield Road, Loanhead, Midlothian, Scotland.

Teaching Exceptional Children, Council for Exceptional Children, 1920 Association Drive, Reston, VA 22091, U.S.A.

Teaching Geography, Geographical Association, 43 Fulwood Road, Sheffield S10 3BP, England.

Teaching History, Historical Association, 59a Kennington Park Road, London SE11 4JH, England.

Teaching Learning and Technology, Centre for Research into Practice, 1718 Conneticut Ave N.W., Washington, D.C. 2009, U.S.A.

Teaching Mathematics and its Applications, Oxford University Press, Walton Street, Oxford OX2 6DP, England.

Teaching of Psychology, Lawrence Erlbaum Associates, Inc., c/o Department of Psychology, Furman University, Greenville, SC 29613, U.S.A.

Teaching Philosophy, Bowling Green State University, Philosophy Documentation Center, Bowling Green, OH 43403, U.S.A.

Teaching Political Science, Heldref Publications, Inc., 4000 Albemarle Street, N.W., Washington, D.C. 20016, U.S.A.

Teaching Science, School Natural Science Society, 29 Alders, Heston, Middlesex TW5 0HP, England.

Teaching Sociology, American Sociological Association, 1722 North Street, N.W., Washington, D.C. 20036, U.S.A.

Teaching Statistics, Applied Probability Trust, Department of Probability and Statistics, University of Sheffield, Sheffield S10 2TN, England.

Tech Trends, Association for Educational Communications and Technology, 1126 16th Street, N.W., Washington, D.C. 20036, U.S.A.

Theory and Research in Social Education, National Council for the Social Studies, University of Wisconsin, Dept. Curriculum & Instruction, 225 North Mills Street, Madison, WI 53706, U.S.A.

Theory into Practice, Ohio State University, College of Education, 149 Arps Hall, 1945 North High Street, Columbus, OH 43210, U.S.A.

Thinking, Montclair State College, Institute for the Advancement of Philosophy for Children, Upper Montclair, NJ 07043, U.S.A.

TOPIC: Practical Applications of Research in Education, NFER-NELSON Publishing Company, Ltd., *Subscription*: Carfax Publishing Company, P.O. Box 25, Abingdon, Oxfordshire OX14 3UE, England.

Topics in Early Childhood Special Education, PRO-ED, Inc., 5341 Industrial Oaks Boulevard, Austin, TX 78735-8809, U.S.A.

Training and Development, Journals Ltd, 5 Baring Road, Beaconsfield, Buckinghamshire HP9 2NX, England.

Training and Education, Personel Training and Education Group of the Library Association, College of Librarianship, Wales, Aberystwyth SY23 3AS, Wales.

Training Officer, Marylebone Press Ltd, Lloyds House, 18 Lloyds Street, Manchester M2 5WA, England.

Transition, Tempus House of Publishers Ltd, 342/362 Corn Exchange Buildings, Manchester M4 3BU, England.

Unicorn, Australian College of Education, 916 Swanston Street, Carlton, Victoria 3053, Australia.

University Affairs, Association of Universities and Colleges of Canada, 151 Slater Street, Ottawa, Ontario K1P 5N1, Canada.

University Computing, Blackwell Scientific Publications Ltd, Osney Mead, Oxford OX2 0EL, England.

Urban Education, Sage Publications, Inc., 275 South Beverly Drive, Beverly Hills, CA 90212, U.S.A.

Vocational Aspect of Education, National Centres for Further Education Teacher Training, Garnett College of Education, Downshire House, Roehampton Lane, London SW15 4HR, England.

Vocational Education Journal, American Vocational Association, Inc., 1410 King Street, Alexandria, VA 22314, U.S.A.

Vocational Training Bulletin, CEDEFOP—European Centre for the Development of Vocational Training, Bundesalle 22, West Berlin, West Germany.

West African Journal of Educational and Vocational Measurement, West African Examination Council, Test Development and Research Office, P.M.B. 1076, Lagos, Nigeria.

Western European Education, M.E. Sharpe, Inc., 80 Business Park Drive, Armonk, N.Y. 10504, U.S.A.

Westminster Studies in Education, Carfax Publishing Company, P.O. Box 25, Abingdon, Oxfordshire OX14 3UE, England.

Workers Education (UK), Workers Education Association, Temple House, 9 Upper Berkeley Street, London W1H 8By, England.

World Englishes, Pergamon Journals Ltd, Headington Hill Hall, Oxford OX3 0BW, England.

World Studies Journal, Centre for Global Education, University of York, Heslington, York YO1 5DD, England.

Young Children, National Association for the Education of Young Children, 1834 Connecticut Avenue, N.W., Washington, D.C. 20009, U.S.A.

Youth and Society, Sage Publications, Inc., 275 South Beverly Drive, Beverly Hills, CA 90212, U.S.A.

Youth Training News, Manpower Services Commission, Distribution Unit, Room E825, Moorfoot, Sheffield S1 4PQ, England.

Zeitschrift für Pädagogik, Verlag Julian Beltz AM, Hauptbahnhof 10, Postfach 1120, 6940 Weinheim, West Germany.

Zimbabwe Journal of Educational Research, HRRC, Faculty of Education, University of Zimbabwe, P.O. Box MP 167, Mount Pleasant, Harare, Zimbabwe.

The University Grants Commission Powers, Functions and Composition

Establishment of the Commission

4. *(1)* With effect from such date as the Central Government may, by notification in the Official Gazette, appoint, there shall be established a Commission by the name of the University Grants Commission.

(2) The said Commission shall be a body corporate having perpetual succession and a common seal, and shall by the said name sue and be sued.

Composition of the Commission

[5. *(1)* The Commission shall consist of—

(i) a Chairman,
(ii) a Vice-Chairman, and
(iii) ten other members,

to be appointed by the Central Government.

(2) The Chairman shall be chosen from among persons who are not officers of the Central Government or of any State Government.

(3) Of the other members referred to in clause (iii) of sub-section *(1)*—

(a) two shall be chosen from among the officers of Central Government to represent that Government;

(b) not less than four shall be chosen from among persons who are, at the time when they are so chosen, teachers of Universities; and

(c) the remainder shall be chosen from among persons—

(i) Who have knowledge of, or experience in, agriculture, commerce, forestry or industry;

(ii) who are members of the engineering, legal, medical or any other learned profession; or

(iii) who are Vice-Chancellors of Universities or who, not being teachers of Universities, are, in the opinion of the Central Government, educationists of repute or have obtained high academic distinctions:

Provided that not less than one-half of the number chosen under this clause shall be from among persons who are not officers of the Central Government or of any State Government.

(4) The Vice-Chairman shall exercise such of the powers, and discharge such of the duties, of the Chairman as may be prescribed.

(5) Every appointment under this section shall take effect from the date on which it is notified by the Central Government in the Official Gazette.]

Terms and Conditions of Service of Members

6.[*(1)* A person appointed as Chairman, Vice-Chairman or other member shall, unless he becomes disqualified for continuing as such under the rules that may be made under this Act,—

(a) in the case of Chairman, hold office for a term of five years; and

(b) in the case of Vice-Chairman or any other member, hold office for a term of three years: Provided that—

(i) a person who has held office as Chairman or Vice-Chairman shall be eligible for further appointment as Chairman, Vice-Chairman or other member, and

(ii) a person who has held office as any other member shall be eligible for further appointment as Chairman, Vice-Chairman or other member:

Provided further that a person who has held office for two terms, in any capacity, whether as Chairman, Vice-Chairman or other member, shall not be eligible for any further appointment as Chairman, Vice-Chairman or other member.]

(2) A member may resign his office by writing under his hand addressed to the Central Government, but he shall continue in office until his resignation is accepted by the Central Government.

[*(3)* If a casual vacancy occurs in the office of the Chairman, whether by reason of his death, resignation or inability to discharge his functions owing to illness or other incapacity, the Vice-Chairman holding office as such for the time being shall, notwithstanding anything contained in sub-section *(2)* of section 5, act as the Chairman and shall, unless any other person is appointed earlier as the Chairman, hold the office of the Chairman for the remainder of the term of office of the person in whose place he is to so act:

Provided that where no Vice-Chairman is holding office at the time when the vacancy in the office of the Chairman occurs, the Central Government shall, notwithstanding anything contained in sub-section *(2)* of section 5, appoint any other member to act as the Chairman and the person so appointed shall not hold the office of the Chairman for a period exceeding six months.

(4) If a casual vacancy occurs in the office of the Vice-Chairman or any other member, whether by reason of his death, resignation or inability to discharge his functions owing to illness or other incapacity, such vacancy shall be filled up by the Central Government by making a fresh appointment and the member so appointed shall hold office for a term of three years.

(5) The office of the Chairman and the Vice-Chairman shall be whole-time salaried and subject thereto, the terms and conditions of service of the Chairman, Vice-Chairman and other members shall be such as may be prescribed.]

Meetings of the Commission

7. The Commission shall meet at such times and places and shall

observe such rules of procedure in regard to the transaction of business at its meetings as may be provided by regulations made under this Act.

Vacancies amongst Members or Defect in Constitution not to Invalidate Acts or Proceedings of the Commission

8. No act or proceedings of the Commission shall be deemed to be invalid by reason merely of any vacancy in, or any defect in the constitution of, the Commission.

Temporary Association of Persons with the Commission for Particular Purposes

9. *(1)* The Commission may associate with itself, in such manner and for such purposes as may be determined by regulations made under this Act, any person whose assistance or advice it may desire in carrying out any of the provisions of this Act.

(2) A person associated with it by the Commission under sub-section *(1)* for any purpose shall have a right to take part in the discussions relevant to that purpose but shall not have a right to vote at a meeting of the Commission, and shall not be a member for any other purpose.

Staff of the Commission

10. Subject to such rules as may be made by the Central Government in this behalf, the Commission may appoint a Secretary and such other employees as it may think necessary for the efficient performance of its functions under this Act and the terms and conditions of service of the employees shall be such as may be determined by the Commission.

Authentication of Orders and other Instruments of the Commission

11. All orders and decisions of the Commission shall be authenticated by the signature of the Chairman or any other member authorised by the Commission in this behalf, and all other instruments issued by the Commission shall be

authenticated by the signature of the Secretary or any other officer of the Commission authorised in like manner in this behalf.

Powers and Functions of the Commission

12. It shall be the general duty of the Commission to take, in consultation with the Universities or other bodies concerned, all such steps as it may think fit for the promotion and co-ordination of University education and for the determination and maintenance of standards of teaching, examination and research in Universities, and for the purpose of performing its functions under this Act, the Commission may—

(a) inquire into the financial needs of Universities;

(b) allocate and disburse, out of the Fund of the Commission, grants to Universities established or incorporated by or under a Central Act for the maintenance and development of such Universities or for any other general or specified purpose;

(c) allocate and disburse, out of the Fund of the Commission, such grants to other Universities as it may deem [necessary or appropriate for the development of such Universities or for the maintenance, or development, or both, of any specified activities of such Universities] or for any other general or specified purpose:

Provided that in making any grant to any such University, the Commission shall give due consideration to the development of the University concerned, its financial needs, the standard attained by it and the national purposes which it may serve,

[(cc) allocate and disburse out of the Fund of the Commission, such grants to institutions deemed to be Universities in pursuance of a declaration made by the Central Government under section 3, as it may deem necessary, for one or more of the following purposes, namely:

(i) for maintenance in special cases,

(ii) for development,

(iii) for any other general or specified purposes;]

["(ccc) establish, in accordance with the regulations made under this Act, institutions for providing common facilities, services and programmes for a group of universities or for the universities in general and maintain such institutions or provide for their maintenance by allocating and disbursing out of the Fund of the Commission such grants as the Commission may deem necessary".]

(d) recommends to any University the measures necessary for the improvement of University education and advise the University upon the action to be taken for the purpose of implementing such recommendation;

(e) advise the Central Government or any State Government on the allocation of any grants to Universities for any general or specified purpose out of the Consolidated Fund of India or the Consolidated Fund of the State, as the case may be;

(f) advise any authority, if such advice is asked for, on the establishment of a new University or on proposals connected with the expansion of the activities of any University;

(g) advise the Central Government or any State Government or University on any question which may be referred to the Commission by the Central Government or the State Government or the University, as the case may be;

(h) collect information on all such matters relating to University education in India and other countries as it thinks fit and make the same available to any University;

(i) require a University to furnish it with such information as may be needed relating to the financial position of the University or the studies in the various branches of learning undertaken in that University, together with all the rules and regulations relating to the standards of teaching and examination in that University respecting each of such branches of learning;

(j) perform such other functions as may be prescribed or as may be deemed necessary by the Commission for advancing the cause of higher education in India or as may be incidental or conducive to the discharge of the above functions.

Regulation of Fees and Prohibition of Donations in Certain Cases

[(12A) *(1)* In this section,—

(a) "affiliation" together with its grammatical variations, includes, in relation to a college, recognition of such college by, association of such college with and admission of such college to the privileges of, a university;
(b) "college" means any institution, whether known as such or by any other name which provides for a course of study for obtaining any qualification from a university and which, in accordance with the rules and regulations of such university, is recognised as competent to provide for such course of study and present students undergoing such course of study for the examination for the award of such qualification;
(c) "prosecution" in relation to a course of study, includes promotion from one part or stage of the course of study to another part or stage of the course of study;
(d) "qualification" means a degree or any other qualification awarded by a university;
(e) "regulations" mean regulations made under this Act;
(f) "specified course of study" means a course of study in respect of which regulations of the nature mentioned in sub-section (2) have been made;
(g) "student" includes a person seeking admission as a student;
(h) "university" means a university or institution referred to in sub-section (1) of section 22,

(2) Without prejudice to the generality of the provisions of section 12 if, having regard to—

(a) the nature of any course of study for obtaining any qualification from any university;
(b) the types of activities in which persons obtaining such qualification are likely to be engaged on the basis of such qualification;
(c) the minimum standards which a person possessing such qualification should be able to maintain in his work relating to such activities and the consequent need for

ensuring, so far as may be, that no candidate secures admission to such course of study by reason of economic power and thereby prevents a more meritorious candidate from securing admission to such course of study; and

(d) all other relevant factors, the Commission is satisfied that it is necessary so to do in the public interest, it may, after consultation with the university or universities concerned specify by regulations the matters in respect of which fees may be charged, and the scale of fees in accordance with which fees shall be charged in respect of those matters on and from such date as may be specified in the regulations in this behalf, by any college providing for such course of study from, or in relation to, any student in connection with his admission to, and prosecution of, such course of study;

Provided that different matters and different scales of fees may be so specified in relation to different universities or different classes of colleges or different areas.

(3) Where regulations of the nature referred to in sub-section (2) have been made in relation to any course of study, no college providing for such course of study shall—

(a) levy or charge fees in respect of any matter other than a matter specified in such regulations;
(b) levy or charge any fees in excess of the scale of fees specified in such regulations, or
(c) accept, either directly or indirectly, any payment otherwise than by way of fees; or any donation or gift (whether in cash or kind),

from, or in relation to, any student in connection with his admission to, and prosecution of, such course of study.

(4) If, after making, in relation to a college providing for a specified course of study, an inquiry in the manner provided by regulations, and after giving such college a reasonable opportunity of being heard, the Commission is satisfied that such college has contravened the provisions of sub-section (3), the Commission may, with the previous approval of the Central

Government, pass an order prohibiting such college from presenting any students then undergoing such course of study therein to any university for the award of the qualification concerned.

(5) The Commission shall forward a copy of the order made by it under sub-section (4) to the university concerned, and on and from the date of receipt by the university of a copy of such order, the affiliation of such college to such university shall, in so far as it relates to the course of study specified in such order, stand terminated and on and from the date of termination of such affiliation and for a period of three years thereafter affiliation shall not be granted to such college in relation to such or similar course of study by that or any other university.

(6) On the termination of the affiliation of any college under sub-section (5), the Commission shall take all such steps as it may consider appropriate for safeguarding the interests of the students concerned.

(7) The provisions of this section and the regulations made for the purposes of this section shall have effect notwithstanding anything inconsistent therewith contained in any other law for the time being in force.]

Prohibition Regarding Giving of any Grant to a University not Declared by the Commission Fit to Receive such Grant

[(12B)No grant shall be given by the Central Government, the Commission, or any other organisation receiving any funds from the Central Government, to a University which is established after the commencement of the University Grants Commission (Amendment) Act, 1972, unless the Commission has, after satisfying itself as to such matters as may be prescribed, declared such University to be fit for receiving such grant.]

Inspection

13. (1) For the purpose of ascertaining the financial needs of a University or its standards of teaching, examination and research, the Commission may, after consultation with the University, cause an inspection of any department or departments thereof to be made in such manner as may be

prescribed and by such person or persons as it may direct.

(2) The Commission shall communicate to the University the date on which any inspection under sub-section (1) is to be made and the University shall be entitled to be associated with the inspection in such manner as may be prescribed.

(3) The Commission shall communicate to the University its views in regard to the results of any such inspection and may, after ascertaining the opinion of the University, recommend to the University the action to be taken as a result of such inspection.

(4) All communications to a University under this section shall be made to the executive authority thereof and the executive authority of the University shall report to the Commission the action, if any, which is proposed to be taken for the purpose of implementing any such recommendation as is referred to in sub-section (3).

Consequences of Failure of Universities to Comply with Recommendations of the Commission

14. If any University (grants affiliation in respect of any course of study to any college referred to in sub-section (5) of section 12A in contravention of the provisions of that sub-section or) fails within a reasonable time to comply with any recommendation made by the Commission under Section 12 or Section 13, [or contravenes the provisions of any rule made under clause (f) or clause (g) of sub-section (2) of Section 25, or of any regulation made under clause (e) or clause (f) or clause (g) of Section 26,] the Commission, after taking into consideration the cause, if any, shown by the University [for such failure or contravention,] may withhold from the University the grants proposed to be made out of the Fund of the Commission.

Payment to the Commission

15. The Central Government may, after due appropriation made by Parliament by law in this behalf, pay to the Commission in each financial year such sums as may be considered necessary for the performance of the functions of the Commission under this Act.

Fund of the Commission

16. (1) The Commission shall have its own Fund; and all sums which may, from time to time, be paid to it by the Central Government and all the receipts of the Commission (including any sum which any State Government or any other authority or person may hand over to the Commission) shall be carried to the Fund and all payments by the Commission shall be made therefrom.

(2) All moneys belonging to the Fund shall be deposited in such banks or invested in such manner as may, subject to the approval of the Central Government, be decided by the Commission.

(3) The Commission may spend such sums as it thinks fit for performing its functions under this Act, and such sums shall be treated as expenditure payable out of the Fund of the Commission.

Budget

17. The Commission shall prepare, in such form and at such time each year as may be prescribed, a budget in respect of the financial year next ensuing showing the estimated receipts and expenditure, and copies thereof shall be forwarded to the Central Government.

Annual Report

18. The Commission shall prepare once every year, in such form and at such time as may be prescribed, an annual report giving a true and full account of its activities during the previous year, and copies thereof shall be forwarded to the Central Government and the Government shall cause the same to be laid before both Houses of Parliament.

Account and Audit

19. (1) The Commission shall cause to be maintained such books of account and other books in relation to its account in such form and in such manner as may, in consultation with the

Comptroller and Auditor-General of India, be prescribed.

(2) The Commission shall, as soon as may be after closing its annual accounts, prepare a statement of accounts in such form, and forward the same to the Comptroller and Auditor-General by such date, as the Central Government may, in consultation with the Comptroller and Auditor-General, determine.

(3) The accounts of the Commission shall be audited by the Comptroller and Auditor-General at such times and in such manner as he thinks fit.

(4) The annual accounts of the Commission together with the audit report thereon shall be forwarded to the Central Government and the Government shall cause the same to be laid before both Houses of Parliament and shall also forward a copy of the audit report to the Commission for taking suitable action on the matters arising out of the audit report.

Miscellaneous

Directions by the Central Government

20. (1) In the discharge of its functions under this Act, the Commission shall be guided by such directions on questions of policy relating to national purposes as may be given to it by the Central Government.

(2) If any dispute arises between the Central Government and the Commission as to whether a question is or is not a question of policy relating to national purposes, the decision of the Central Government shall be final.

Returns and Information

21. The Commission shall furnish to the Central Government such returns or other information with respect to its property or activities as the Central Government may, from time to time, require.

Right to Confer Degrees

22. (1) The right of conferring or granting degrees shall be

exercised only by a University established or incorporated by or under a Central Act, a Provincial Act or a State Act or an institution deemed to be a University under section 3 or an institution specially empowered by an Act of Parliament to confer or grant degrees.

(2) Save as provided in sub-section (1), no person or authority shall confer, or grant, or hold himself or itself out as entitled to confer or grant, any degree.

(3) For the purposes of this section, "degree" means any such degree as may, with the previous approval of the Central Government, be specified in this behalf by the Commission by notification in the Official Gazette.

Prohibition of the Use of the Word "University" in Certain Cases

23. No institution, whether a corporate body or not, other than a University established or incorporated by or under a Central Act, a Provincial Act or a State Act shall be entitled to have the word "University" associated with its name in any manner whatsoever:

Provided that nothing in this section shall, for a period of two years from the commencement of this Act, apply to an institution which, immediately before such commencement, had the word "University" associated with its name.

Penalties

24. Whoever contravenes the provisions of section 22 or section 23 shall be punishable with fine which may extend to one thousand rupees, and if the person contravening is an association or other body of individuals, every member of such association or other body who knowingly or wilfully authorises or permits the contravention shall be punishable with fine which may extend to one thousand rupees.

Power to Make Rules

25. (1) The Central Government may, by notification in the Official Gazette, make rules to carry out the purposes of this Act.

(2) In particular, and without prejudice to the generality of the

foregoing power, such rules may provide for all or any of the following matters, namely: –

(a) the procedure for the retirement of members under section 6;
(b) the disqualifications for continuing as a member of the Commission;
(c) the terms and conditions of service of members of the Commission;
(d) the terms and conditions of service of employees appointed by the Commission;
(e) the additional functions which may be performed by the Commission under clause (j) of section 12;
(f) the returns and information which are to be furnished by Universities in respect of their financial position or standards of teaching and examination maintained therein;
(g) the inspection of Universities;
(h) the form and manner in which the budget and reports are to be prepared by the Commission;
(i) the manner in which the accounts of the Commission are to be maintained;
(j) the form and manner in which returns or other information are to be furnished by the Commission to the Central Government;
(k) any other matter which has to be, or may be, prescribed.

["(3) The power to make rules conferred by this section shall include the power to give retrospective effect from a date not earlier than the date of commencement of this Act, to the rules or any of them but no retrospective effect shall be given to any rule so as to prejudicially affect the interests of any person to whom such rule may be applicable."]

Power to make Regulations

26. (1) The Commission [may, by notification in the Official Gazette, make regulations] consistent with this Act and the rules made thereunder—

(a) regulating the meetings of the Commission and the procedure for conducting business thereat;

(b) regulating the manner in which and the purposes for which persons may be associated with the Commission under section 9;

(c) specifying the terms and conditions of service of the employees appointed by the Commission;

(d) specifying the institutions or class of institutions which may be recognised by the Commission under clause (f) of section 2;

(e) defining the qualifications that should ordinarily be required of any person to be appointed to the teaching staff of the University, having regard to the branch of education in which he is expected to give instruction;

(f) defining the minimum standards of instruction for the grant of any degree by any University;

(g) regulating the maintenance of standards and the co-ordination of work or facilities in Universities.

["(h) regulating the establishment of institutions referred to in clause (ccc) of Section 12 and other matters relating to such institutions;

(i) specifying the matters in respect of which fees may be charged, and scales of fees in accordance with which fees may be charged, by a college under sub-section (2) of Section 12A;

(j) specifying the manner in which an inquiry may be conducted under sub-section (4) of Section 12A.";]

(2) No regulation shall be made under clause (a) or clause (b) or clause (c) or clause (d) [or clause (h) or clause (i) or clause (j)] of sub-section (1) except with the previous approval of the Central Government,

[(3) The power to make regulations conferred by this section [except clause (i) and clause (j) of sub-section (1)] shall include the power to give retrospective effect from a date not earlier than the date of commencement of this Act, to the regulations or any of them but no retrospective effect shall be given to any regulation so as to prejudicially affect the interests of any person to whom such regulation may be applicable."]

Power to Delegate

[27 (1) The Commission may, [by regulations made, by notification in the Official Gazette,] under this Act, delegate to its Chairman, Vice-Chairman or any of its officers, its power of general superintendence and direction over the business transacted by, or in, the Commission, including the powers with regard to the expenditure incurred in connection with the maintenance of the office and internal administration of the Commission.

(2) No regulation shall be made under this section except with the previous approval of the Central Government]

Laying of Rules and Regulations before Parliament

["28. Every rule and every regulation made under this Act shall be laid, as soon as may be after it is made, before each House of Parliament while it is in session, for a total period of thirty days which may be comprised in one session or in two or more successive sessions, and if, before the expiry of the session immediately following the session, or the successive sessions aforesaid, both Houses agree in making any modification in the rule or regulation or both Houses agree that the rule or regulation should not be made, the rule or regulation shall thereafter have effect only in such modified form or be of no effect, as the case may, be; so, however, that any such modification or annulment shall be without prejudice to the validity of anything previously done under that rule or regulation,"]

Validation

No rule made or purporting to have been made, with retrospective effect, under section 25 of the principal Act before the commencement of this Act shall be deemed to have been invalid or ever to have been invalid merely on the ground that such rule was made with retrospective effect and accordingly every such rule and every action taken or thing done thereunder shall be as valid and effective as if the provisions of section 25 of the principal Act, as amended by this Act, were in force at all material times when such rule was made or action or thing was taken or done.]

APPENDIX-VII

List of Centres of Advance Study

University	*Subject with thrust area*	
Allahabad Uni.	Psychology	: Applied and experimental social psychology
		: Organisational psychology
AMU, Aligarh	History	: Indian Medieval
Annamalai	Biology	: Marine
	Linguistics	: Dravidian
Banaras Hindu University	Zoology	
	Botany	
	Met. Engn.	
Bombay	Chemistry	: Applied
	Mathematics	
	Economics	: Public Finance and Industrial Eco.
Calcutta	Botany	
	Chemistry	
	Physics	: Radio & Electronics
	Maths.	: Applied
Delhi	Botany	
	Zoology	
	Physics	
	Chemistry	
	Economics	: Economics of development and Economic History
Gokhale Institute	Sociology	
	Economics	: Agricultural
Indian Institute of Sciencces, Bangalore	Biophysics	: Molecular
	Bio-Chemistry	
	Chemistry	: Inorganic, Physical and Solid State
	Physics	
Jadavpur	Geology	

University	Philosophy	: Theory of knowledge and reality: Indian and Western logic and language – Indian and Western Ethics, Religion, Social and Political Philosophy – Indian and Western Philosophy of mind.
Madras University	Botany	
	Math	
	Philosophy	: Advaita and Allied System
M.S. University Baroda	Education	: Research
Osmania University	Linguistics	: Historical and Comparative method (Indo-Aryan and Dravidian)
		: Phonetics (Linguistics and Experimental)
		: Contact and Convergence study with special reference to Munda, Dravidian and Indo-Aryan languages in Central India.
		: Socio-lingustics and applied socio-linguistics W.S.T.I. language teaching, literacy and trans- lation.
		: Psycholinguistics
Punjab	Chemistry	
	Geology	
	Math	
Poona	Physics	
	Sanskrit	: Literature
Pune		
Daccan College	Archaeology	: Indian
Ranchi University	Anthropology	: Advanced Anthropological Theory and Methodology;
		: Macro analysis qualification Method and system analysis.
Utkal University	Psychology	: Educational
		: Social

Universities, Deemed Universities and Institutions of National Importance

S. No.	University Name & Address	Estd. Year
1.	Agra Agra-282004, Uttar Pradesh	1927
2.	Ajmer Ajmer-305001, Rajasthan	1987
3.	Alagappa Karaikudi-623004, Tamil Nadu	1985
4.	Allahabad Allahabad-211002, U.P.	1857
5.	Amravati Amravati-444604, Maharashtra	1983
6.	Andhra Waltair-530003, Visakhapatnam, A.P.	1926
7.	Arunachal Itanagar-791111, Arunachal Pradesh	1985
8.	Avadh Faizabad-224001, Uttar Pradesh	1975
9.	Awadesh Pratap Singh Rewa-486003, Madhya Pradesh	1968
10.	Bangalore Janana Bharati-560056, Bangalore	1964
11.	Barkatullah Bhopal-462006, Madhya Pradesh	1970
12.	Berhampur Berhampur-760007, Orissa	1967
13.	Bhagalpur Bhagalpur-812007, Bihar	1960

(Contd.)

(*Contd.*)

S. No.	University Name & Address	Estd. Year
14.	Bharathidasan Tiruchirapalli-620024, T.N.	1982
15.	Bharathiyar Coimbatore-641046, Tamil Nadu	1982
16.	Bhavnagar Bhavnagar-364002, Gujarat	1978
17.	Bihar Muzaffarpur-842001, Bihar	1952
18.	Bombay Bombay-400032, Maharashtra	1857
19.	Bundelkhand Jhansi 284001, Uttar Pradesh	1975
20.	Burdwan Burdwan-713104, West Bengal	1960
21.	Calcutta Calcutta-700073, West Bengal	1857
22.	Calicut Calicut-673635, Kerala	1968
23.	Devi Ahilya Indore-452001, Madhya Pradesh	1964
24.	Dibrugarh Dibrugarh-786004, Assam	1965
25.	Dr. Hari Singh Gaur Sagar-470003, Madhya Pradesh	1946
26.	Gauhati Gauhati-781014, Assam	1948
27.	Goa Bambolim, Panaji-403005, Goa	1985
28.	Gorakhpur Gorakhpur-273001, Uttar Pradesh	1957
29.	Gujarat Ahmedabad-380009, Gujarat	1950
30.	Gulbarga Gulbarga-585106, Karnataka	1980

(Contd.)

(*Contd.*)

S. No.	University Name & Address	Estd. Year
31.	Guru Ghasi Dass Bilaspur-495001, Madhya Pradesh	1983
32.	Guru Nanak Dev Amritsar-143005, Punjab	1969
33.	H.N. Bahuguna Srinagar-246174, Uttar Pradesh	1973
34.	Himachal Pradesh Shimla-171005, Himachal Pradesh	1970
35.	Indira Kala Sangeet Kharaigarh-491881, Madhya Pradesh	1956
36.	Jadavpur Calcutta-700032, West Bengal	1955
37.	Jammu Jammu-180001, J & K	1969
38.	Jiwaji Gwalior-474001, Madhya Pradesh	1964
39.	Jodhpur Jodhpur-342003, Rajasthan	1962
40.	K.S.D. Sanskrit Darbhanga-846004, Bihar	1961
41.	Kakatiya Warangal-506009, Andhra Pradesh	1976
42.	Kalyani Kalyani-741235, West Bengal	1960
43.	Kanpur Kanpur-208024, U.P.	1965
44.	Karnatak Dharwad-580003, Karnataka	1949
45.	Kashmir Srinagar-190006, Jammu & Kashmir	1949
46.	Kerala Trivandrum-695034, Kerala	1937
47.	Kumaon Nainital-263001, Uttar Pradesh	1973

(*Contd.*)

(*Contd.*)

S. No.	University Name & Address	Estd. Year
48.	Kurukshetra Kurukshetra-132119, Haryana	1956
49.	Kuvempu B.R. Project, Shimoga-577115, Karnataka	1988
50.	L.N. Mithila Darbhanga-846004, Bihar	1972
51.	Lucknow Lucknow-226007, Uttar Pradesh	1921
52.	M.S. Baroda Baroda-390002, Gujarat	1949
53.	Madras Madras-600005, Tamil Nadu	1857
54.	Madurai Kamraj Madurai-625021, Tamil Nadu	1965
55.	Magadh Bodhgaya-824234, Bihar	1962
56.	Maharishi Dayanand Rohtak-124001, Haryana	1976
57.	Mahatma Gandhi Kottayam-686002, Kerala	1983
58.	Mangalore Light House Hills-574119, Mangalore	1980
59.	Manipur Chanchipur, Imphal-795003, Manipur	1980
60.	Marathwada Aurangabad-431004, Maharashtra	1958
61.	Meerut Meerut-250001, Uttar Pradesh	1965
62.	Mysore Mysore-570005, Karnataka	1916
63.	Nagarjuna Nagarjuna Nagar, Guntur-522510, A.P.	1976
64.	Nagpur Nagpur-440001, Maharashtra	1923

(*Contd.*)

(*Contd.*)

S. No.	University Name & Address	Estd. Year
65.	North Bengal Raja Ram Mohanpur, Darjeeling-734430	1962
66.	North Gujarat Patan-384265, Gujarat	1986
67.	Osmania Hyderabad-500007, Andhra Pradesh	1918
68.	Panjab Chandigarh-160014	1947
69.	Panjab Rao Krishi Akola-444104, Maharashtra	1969
70.	Patna Patna-800003, Bihar	1917
71.	Poona Pune-411007, Maharashtra	1949
72.	Punjabi Patiala-147002, Punjab	1962
73.	Purvanchal Jaunpur-222002, Uttar Pradesh	1987
74.	Rajasthan Jaipur-302004, Rajasthan	1947
75.	Rajindra Agricultural Pusa, Samastipur-848125, Bihar	1970
76.	Ranchi Ranchi-843001, Bihar	1960
77.	Rani Durgawati Jabalpur-482001, Madhya Pradesh	1957
78.	Ravi Shankar Raipur-492002, Madhya Pradesh	1975
79.	Rohilkhand Bareilly-243001, Uttar Pradesh	1975
80.	S.N.D.T. Women's Nathi Bai T. Road, Bombay-400020	1951
81.	S.N. Sanskrit Varanasi-221002, Uttar Pradesh	1958

(*Contd.*)

(*Contd.*)

S. No.	University Name & Address	Estd. Year
82.	Sambalpur Jyoti Vihar, Sambalpur-768001	1967
83.	Sardar Patel Vallabh Vidyanagar-388120	1955
84.	Saurashtra Rajkot-360005, Gujarat	1965
85.	Sh. Jagan Nath Sanskrit Puri-752002, Orissa	1981
86.	Shivaji Kolhapur-416004, Maharashtra	1962
87.	South Gujarat Surat-395007, Gujarat	1965
88.	Sri Venkateswara Tirupati-517502, Andhra Pradesh	1954
89.	Tripura Agartala-799004, West Tripura	1987
90.	Utkal Bhubaneshwar-751004, Orissa	1943
91.	Vidyasagar Midnapore-721001, West Bengal	1981
92.	Vikram Ujjain-456010, Madhya Pradesh	1957
93.	Aligarh Muslim Aligarh-202001, Uttar Pradesh	1921
94.	Banaras Hindu Varanasi-221005, Uttar Pradesh	1916
95.	Delhi Maurice Nagar, Delhi-110007	1922
96.	Hyderabad Hyderabad-500134, Andhra Pradesh	1974
97.	Indira Gandhi National Open Y.M.C.A. Cultural Centre, New Delhi-110001	1985
98.	Jamia Millia Islamia New Delhi-110025	1962

(*Contd.*)

(*Contd.*)

S. No.	University Name & Address	Estd. Year
99.	Jawaharlal Nehru New Mehrauli Road, New Delhi-110067	1968
100.	North Eastern Hill P.O. Lower Lachumiers, Shillong-793001	1973
101.	Pondicherry Pondicherry-605001, Tamil Nadu	1985
102.	Visva Bharati Santiniketan-731235, West Bengal	1951
103.	Avinashlingam Institution for Home Science & Higher Education for Women, Coimbatore-641043, Tamil Nadu	1988
104.	Banasthali Vidyapith Banasthali-304022, Rajasthan	1983
105.	Birla Institute of Technology & Science, Pilani-333031	1964
106.	Birla Institute of Technology Mesra, Ranchi- 835215, Bihar	1986
107.	Central Institute of English & Foreign Languages, Hyderabad-500007	1973
108.	Central Institute of Fisheries Education Versova, Bombay-400061	1989
109.	Central Instt. of Higher Tibetan Studies, Sarnath, Varanasi-221007	1958
110.	Dayalbagh Educational Institute Agra-282005, Uttar Pradesh	1981
111.	Gandhi Gram Rural Institute Dindigul, Gandhi Gram-624302, TN	1976
112.	Gujarat Vidyapith Ahmedabad-380014, Gujarat	1963
113.	Gurukul Kangri Hardwar-249404, Uttar Pradesh	1962
114.	Indian Agricultural Research Institute, Pusa, New Delhi-110012	1958

(*Contd.*)

(*Contd.*)

S. No.	University Name & Address	Estd. Year
115.	Indian Veterinary Research Institute, Izatnagar-2443122, U.P.	1983
116.	Indian Institute of Science Bangalore-560012, Karnataka	1958
117.	Indian School of Mines Dhanbad-826004, Bihar	1967
118.	International Institute for Population Sciences, Bombay-400088	1985
119.	Jamia Hamdard Hamdard Nagar, New Delhi-110062	1989
120.	National Dairy Research Institute Karnal-132001, Haryana	N.A.
121.	National Museum Institute of History of Arts, Consn. & Museology, New Delhi-110011	1989
122.	Rajasthan Vidyapeeth Udaipur-313001, Rajasthan	1987
123.	Rashtriya Sanskrit Vidyapeeth Tirupati-517507, Andhra Pradesh	1961
124.	School of Planning & Architecture, No. 4, Block-8, New Delhi-110002	1979
125.	Sh. Satya Sai Instt. of Higher Learning, P. Nilayam-515134, Anantpur	1981
126.	Shri Lal B. Shastri Rashtriya Sanskrit Vidyapeeth, Kathodia Sarai, New Delhi-110016	1962
127.	Tata Instt. of Social Sciences Trombay, Deonar, Bombay-400088	1964
128.	Thapar Instt. of Engineering & Technology, Patiala-147001	1985
129.	Tilak Maharashtra Vidyapeeth Pune-411037, Maharashtra	1987
130.	All India Institute of Medical Sciences, Ansari Nagar, New Delhi-110029	1956
131.	Dakshina Bharat Hindi Prachar Sabha, Hyderabad-600017, Andhra Pradesh	1918

(*Contd.*)

(*Contd.*)

S. No.	University Name & Address	Estd. Year
132.	Indian Statistical Institute 203, Barackpore, T. Road, Calcutta-700035	1932
133.	Indian Institute of Technology Hauz Khas, New Delhi-110016	1961
134.	Indian Institute of Technology Agriculture Garden, Kanpur-208016, U.P.	1959
135.	Indian Institute of Technology Kharagpur-721302, West Bengal	1950
136.	Indian Institute of Technology Madras-600036, Tamil Nadu	1959
137.	Indian Institute of Technology Powai, Bombay-400076	1958
138.	Post Graduate Instt. of Medical Education & Research, Chandigarh-160012	1962
139.	Sree Chitra Tirunal Instt. for Medical Sci. & Tech., Trivandrum-695011	1973
140.	A.P. Agricultural Rajendra Nagar, Hyderabad-500030, A.P.	1964
141.	A.P. University of Health Sciences Vijayawada-520005, A. Pradesh	1986
142.	Andhra Pradesh Open 6-3-345, Somajiguda, Hyderabad-500482	1982
143.	Anna Sardar Patel Road, Madras-600025	1978
144.	Annamalai Annamalai Nagar-608002, T.N.	1929
145.	Assam Agricultural Jorhat-785013, Assam	1968
146.	Bidhan Chandra Krishi Mohanpur, Nadia-741252, West Bengal	1974
147.	Birsa Agricultural Kanke, Ranchi-834006, Bihar	1980
148.	C. Azad University of Agriculture & Tech. Kanpur-208002, U.P.	1974

(*Contd.*)

(*Contd.*)

S. No.	University Name & Address	Estd. Year
149.	Cochin University of Science & Technology Cochin-682022	1971
150.	Dr. M.G.R. Medical Madras, Tamil Nadu-600007	1987
151.	Dr. Yashwant Singh Parmar Univ. of Hort. & Forest Solan-173230	1985
152.	G.B. Pant University of Agri. & Technology, Pant Nagar, Nainital-263145, U.P.	1960
153.	Gujarat Agricultural S.K. Nagar, Dantiwada, Banas Kantha-385506	1972
154.	Gujarat Ayurveda Dhanvantri Mandir, Jamnagar-361008	1968
155.	Haryana Agricultural Hissar-125004, Haryana	1970
156.	Himachal Pradesh Krishi Palampur-176062, Himachal Pradesh	1978
157.	Indira Gandhi Krishi Raipur-492012, Madhya Pradesh	1987
158.	J.N. Technological Mahavir Marg, Hyderabad-500028, A.P.	1972
159.	Jawaharlal Nehru Krishi Jabalpur-482004, Madhya Pradesh	1964
160.	Kashi Vidyapith, Varanasi-221002, U.P.	1974
161.	Kerala Agricultural M. Campus, Vellanikkapa-680654, Trichur	1972
162.	Konkan Krishi Deopali-415712, Ratnagiri	1972
163.	Kota Open Kota-324001, Rajasthan	1988
164.	Mahatma, Phule Krishi Rahuri, Ahmednagar-413772	1968
165.	Marathawada Agricultural Parbhani-431402, Maharashtra	1972

(*Contd.*)

(*Contd.*)

S. No.	University Name & Address	Estd. Year
166.	Mohan Lal Sukhadia Udaipur-313001, Rajasthan	1972
167.	Mother Teressa Women's Kudai Kanal-624102, Tamil Nadu	1984
168.	Narendra Dev University of Agriculture & Tech. Faizabad-2242299	1974
169.	Orissa University of Agriculture & Tech., Bhubaneswar-751003.	1962
170.	Panjab Agricultural Ludhiana-141004, Punjab	1962
171.	Rabindra Bharati Calcutta-700050, West Bengal	1962
172.	Rajasthan Agriculture Bikaner-334001, Rajasthan	1987
173.	Roorkee Roorkee-247667, Uttar Pradesh	1949
174.	Sanjay Gandhi PG. Institute of Medical Sciences Lucknow-226001, U.P.	1983
175.	Shere Kashmir Instt. of Medical Sciences, P.B. 27, Srinagar	1989
176.	Shere Kashmir Univ. of Agricultural Sciences & Tech., Srinagar-190001	1982
177.	Sri Krishnavevarya Anantpur-515003, Andhra Pradesh	1981
178.	Shri Padmavathy Mahila Tirupati-517502, Andhra Pradesh	1983
179.	Tamil Thanjavur-613001, Tamil Nadu	1971
180.	Tamilnadu Agricultural Coimbatore-641003, Tamil Nadu	1971
181.	Telugu K. Bhawan, Saifabad, Hyderabad-500004	1985
182.	University of Agricultural Sciences Bangalore-560065	1964
183.	University of Agricultural Sc. Krishi Nagar, Dharwad-580005.	1986

APPENDIX-IX

List of Autonomous Colleges

State	*University*	*College*
Tamil Nadu	Madurai Kamraj University	1. Arul Anandar College, Karumathur. 2. GTN Arts College, Dindigul. 3. Thiagarajan College, Madurai. 4. Vivekanand College, Tiruvedagam. 5. Ayya Nadar Janaki Ammal College, Sivakasi. 6. St. Xavier's College, Palayankottai. 7. Thiagarajan College of Engineering, Madurai.
Tamil Nadu	Madras University	1. Stella Maris College, Madras. 2. Presidency College, Madras. 3. Queen Mary's College, Madras. 4. Sacred Heart College, Tirupattur. 5. Meston College of Education, Madras. 6. Technical Teachers Training Institute, Madras.
Tamil Nadu	Bharathidasan University	1. Holly Cross College, Tiruchirapalli. 2. A.V.C. College, Mayuram. 3. Sri Pushpam College, Pondi. 4. Government College for Men, Kumbahenam. 5. Seetha Lakshmi Ramaswami College, Tiruchirapalli.
Tamil Nadu	Bharathiar University	1. Erode Arts College, Erode. 2. Nallamuthu Gunder Mahalingam College, Pollanchi. 3. Gobi Arts College, Gobichettipalayam. 4. Govt. Arts College, Coimbatore.

(Contd.)

(Contd.)

State	*University*	*College*
Tamil Nadu	Bharathiar University	5. Coimbatore Instt. of Technology, Coimbatore. 6. Govt. College of Technology, Coimbatore.
Madhya Pradesh	Ravi Shanker University	1. Govt. Science College, Raipur.
Madhya Pradesh	Dr. Hari Singh Gour University	1. Govt. S.N. Postgraduate College, Khandwa. 2. Govt. PG College, Chindwara.
Madhya Pradesh	Devi Ahilya Vishwavidyalaya	1. Holkar Science College, Indore. 2. Kasturbagram Rural Instt. Indore.
Madhya Pradesh	Bhopal University	1. Govt. Motilal Vigyan Mahavidyalaya, Bhopal.
Madhya Pradesh	Guru Ghasidas University	1. Govt. Model PG Science College, Bilaspur. 2. Govt. PG College, Ambikapur. 3. K.G. Arts and Science College, Raigarh.
Madhya Pradesh	Jiwaji University	1. Govt. Science College, Gwalior. 2. MLB Arts & Commerce College, Gwalior.
Andhra Pradesh	Andhra University	1. DNR College, Bhimavaram. 2. Sir C.R.R. College, Eluru. 3. Ch. S.D. St. Theresa's College for Women, Eluru. 4. S.R.V.S.S.J.R. Maharance College, Paddapuram. 5. S.D.S. College of Arts & Applied Science, Shreeram Nagar. 6. M.R. College for Men, Vizianagar. 7. St. Joseph's College for Women.
Andhra Pradesh	Nagar Nagarjuna University	1. Andhra Loyola College, Vijayawada. 2. P.B. Sidhartha College of Arts & Science, Vijayawada.

(Contd.)

(Contd.)

State	*University*	*College*
Rajasthan	Rajasthan University	1. Govt. College, Ajmer. 2. M.S.J. College, Bharatpur. 3. Dungar College, Bikaner. 4. Arts & Science College, Kota.
Andhra Pradesh	Osmania University	1. University College for Women, Hyderabad. 2. Nizam College, Hyderabad. 3. R.B.V.R.R. Women's College, Hyderabad. 4. Anwar-ul-Uloom College, Hyderabad. 5. S.S.R. Jyothi Arts & Sci. College, Khammam. 6. St. Francis College for Women, Secunderabad.
Andhra Pradesh	Sri Venkateshwara	1. Sri Padmavathi College for Women, Tirupati. 2. S.V. College for Men, Tirupati. 3. B.T. College, Madanapalle. 4. Jawahar Bharati, Kaveli.
Madhya Pradesh	Ravi Shanker University	1. Govt. Arts & Science College, Durg. 2. Govt. D.B. Girls College, Raipur. 3. Durga Mahavidyalaya, Raipur. 4. Govt. Digvijai Mahavidyalaya, Rajnandgaon. 5. Govt. Degree College, Jabalpur. 6. Kalyan Arts & Commerce College, Bhilai Nagar.
Madhya Pradesh	Guru Ghasidas	1. Govt. Girls PG College, Bilaspur. 2. CMD Postgraduate College, Bilaspur.
Madhya Pradesh	Jiwaji University	1. Ambah PG College, Ambah (Morena).
Madhya Pradesh	Rani Durgavati Vishwavidyalaya	1. Govt. Science College, Jabalpur. 2. Govt. M.H. College of Home Science for Women, Jabalpur.

(Contd.)

(Contd.)

State	*University*	*College*
		3. Govt. Mahakaoshal Arts & Commerce College, Jabalpur.
Madhya Pradesh	Vikram University	1. Madhav Vigyan Mahavidyalaya, Ujjain.
Madhya Pradesh	A.P. Singh	1. Govt. Science College, Rewa.
Tamil Nadu	Madras University	1. Sri Sarada College for Women, Fairlands, Salem.
Tamil Nadu	Madras University	2. Sri Sarada College of Education, Salem. 3. NKT National College of Education, Madras. 4. St. Christopher's College of Education, Vepery, Madras.
Rajas-than	Ajmer University	1. M.L.V. Government College, Bhilwara.

APPENDIX-X

Departments of Special Assistance as on 31.3.1989

Commerce	AMU/Andhra/Allahabad/Banaras Hindu/Calcutta/Delhi/Gauhati/ Rajasthan
Economics	Andhra/Calcutta/Jadavpur/M.S. Uni. Baroda/Marathwada/Presidency College Calcutta/Punjabi S.V. Uni. Tirupati/Sardar Patel/Osmania/ Madras/Utkal
Political Science	Calcutta/Delhi/Jadavpur/M.S. University of Baroda/Rajasthan
Ancient History	Allahabad
Modern History	Calcutta
History	M.S. Uni. Baroda/Mysore/JNU/Patna/ Hyderabad
Art History	M.S. Uni. Baroda
Philosophy	Banaras/Delhi/Punjab/Rajasthan/ Visva-Bharati/Utkal/Allahabad/ Andhra/Poona
Sociology	JNU/Punjab/Ravi Shankar/Bangalore/ Osmania/Poona
Psychology	Delhi/Gorakhpur
Anthropology	Delhi/Punjabi/Utkal
Education	Himachal/Kerala/Kurukshetra
Linguistics	Delhi/Deccan College, Pune
Sanskrit	Jadavpur/Karnataka
Comparative literature	Jadavpur
Urdu	Kashmir
Telugu	S.V. Uni.
Tamil	Madurai Kamaraj
Punjabi	Punjabi
Hindi	Sardar Patel/Allahabad

Gujarati	S N D T
Bengali	Burdwan
Kannada	Mysore
Malayalam	Kerala
Mass Communication and Journalism	Osmania/Bangalore
Geography	AMU, Aligarh/BHU/Osmania
Mathematics	AMU, Aligarh/Allahabad/Bangalore/II Sc., Bangalore/Jadavpur/M.K. University/Poona
Statistics	Poona
Physics	Andhra/AMU, Aligarh/Allahabad/Banaras Hindu Uni./Calcutta/Hyderabad/Jammu/ Madras/Punjab/Roorkee
Nuclear Physics	Andhra
Bio-Physics	Madras
Chemistry	Allahabad/Jadavpur/Madras/Osmania/ Poona/Rajasthan/Sardar Patel Uni.
Organic Chemistry	Hyderabad
Inorganic Chemistry	-do-
Physical Chemistry	-do-
Bio-Chemistry	Lucknow/M.S. Uni., Baroda
Geology	Andhra/Calcutta/Delhi/Kumaon/M.L. Sukhadia/Mysore/M.S. Uni., Baroda/ Presidency College, Calcutta/Roorkee
Botany	Andhra/Allahabad/Kalyani/Kerala/ Lucknow/Patna/Punjab/Rajasthan
Bio-Science	BHU/Kerala/MK University, Saurashtra
Life Science	JNU
Micro-Biology	M.S. Uni. Baroda
Pharmacy	Nagpur/Punjab
Genetics	Osmania
Zoology	Andhra/AMU, Aligarh/Bangalore/Calcutta/ Gujarat/Marathwada/Mysore/Punjab- / Poona/Rajasthan
Aerospace Engg.	II Sc., Bangalore
Automation Engg.	II Sc., Bangalore
Mechanical Engg.	II Sc., Bangalore

Chemical Engg.	Anna, Bombay
Water Resource Engg.	Anna
Environ Engg.	Anna
Civil Engg.	Anna/II Sc., Bangalore/Roorkee
Electrical Engg.	Anna/BHU/II Sc., Bangalore/Jadavpur
Mining Engg.	BHU/ISM, Dhanbad
Ceramic Engg.	BHU
Electronic Engg.	BHU/II Sc., Bangalore
Metallurgical Engg.	II Sc., Bangalore
Production Engg.	Jadavpur
Earth Quake Engg.	Roorkee

APPENDIX-XI

Institutions Imparting Distance Education

Degree Courses

B.A.	Allahabad, AP Open, Andhra, Annamalai, Bangalore, Bhopal, Bombay, Calcutta, Delhi, Himachal, IGNOU, Jammu, Kashmir, Kota Open, Kerala, Kurukshetra, Madras, Madurai Kamraj, Meerut, Mysore, Osmania, Punjab, Patna, Poona, Panjabi, SNDT, Shri Venkateswara, Utkal.
B.A. (External in one sitting)	Kakatiya, Osmania
B.A. (Hons)	Delhi
B.A. (Open)	AP Open, Andhra, IGNOU, Kota Open, Madras, Mysore, Poona, SNDT
B.A. (Law) (Bachelor of Academic Law)	Annamalai
B.Com.	Allahabad, AP Open, Andhra, Annamalai, Bhopal, Bombay, Calicut, Delhi, IGNOU, Jammu, Kashmir, Kota Open, Kerala, Madras, Madurai Kamraj, Meerut, Mysore, Osmania, Punjab, Patna, Poona, Panjabi, SNDT, Shri Venkateswara, Utkal
B.Com. (External in one setting)	Kakatiya, Osmania
B.Com. (Hons)	Delhi
B.Com. (Open)	AP Open, Andhra, IGNOU, Kota Open, Madras, Mysore, Poona, SNDT
B. Ed.	Andhra, Annamalai, Jammu, Kakatiya, Kashmir, Kota Open, Madras, Madurai, MDU, Mysore, Osmania, Punjabi, Shri Venkateswara, Utkal

B.G.L. (Bachelor of General Laws)	Annamalai, Cochin, Madurai Kamraj
B.J.M.C. (Bachelor of Journalism and Mass Communication)	Kota Open
B.L.I.S. (Bachelor of Library and Information Science)	AP Open, IGNOU, Madras
B.Litt. (Tamil)	Annamalai, Madras
B.Litt. (Tamil) Open	Madras
B.Sc.	AP Open, Andhra, Annamalai, Kota Open, Madras, Madurai Kamraj
B.S.	BITS
B.Tech.	J.N. Tech.
B.B.C. (Banking)	Cochin
L.L.B. (Academic)	Jammu, Kashmir

Master Degree Courses

Ancient History of Culture	Osmania
History	Annamalai, Delhi, Himachal, Kerala, Kota Open, Madras, Madurai Kamraj, Mysore, Osmania, Punjab, Panjabi
Arabic	Osmania
English	Andhra, Annamalai, Himachal Pradesh, Madras, Madurai Kamraj, Meerut, Mysore, Osmania, Punjab, Panjabi
French	CIEFL, Hyderabad
German	CIEFL, Hyderabad
Hindi	Delhi, Himachal Pradesh, Kota Open Meerut, Mysore, Osmania, Punjab, Panjabi
Islamic Studies	Osmania
Kannada	Mysore, Osmania
Marathi	Osmania
Persian	Osmania
Punjabi	Punjab, Panjabi
Russian	CIEFL, Hyderabad
Sanskrit	Delhi, Himachal Pradesh, Meerut, Mysore, Osmania

Tamil	Annamalai, Madras, Madurai Kamraj, Osmania
Telugu	Osmania
Urdu	Kashmir, Mysore, Osmania, Punjab
Botany	Annamalai
Chemistry	Annamalai
Maths	Annamalai, Cochin, Kakatiya, Kashmir, Meerut, Osmania, Shri Venkateswara
Physics	Annamalai
Zoology	Annamalai
Commerce	Andhra, Annamalai, Delhi, Himachal, Kakatiya, Kashmir, Kerala, Kota Open, Kurukshetra, Madras, Madurai Kamraj, Osmania, Shri Venkateswara
Defence Studies	Madras
Economics	Andhra, Annamalai, Himachal, Kashmir, Kerala, Kota Open, Madras, Madurai Kamraj, Meerut, Osmania, Punjab, Panjabi, Shri Venkateswara
Education	Andhra, Annamalai, Gujarat Vidyapeeth, Himachal, Madras, Madurai Kamraj, Osmania, Panjabi
Gandhian Thought	Gujarat Vidyapeeth, Madurai Kamraj
Library and Information Science	Madras
Philosophy	Osmania
Political Science	Delhi, Himachal, Kerala, Kota Open, Madras, Madurai Kamraj, Meerut, Mysore, Osmania, Punjab, Panjabi
Psychology	Annamalai
Public Administration	Andhra, Kota Open, Madurai, Osmania, Punjab
Sociology	Annamalai, Kota Open, Meerut, Mysore, Osmania
M.S.	BITST
M.V.S.	BITST

University Test Centres for (NET) Examinations

1. Agra University
2. Aligarh Muslim University
3. Allahabad University
4. Amravati University
5. Andhra University
6. Annamalai University
7. Avadh University
8. Awadesh Pratap Singh University
9. Banaras Hindu University
10. Bangalore University
11. Berhampur University
12. Bhagalpur University
13. Bharathiar University
14. Bharathidasan University
15. Bhavnagar University
16. Bhopal University
17. Bihar University
18. Bombay University
19. Bundelkhand University
20. Burdwan University
21. Calcutta University
22. Calicut University
23. Cochin University
24. Delhi University
25. Devi Ahilya Vishwavidyalaya
26. Dibrugarh University
27. Dr. H.S. Gaur Vishwavidyalaya
28. Gauhati University
29. Goa University
30. Gorakhpur University
31. Gujarat University
32. Gulbarga University
33. Guru Nanak Dev University
34. Himachal Pradesh University
35. Jammu University
36. Jiwaji University
37. Jodhpur University
38. Kakatiya University
39. Kalyani University
40. Kanpur University
41. Karnatak University
42. Kashmir University
43. Kerala University
44. Kumaon University
45. Kurukshetra University
46. L.N. Mithila University
47. Lucknow University
48. Madras University
49. Madurai Kamraj University
50. Magadh University
51. M.D. University
52. Mangalore University
53. Manipur University
54. Marathwada University
55. Meerut University
56. Mohanlal Sukhadia University
57. M.S. University of Baroda
58. Mysore University
59. Nagarjuna University
60. Nagpur University

61. North Bengal University
62. North Eastern Hill University
63. Osmania University
64. Panjab University
65. Patna University
66. Poona University
67. Punjabi University
68. Rajasthan University
69. Ranchi University
70. Rani Durgavati Vishwavidyalaya
71. Ravi Shankar University
72. Rohilkhand University
73. Roorkee University
74. Sardar Patel University
75. Saurashtra University
76. Shivaji University
77. South Gujarat University
78. Sri Krishnadevaraya University
79. Sri Venkateswara University
80. Tripura University
81. Utkal University
82. Vikram University
83. Viswa Bharati University

APPENDIX-XIII

The Accreditation and Assessment Council Committee – Report (1987)

I. Background

Programme of Action of National Policy on Education, 1986 inter-alia recommended that:

> "Excellence of institutions of higher education is a function of many aspects: self-evaluation and self-improvement are important among them. If a mechanism is set up which will encourage self-assessment in institutions and also assessment and accreditation by a Council of which these institutions are corporate members, the quality of process, participation, achievements, etc. will be constantly monitored and improved.

It is proposed to develop a mechanism for accreditation and assessment for maintaining and raising the quality of institutions of higher education. As a part of its responsibility for the maintenance and promotion of standards of education, the UGC will, to begin with, take the initiative to establish Accreditation and Assessment Council as autonomous body. It will evolve its own criteria and methodology for accreditation and assessment. Its main functions will be catalytic; it will analyse and evaluate institutions and their performance to facilitate self-improvement. This Council will be supported by a professional secretariat in the performance of its functions".
[Programme of Action, page 47, paras (27) and (28)].

II. Committee

The University Grants Commission in view of the above directives of NPE/POA has constituted a Committee. The list of the members of the Committee is given in Annexure I.

III. Terms of Reference

To make recommendations regarding setting up of Accreditation and Assessment Council in order to develop a mechanism for maintenance and raising of quality of institutions of higher education, while keeping in view the objectives, uses and various methods/procedures that are currently being followed by different countries or that can be adopted.

IV. Sub-Committee

The Committee desired that a sub-Committee consisting of the following members may be constituted under the convenership of Dr. Vasant Gowariker, Secretary, Ministry of Science and Technology, New Delhi, who shall bring out a working paper on the above terms of reference:

1. Dr. Vasant Gowariker — Convener
2. Professor Irfan Habib
3. Professor S.A.R. Zaidi
4. Shri C.R. Pillai
5. Shri R.P. Gangurde — Member-Secretary

The Committee at its meeting held on 4th November, 1986, also desired that the members may send a note on accreditation to the sub-Committee giving their views, so as to enable it to prepare the background paper, and in this regard the members were also provided the copy of the document 'Accreditation Handbook' published by the Commission on Institutions of Higher Education (U.S.A.).

The sub-Committee met on 24th December, 1986, and after a great deal of discussions on various aspects of accreditation and assessment of education institutions as well as considering the notes of (i) Professor Irfan Habib (ii) Dr. Jagdish Narain, Secretary, AIU and (iii) Dr. B.B. Sundaresan, it was decided to constitute a working group consisting of the following members to prepare a draft document suggesting practical steps towards setting up of Accreditation and Assessment Council indicating therein the objective, functions, structure and the methodology of assessing the performance of educational institutions:

(i) Professor S.A.R. Zaidi

(ii) Dr. Narender K. Sehgal,
Director,
NCSTC, DST.
New Delhi.

(iii) Mr. K. Gunasekaran,
Education Officer,
U.G.C.
New Delhi

The Working group submitted the above-mentioned draft document to the sub-Committee who placed the same before the main Committee on 9th December, 1987. The main Committee accepted the draft. The approved report is given in Annexure II.

Annexure-I

List of Members of the Committee on Accreditation and Assessment Council

1. Dr. Vasant Gowariker
   Secretary
   Ministry of Science and Technology
   New Delhi

2. Professor K. Satchidananda Murty
   Vice-Chairman
   University Grants Commission
   New Delhi

3. Shri J. Veera Raghavan
   Secretary
   Ministry of Human Resource Development
   Department of Education (Coordination and Planning)
   New Delhi

4. Shri Kireet Joshi
   Secretary
   Ministry of Human Resource Development
   Department of Education
   New Delhi

5. Professor G. Padmanabhan
   Department of Bio-Chemistry
   Indian Institute of Science
   Bangalore

6. Professor C.N.R. Rao
   Director
   Indian Institute of Science
   Bangalore

7. Professor Navanita Rao
   Vice-Chancellor
   Osmania University
   Hyderabad

8. Dr. B.B. Sundaresan
   Vice-Chancellor
   Madras University
   Madras

9. Professor Irfan Habib
   Chairman
   Indian Council for Historical Research
   35, Ferozeshah Road
   New Delhi

10. Shri J.D. Gupta
    Joint Secretary
    Ministry of Human
    Resource Development
    Department of Education
    New Delhi

11. Shri C.R. Pillai
    Deputy Secretary
    Ministry of Human
    Resource Development
    Department of Education
    New Delhi

12. Dr. Jagdish Narain
    Secretary
    Association of Indian
    Universities
    16, Kotla Road
    New Delhi

13. Professor Syed A.R. Zaidi
    238, Sector 28
    NOIDA (U.P.)

14. Shri R.P. Gangurde
    Joint Secretary
    University Grants
    Commission
    New Delhi

15. K. Gunasekaran
    Education Officer
    University Grants
    Commission
    New Delhi

Annexure-II

Accreditation and Assessment of Institutions of Higher Learning

I. Introduction

In brief, what is wrong with Indian universities is that they are not generative. They do not give rise to a vital and self-supporting intellectual life. Though it is true that they do not have realistic funding, their achievement is still not proportionate to the time, effort and intellectual resources expended on them. Perhaps the major cause of their failure is the manner of their governance, which does violence to the operations of mind and the growth of knowledge. Academic institutions must be built around the principle of intellectual autonomy. Most of ours are not.

Historical roots of the mediocrity of Indian higher education can be traced to the exigencies of British rule, in the need to contain the dangerous potential of self-rule in the realm of ideas. The present structures are descended practically unaltered from that time. The governance of universities is part of a larger pattern, the command-and-control style of bureaucracy, which was established in the interests of British supremacy and which still continues to dominate our public life.

II. Management of Higher Education

Command-and-control management entails a hierarchical notion of "accountability" and top-down initiative. Goals and values are formulated from the outside, and the various ways in which their implementation can go wrong are taken into account and sanctions are provided against these. The governing attitude is suspicion. Dignity and authority are vested largely in the supervisory levels, most of all in the remote government bureaucracy, and next to none with working academics. Intellectual and pedagogical initiative are stifled, and experimentation, innovation and the finding of appropriate responses to local circumstances become impossible. The goals of universities get pitched at a very modest level, to achievements peripheral to the real purpose of a university such as the regular holding of examinations and the announcement of results. The management of universities gets reduced to a law-and-order problem, with a limited and crude repertoire of political-bureaucratic actions to bring them to a semblance of control.

The situation of colleges is particularly bad, because of their subordination to affiliating universities. This suffocates the initiative of college faculty and denies them the necessary control over the circumstances of their work. On the other hand, factors like the recent raising of the college entrance age with the addition of two years of secondary education and the raising of lecturer qualification to the doctoral level have made the issue of academic autonomy at the college level both more urgent and more promising.

There is an alternative style of management to the command-and-control, hierarchical bureaucratic method. It is a style which has been demonstrating its superiority world-wide, not just in the academic realm but in business and government as well. It means putting people first. In the words of one of the leaders of the Japanese ascendancy, "To motivate people, you must bring them into the family and treat them like respected members of it." A system which does this is decentralised, democratic and facilitative.

In the academic sphere the first postulate of the new system is the authority and dignity of the working academic. Once this is conceded, the organisational patterns that are coherent with it follow naturally. These include collegiality in the life of the department and of the institution, and the derivation of administrative authority from departmental and faculty councils.

Though it is widely conceded that nothing worthwhile can be accomplished without academic autonomy, the tendency is to let the fear of potential abuse lead back to the bureaucratic-hierarchical system.

III. Accreditation

As a way to assure the effectiveness of academic institutions while maximally supporting academic self-regulation, the programme of action of the National Policy on Education 1986 has called for the setting up of an autonomous Council on Accreditation and

Assessment. The accreditation policy forms part of a reform which must be viewed as a whole and whose other important aspects include the provision for autonomy of colleges and the projected National Testing Service.

While the central motive to the accreditation system has come from the requirements of college autonomy, it also answers the need for a systematic and regular means for assuring that colleges and universities are functioning effectively.

The hierarchical-bureaucratic approach to possible academic abuses is like administering a dope-test while the race is still on. The system of institutional accreditation, on the other hand, is based on first giving an institution the maximum freedom in defining its goals and the means to achieve them, and then examining it closely, as a whole. The crucial difference from the bureaucratic system with its cumbersomeness and enforced uniformity is made possible by reliance on the faculty of judgment, in particular the judgment of responsible educators who know what academic excellence is through their own participation in it. They are able to evaluate the institution as a whole and to assess its parts in terms of their functional relation to this, and they are not constrained to see those parts only in terms of adherence to some preconceived bureaucratic prescription.

Operationalisation of an effective system of accreditation in the country will gradually lead to the establishment of norms and criteria for institutional performance assessment, and methodologies and tools for systematic institutional self-study and self-evaluation. Moreover, institutions themselves will collectively benefit through integration of this element of assessment into the institutional culture.

IV. Important Features of an Accreditation System

Institutional accreditation originated in the United States and has existed there in close to the present form for some decades and is also to be found in Canada and Japan among others. The division of authority and responsibility between Central Government and States in the field of higher education is similar in North America and India. Some of the main features of an operational institutional accreditation system which commend themselves are the following:

(1) Institutional accreditation, the recognition of the performance and integrity of an educational institution, is granted by an

association of institutions of higher education. Accreditation means membership in the association, and the accrediting commission of the association is elected by the institutional members.

Accreditation, which is the assurance by a non-governmental body of the quality of an educational institution, must be distinguished from the granting by the (state or federal) government of a charter or licence to an institution, legally enabling it to award degrees. An institution must have a charter before it can be accredited.

(2) Institutional accreditation is a means for the self-regulation of the academic profession, with minimal political and bureaucratic interference.

(3) Institutional accreditation does not imply that accredited institutions have a similarity of goals or uniformity of process or that they are comparable. It permits diversity and innovation.

(4) The first part of the accreditation process is a self-study by the institution, involving in this activity all of its major constituents including faculty, students and administration. Included in this process is the sharp defining by the institution of its primary mission or goals. This must be soundly conceived; it must be realistic as well as appropriate to the collegiate level.

(5) The second part of the accreditation process is an on-site evaluation by a team of professional educators (faculty and administrator). Though they have the help of published association policies, their main reliance is upon their own experienced judgment. Institutional evaluation is ultimately subjective.

(6) Institutional accreditation indicates that, in the judgment of responsible members of the academic community, an institution's own goals are soundly conceived and appropriate, that its educational programmes have been intelligently planned and are competently conducted, and that the institution is accomplishing the majority of its goals substantially and has the resources to continue to do so for the foreseeable future.

(7) Institutional accreditation is a matter of "yes" or "no" to the institution as a whole. It embraces all educational endeavours conducted by a single institution regardless of its complexity. Institutional accreditation must be distinguished from specialised or professional accreditation; where the latter applies, institutional accreditation is usually a prior necessity. Institutional accreditation must also be distinguished from the nationwide comparative

assessments of departments in a particular discipline. This is usually carried out by a professional association in that discipline.

(8) In order to be accredited an institution must meet the Association's qualitative criteria for the assessment of institutional effectiveness in each of the principal areas of institutional activity and responsibility, as follows:

(a) Institutional Mission and Objectives
(b) Evaluation and Planning
(c) Organisation and Governance
(d) Programmes and Instruction
(e) Special Activities
(f) Faculty
(g) Student Services
(h) Library and Learning Resources
(i) Physical Facilities
(j) Financial Resources
(k) Ethical Practices
(l) Publications and Advertising.

(9) The accreditation agency is not simply a body for the assurance of educational quality. The process of accreditation encourages institutional improvement through continual self-study and evaluation. Accreditation agencies develop criteria and guidelines for assessing institutional effectiveness. And the expert criticism and suggestions of the evaluating team are invaluable.

(10) Developing or newly applying institutions can, prior to accreditation, be awarded candidate status on satisfying certain criteria. *These Requirements of Candidature* concern institutional characteristics largely capable of objective verification. Candidature is usually granted for a two-year term. If progress is being made, candidacy can be extended for up to six years.

(11) Accreditation must be periodically reaffirmed, within a period of five years after initial accreditation, and within ten years thereafter. Accrediting bodies reserve the right to review member institutions any time for cause. They also reserve the right to review any substantive change in the institution; such changes are reviewed within two years after the changes become effective. An accredited institution which shows serious weakness in one or more areas, but which also shows firm potential for remedying the deficiencies, may

be put on probation. Accreditation continues, but generally for a sharply reduced term.

(12) The accrediting associations are institutional-membership organisations supported by annual dues, from the candidate and accredited institutions. They elect the accreditation commissions, the bodies which make the final decision on accreditation after receiving the institution's self-study report and the report of the evaluation team.

Expenses for accrediting activities are borne by the institution on a cost basis. This is kept low by the extensive use of volunteers on evaluation visits.

A typical Commission consists of sixteen members who are elected at the Annual Meeting for staggered three-year terms. Provision is made for different types of institutions and the general public to be represented on the Commission. Commissioners serve without compensation, and those who are institutional representatives are currently active on the faculties or staffs of institutions accredited through the Commission. The Commission normally meets four times a year, but various committees may meet more frequently. The day-to-day activities of the Commission are conducted by a Director of Evaluation, professional staff, and support staff.

(13) Though accreditation agencies are non-governmental their accreditation has come to be recognised as a necessary qualification for eligibility to receive federal funds. The federal government in turn recognises, for a four-year duration, those accrediting agencies which it finds to be a reliable indicator of educational quality.

(14) Despite the diversity of accredited institutions, there are some substantive curricular requirements that they must all meet, most notably a coherent and substantial programme of liberal or general studies, amounting to not less than a quarter of all course-work in a four-year undergraduate programme. This requirement is also extended to post-baccalaureate degrees, in the sense that undergraduate work with a sufficient general education component must at least be a prerequisite to those post-baccalaureate programmes.

V. Steps Toward an Accreditation System in India

(1) These above features of an operational accreditation system will

serve as benchmarks in establishing a system of institutional accreditation in the Indian context as a means of reorganising the assurance of educational quality, of making expert academic consultation widely available, and as a way of mobilising local initiative and energy through self-definition and continual self-appraisal.

(2) The initial impetus for an accreditation system will come from the UGC, through its selection of a group of about twenty good autonomous institutions for initial candidature.

Until such time as twenty institutions are accredited, there will be a provisional *Accreditation Association* made up of candidate institutions, the original twenty plus those that are later admitted into candidature. After twenty institutions are accredited they will constitute the core of the *Accreditation Association* or *Accreditation Council*, and candidate institutions will thereafter have observer status. The Association will be an autonomous, self-governing body – to begin with, a registered society. It will meet once a year.

Each institution's representative to the Annual Meeting of the Association will be appointed by the administrative head of the institution, the Vice-Chancellor or the Principal. At the Annual Meeting the representatives will elect *Commissioners*, the members of the *Accreditation Commission*, the body which will make the final decision on accreditation. The Commission will comprise fifteen members, serving three-year terms. Eventually, the appointments will be staggered, with about one-third of the positions being vacated each year. Commissioners will be drawn from institutions of different types as well as from outside the academic world. From among these the Association representatives will at their first meeting elect a *Chairman of the Commission* and an *Associate Chairman* for one-year terms. Subsequently, the Associate Chairman will succeed the Chairman, and a new Associate Chairman will be elected annually. The Commission will meet about four times a year.

The Accreditation Commission will, with the consent of the University Grants Commission, initially and then whenever necessary appoint a Director of Evaluation, who will conduct the day-to-day activities of the Commission with the help of a secretariat of professional and support staff. The Director's term will normally be five years, but can be terminated earlier for valid reasons by the Accreditation Commission. His status, method of appointment and terms and conditions of service will be comparable with those of a

Vice-Chancellor of a University.

The Commission will also, with the consent of the University Grants Commission, appoint an *Associate Director of Evaluation*, who will report to the Director. He will normally succeed the Director.

The Director will supervise the codification of the principles, guidelines, methods and observations of the accreditation agency into a Handbook, and will submit these to the Commission for its approval.

The Director will draw up a list of potential evaluators, with critical biographies, for the approval of the Commission. The accreditation agency will keep on file a list of at least a hundred approved evaluators. They will serve in an honourary capacity. The other terms of their association with the Commission, will be determined by the Commission.

The ultimate decision on accreditation will be made by the Commission after seeing the self-appraisal and evaluation reports and related material.

The Accreditation Association will eventually be encouraged to function on a zonal basis, for reasons of tractability and economy.

(3) The following are some of the major points on which an institution will face scrutiny in the process of accreditation, and which it will address in its self-appraisal:

(a) *Institutional Mission and Objectives*

These should be practical, appropriate to the university/collegiate level, and socially responsible.

(b) *Evaluation and Planning*

There should be sharply defined institutional goals and effective mechanisms for periodic, systematic self-evaluation, planning and review of objectives. The process should take into account state and central plans.

(c) *Organisation and Governance*

There should be published a clear statement based on the acts and statutes defining the respective powers, functions, responsibilities of each organisational component (Senates, Executive Council, Academic Council, governing board, administrative officers, faculty, departments, students and other constituencies) and their inter-relationships. Provisions for the distribution of authority and responsibility should be depicted in an organisational chart that represents the actual working of the institution. The faculty must have a major role in shaping and conducting academic policy. There should be provision for the consideration of student views in matters of direct and reasonable interest to them. The public interest should be adequately represented in the determination of the overall policies of the institutions.

(d) *Programmes and Instruction*

Every undergraduate programme whether professional, specialised or general ought to show an appropriate regard for the humanities, natural sciences and social sciences. Usually, at least a quarter of each student's programme should consist of courses in these areas, but experimentation with other ways of meeting the end of well-roundedness should be encouraged. Courses should adhere to clearly defined institutional standards of scholarship. There ought to be appropriate means for monitoring the effectiveness of the educational programmes. (The development of some of these, such as a National Testing Service, will be the job of educational bodies and authorities outside the institution.) There should be some systematic procedures that tend to assure that assessments are fairly awarded while at the same time preserving the integrity of the educational process. There should be some means of assuring that the number of sessions planned for a course are actually held, and that the students and teachers are fulfilling their responsibilities in respect of the course.

(e) *Faculty*

The qualifications and numbers of the faculty should be adequate to discharge their academic responsibilities. Their recruitment, promotion, retention and security of tenure and other conditions of service, particularly the teacher's academic autonomy, in determining the content of the course, the teaching method and the method of evaluation, should be at a level consonant with the dignity of the academic profession. There ought to be formal or informal forums for open communication amongst the faculty and between faculty and administrative officers.

(f) *Student Services*

There should be an orderly and ethical admissions procedure, and compliance in spirit as well as law with special provisions for disadvantaged groups. Academic, personal and career counseling services, grievance-redressal services, health services and services for foreign students and the handicapped should be available. There should be clear published statements on students rights and responsibilities. Current information about graduates and their progress in careers should be maintained, and the interest of alumni in the development of the institution encouraged.

(g) *Library and Learning Resources*

Books and non-print materials and library services, study space and staff should be adequate to the educational programme and there should be systematic planning for future needs.

(h) *Physical Facilities*

Buildings, grounds and equipment should be adequate to meet the needs of the institution. They should be well-maintained and aesthetically pleasing. Classrooms and laboratories ought to be properly equipped and adequate in number and size.

(i) *Financial Resources*

The institution should be financially stable, with sufficient resources to carry out its objectives into the foreseeable future. It should have control of its financial resources and budgetary procedures, and be free from undue influence or pressure from external funding sources. There should be a clearly defined and consistently implemented process by which the budget is established and resources are allocated. There should be a yearly external audit, reviewed by the appropriate individuals or groups in the institution.

(j) *Ethical Practices*

In all its dealings the institution should show concern for basic values and observe the spirit as well as the letter of legal requirements.

(k) *Publications and Advertising*

The institution should publish a catalogue or handbook describing clearly and accurately its objectives, its admission policies, each academic programme or course of study, the requirements for a degree or other recognition, the members of the faculty with their academic qualifications, the fees and charges, the refund policy, the learning and physical resources, and other information the institution considers significant.

(4) The Accreditation Agency should be a self-financing institution. Its recurring expenditure should be met entirely from the membership fees paid by member-institutions. The fees paid by the institutions should be accepted as an admissible item of expenditure for purposes of grants-in-aid to them. The initial expenditure on setting up the Accreditation Council should be met by the UGC for a period of three years.

(5) Within five years of the setting up of the Accreditation Council, only accredited institutions will be eligible for Central funding. Some painful decisions will have to be made, but if there is to be any point to an accreditation system, it must be operated with great integrity, and therefore, there must be no exceptions.

State Governments will be free, as before, to found, charter or recognise, and to fund, new institutions, but those institutions will not receive any Central funds until they become accredited. Funding, development or support of as yet unaccredited state institutions will be entirely the concern of the states.

For the founding of a new Central Institution, separate funds will be allocated to sustain it until it wins accreditation, and planning for the new institution will be undertaken with the Requirements of Candidature in mind. If a Central institution fails to win accreditation, even after a reasonable period of time and investment of funds, the Accreditation Council will recommend its closure.

(6) The implications of non-accreditation and loss of accreditation, including the consequences for faculty and past and present students, must be spelled out in advance and publicised.

Denial or loss of accreditation must not come as a surprise. Consultancy services recognised by the Association should also be available to provide an early warning of deficiencies and advice in dealing with them.

(7) The right to academic self-determination of the individual academic, the department, and the college or university is fundamental. The prima facie satisfaction of it (as evidenced, for example, by the rules and composition of the statutory bodies of the institution) will be a Requirement of Candidature.

(8) Autonomy is not a prize for the deserving. It is a precondition for any worthwhile work. So it cannot be made a consequent to accreditation or even to candidature, but must precede them.

The accreditation system is designed, above all, to make college (and university) autonomy possible by shifting to a mode of accountability that is horizontally rather than vertically organised, and which, therefore, does not stifle local initiative.

The current UGC guidelines on autonomy envision two degrees of autonomy for colleges. The first, more properly designated "semi-autonomy", is under the aegis of the erstwhile affiliating university, which, along with other external agencies, has its representation on all the colleges' statutory bodies. Semi-autonomy does not go far enough in enabling teachers to determine their work situation, alienating them from their jobs. And it makes the statutory bodies cumbersome and open to manipulation by persons without a legitimate stake in them. Semi-autonomy, then, though it is a great improvement over affiliation, should be seen as a stop-gap arrangement.

After the accreditation system is in place, colleges should be in a position to avail of the second, more complete degree of autonomy, under conferment of "deemed university" status from the UGC, a possibility envisioned by the UGC guidelines and also by the National Policy on Education, 1986.

As for affiliated colleges proper, as distinct from semi-autonomous ones, none of them can be granted candidature by the accreditation system because their set-up is by its nature too violative of individual and departmental academic autonomy. Since accreditation involves a "yes" or "no" to the institution as a whole, no matter how complex it is, affiliating universities will themselves not be eligible for candidature until they have divested themselves of these colleges at least to the extent of semi-autonomy.

Since, within five years of the setting up of the Accreditation Council, only accredited institutions will be eligible for Central funds, the goal of autonomy (or semi-autonomy) is envisioned for all colleges by then.

The UGC has decided to grant autonomous status to 500 colleges by the end of the current Five-Year Plan (1990). Special funds will have to be made available by the UGC during the intervening period to facilitate the transition of the remaining colleges, so that they may all have a fair chance to qualify for accreditation before the deadline.

Some of the conditions for the granting of autonomous status by the UGC will be similar to the conditions for the granting of candidature by the Accreditation Council. Nevertheless, these conferments by two distinct bodies should be kept distinct.

(9) There are a variety of causes which will keep an institution from accreditation, and the appropriate response of the concerned authority will vary accordingly. In most cases what is called for will be a matter of reorganisation and some additional finances, but not very substantial expansion of faculty and facilities. But some present institutions are simply too small to be able to offer a satisfactory educational programme particularly in light of the claims of general education. In such cases, consolidation with other institutions would be called for.

(10) An emphasis on general education will be a primary concern of the accreditation system and will be enforced as a Requirement of Candidature. There is no other way to realize a large number of the curricular goals enunciated in the National Policy on Education, 1986. Every college must make the student aware of the range of human knowledge; it must increase the student's capacity for the organisation and expression of thought; it should provide an opportunity for the development of basic learning skills and foundations necessary for success in mastering advanced specialised subject matter; it should develop within students the capabilities of forming independent judgments, weighing values, and understanding fundamental theory and it should encourage the pursuit of lifelong learning.

The value of elective courses, within the field of specialisation but more especially outside of it, should be emphasised, as this is the primary foundation of interdisciplinary study, which the new education policy is committed to. It will also give new life to some of the fields of study that few would like to specialise in but many would like to study, which are presently wasting away.

The mode of implementing general education, whether through distribution requirements, foundation courses or some other modality, will be left up to the institution.

The system of credits and internal evaluation (not necessarily examination based), modularity of courses of study, and admission to the college as a whole rather than to a department, will be included in the Requirements of Candidature.

VI. Linkages

(1) The Association of accredited institutions of higher education can exert a positive influence on the standards of secondary education, through recognition of the certificates of various boards. They can also recognise independent schools, and help them to establish an accrediting Association of Secondary Schools with strong linkages to the Higher Education Association.

(2) Professional institutions in fields such as engineering, medicine, architecture, management and law should be brought under the scope of institutional accreditation through the aegis of the proposed National Apex Body for Higher Education. Institutional accreditation should be made a prerequisite to professional accreditation.

(3) In assessing the educational effectiveness of an institution, evaluator will want to have some concrete measure of educational outcomes. For this the development of the National Testing Services, providing objective and up-to-date certification in a wide variety of subjects, will be extremely helpful.

VII. Financial Implications

The financial (and political) implications of bringing most of the nation's institutions of higher education upto the level necessary for accreditation must be squarely faced. Even though the implementation of accreditation is in itself bound to improve the cost-benefit ratio, effective education cannot possibly come so cheaply as what is now prevalent.

VIII. Recommendations

This report should be widely circulated in the academic community for a full scale discussion on the idea of an Accreditation and Assessment Council.

APPENDIX-XIV

State Council of Higher Education — Committee Report (1988)

I. Background

National Policy on Education, 1986, inter-alia recommended that:

> "State Level Planning and Coordination of higher education will be done through Councils of Higher Education. The UGC and these Councils will develop coordinative methods to keep a watch on standards".

The above mentioned policy was further elaborated in the Programme of Action as under:

> "There is at present no effective machinery for Planning and Coordination of Higher Education at the State level and coordination of State level programme with those of the UGC". In order to fill this gap, it is proposed:
>
> (a) to set-up State Councils of Higher Education as statutory bodies;
>
> (b) to have for the guidance of State Government, model provision framed by the UGC setting out the composition and Powers of the State Councils; and
>
> (c) The major functions of the Council will include:
>
> (1) Preparation of consolidation programmes of higher education in each State;
>
> (2) initial scrutiny of the development programmes of universities and colleges;
>
> (3) assistance and advice to UGC in respect of maintenance of standards;
>
> (4) assistance to State Governments in determining the

block maintenance grants;

(5) encouragement of the programmes of autonomous colleges;

(6) monitoring the progress of implementation of programmes and assessment of performance of institutions;

(7) advising the State Governments in setting up new institutions.

II. Committee

The University Grants Commission, in view of the above directives of NPE and POA, has constituted a committee. The list of the members of the committee is given in Annexure-I.

III. Terms of Reference

To make the recommendations regarding setting up the State Councils of Higher Education as per National Policy on Education, 1986 and the Programme of Action in this regard.

IV. *Sub-Committee*

The committee desired that a sub-committee consisting of the following may be constituted to formulate draft guidelines.

1. Prof Satish Chandra — *Chairman*
2. Shri S.C. Gupta
3. Shri J.D. Gupta
4. Prof. K.R. Rao
5. Shri R.P. Gangurde — *Member-Secretary*
6. Shri K. Gunasekaran

The guidelines formulated by the sub-committee were accepted by the Committee with some modifications. The Report of the Committee was also approved by the Commission in July, 1987. Meanwhile, the Supreme Court had struck down the Andhra Pradesh Commissionerate of Higher Education Act, 1986. In the light of the above judgement, the Department of Education, Government of India, requested the Commission to review the guidelines. Accordingly, the guidelines were reviewed with the help of the law panel of the Commission. Annexure-II gives the revised guidelines as approved by the Commission in January, 1988.

Annexure-I

List of the Members of the Committee

1. Professor Satish Chandra
   Department of History,
   Jawaharlal Nehru
   University,
   New Delhi.

2. Shri J. Veera Raghavan
   Special Secretary,
   Ministry of Human
   Resource Development,
   New Delhi.

3. Shri Kireet Joshi
   Special Secretary,
   Ministry of Human
   Resource Development,
   New Delhi.

4. Professor Moonis Raza
   Vice-Chancellor,
   Delhi University,
   Delhi.

5. Professor G. Ram Reddy
   Vice-Chancellor,
   Indira Gandhi National
   Open University,
   New Delhi.

6. Professor R.P. Bambah
   Vice-Chancellor,
   Punjab University,
   Chandigarh.

7. Professor K.R. Rao
   Vice-Chancellor,
   Andhra University,
   Visakhapatnam (A.P.)

8. Dr. Jagdish Narain
   Secretary,
   Association of Indian
   Universities,
   Kotla Road,
   New Delhi.

9. Shri M.R. Kolhatkar
   Secretary,
   (Education and
   Employment Department),
   Central Administration
   Department,
   Government of
   Maharashtra,
   Bombay.

10. Shri Parmanand Mishra
    Special Secretary,
    Education Department,
    Government of Uttar
    Pradesh,
    Lucknow.

11. Shri T.D. Sundar Raj
Commissioner & Secretary,
(Education Department),
Government of Tamil
Nadu,
Fort St. George,
Madras.

12. Shri A. Chatterjee
Secretary,
(Education Department),
Government of West
Bengal,
Writer's Building,
Calcutta.

13. Shri S.C. Gupta,
Principal Secretary,
Government of Madhya
Pradesh,
Department of Higher
Education,
Bhopal.

14. Dr. J.N. Kaul
D/121, Saket,
New Delhi.

15. Shri R.P. Gangurde,
Member-Secretary
Joint Secretary,
University Grants
Commission,
New Delhi.

Special Invites

16. Shri J.D. Gupta
Joint Secretary,
Ministry of Human
Resource Development,
Department of Education,
Government of India
New Delhi.

17. Shri V.S. Pathak
Deputy Secretary,
Department of Education,
Government of Madhya
Pradesh,
Bhopal.

18. Shri C.R. Pillai
Deputy Secretary,
Department of Education,
Ministry of Human
Resource Development,
Government of India,
New Delhi.

Annexure-II

Guidelines for Setting up of State Council of Higher Education

(Modified in January, 1988

1. Objectives

Higher Education aims at educating young men and women for fulfilling national objectives, and plays a crucial role in fostering national integration on the basis of the principle of the unity in diversity. There is a felt need for Councils of Higher Education at State level in order to enable the UGC to fulfil its statutory responsibility for the promotion and coordination of University education and for the determination and maintenance of standards of teaching, examination and research in universities. Coordination at the local and regional level would enable expensive facilities to be shared and research projects of an inter-disciplinary basis to be undertaken in keeping with the needs of regional developments. The monitoring of the performance of the colleges which are more than 5,000 in number could also be carried out more easily at the regional level. It denies that there is an urgent need to strengthen planning and coordination of education programmes in higher education. Planning is essential so as to: (a) foresee the needs of future development in the country as a whole, (b) to control unplanned expansion, and (c) to channelise it in desirable directions on the basis of socio-economic needs and academic requirements.

The State Council for Higher Education would act as a link between the universities and colleges and the State Governments and to work closely with the UGC in view of its statutory responsibility for the maintenance and co-ordination of standards of higher education at the all-India level.

2. Setting up of the Council

In order to achieve the objectives set out above, the Central

Government may advise State Governments for enacting legislation for setting up of State Councils of Higher Education in the States. In an Indian state where the number of universities are too few, an advisory body may be set up to fulfil the above objectives.

3. Composition

A State Council of Higher Education may consist of 10-13 members as follows:–

(i) A Chairman

(ii) Not less than two and not more than four members drawn on all-India basis from the following who have:

- (a) obtained high academic distinction in teaching, engineering, medicine, agricultural sciences or law;
- (b) who are industrialists or educationists of high repute.

(iii) Not more than two from among the Vice-Chancellors of the Universities in the area including Vice-Chancellors of Central Universities, if any;

(iv) Not more than two from among the teachers of universities/ colleges in the State;

(v) Secretary, UGC or an officer of the UGC not below the rank of Joint Secretary nominated by the Chairman, UGC;

(vi) Secretary, Education (Ex-officio); and

(vii) Secretary, Finance (Ex-officio).

If any state so desires it may include the Director of Higher Education as an ex-officio member.

4. Terms and Conditions of Service of Chairman and Members

(i) The Chairman shall hold office for a term of five years and other members shall hold office for a term of three years.

(ii) The office of the Chairman shall be a whole-time and salaried one and subject thereto, the terms and conditions of service shall be as prescribed.

(iii) The salary of the Chairman shall not be less than that of a Vice-Chancellor of a University.

(iv) A person who has not attained the age of 65 years shall be eligible for appointment as a Chairman.

5. Staff of the Council

The Council shall appoint a Secretary and such other employees as it may think necessary for the efficient performance of its functions. The Secretary shall be a whole-time one. The terms and conditions of service of the employees shall be determined by the council.

6. Temporary Association of a Person with State Council of Higher Education for Particular Purpose

The Council may associate with itself in such a manner and for such a purpose, any person whose assistance of advice it may desire in carrying out its work. A person associated with council for any purpose shall have a right to take part in the discussions relevant to that purpose but shall not have a right to vote at a meeting of the council and shall not be a member for any other purpose. The council may associate with it members of Medical, Engineering and Agricultural universities with a view of developing coordination amongst universities.

7. Meeting of the Council

The Council shall meet at such times and places and shall observe such rules of procedures in regard to the transaction of business at its meetings as may be provided by regulations.

8. Powers and Functions of the Council

The Council shall function for co-ordination and determination of standards in institutions for higher education or research and scientific and technical institution in accordance with the guidelines issued by the UGC from time to time.

(a) *Planning and Co-ordination*

(i) To prepare consolidated programmes in the sphere of higher education in the State in accordance with the guidelines that may be issued by the UGC from time to time, and to assist in their implementation;

(ii) To forward the development programmes of universities and colleges in the State to UGC along with its comments and recommendations;

(iii) To assist UGC in respect of determination and maintenance of standards and suggest remedial action wherever necessary, in accordance with the guidelines;

(iv) To evolve perspective plans for development of higher education in the State; and

(v) To monitor the progress of implementation of such development programmes.

(b) *Academic Functions*

(i) To encourage and promote innovations in curricular development, restructing of course and updating of syllabi in the universities/colleges;

(ii) To promote and coordinate the programmes of autonomous colleges and to monitor its implementation;

(iii) To devise steps to improve the standards of examinations conducted by the universities and suggest necessary reforms;

(iv) To facilitate training of teachers in colleges/universities;

(v) To promote publication of quality text books, monographs and reference books;

(vi) To develop programmes for greater academic co-operation and inter-action between university teachers and college teachers and to facilitate mobility of students and teachers within and outside the state;

(vii) To regulate admission on the basis of physical facilities and to develop entrance examination for admission to institutions of higher education;

(viii) To encourage sports, games, physical education and cultural activities in the universities and colleges;

(ix) To encourage extension activities and promote inter-action with agencies concerned with regional planning and development; and

(x) To prepare an overview report on the working of the universities in the State. A copy of the report should be sent to the UGC.

(c) *Advisory Functions*

(i) To advice State Government in determining the block maintenance grants and to lay down the basis for such grants;
(ii) To set up a State Research Board so as to link educational institutions research with that of the research agencies and also with research needs of the State;
(iii) To examine the statutes and ordinances in various universities in the State (excluding Central universities) and suggest modifications wherever required;
(iv) To advise State Government regarding the statutes proposed by the universities in a State; and
(v) To perform any other functions necessary for furtherance of higher education in a State.

(d) *Administrative Functions*

To administer and release grant-in-aid from State Government to universities and colleges in the State. For this purpose, the State Government should place the grants meant for the universities and colleges at the disposal of the council.

9. **Payment to the Council**

The State Government may, after due appropriation made by the Legislative Assembly by law in this behalf, pay to the Council in each financial year such sums as may be considered necessary for the functioning of the council.

10. **Budget**

The Council shall prepare, in such form and at such time each year as may be prescribed, and a budget in respect of the financial year next ensung showing the estimated receipts and expenditure, and copies thereof shall be forwarded to the State Governments.

11. **Annual Report**

The Council shall prepare an Annual Report giving an account of its activities during the previous year and copies thereof shall be forwarded to the State Government and the Government shall cause the same to be laid before the Legislative Assembly. A copy of the Annual Report should be sent to University Grants Commission.

SECTION IV

INDICES

NAME INDEX

Zwerling, L. Steven, 188

SUBJECT INDEX

Subject Index to Annotated Bibliography

CICIL LIST

CONCEPTS IN COMMUNICATION, INFORMATICS & LIBRARIANSHIP

(CICIL)

General Editor: **S.P. AGRAWAL**

CICIL-1 Development of Library Services in India: Social Science Information
S.P. Agrawal Rs. 150

CICIL-2 Development of Documentation in India: Social Science Information
S.P. Agrawal Rs. 250

CICIL-3 UNESCO and Social Sciences: Retrospect and Prospect
S.P. Agrawal and **J.C. Aggarwal** Rs. 250

CICIL-4 INDIANA : A Bibliography of Bibliographical Sources
M.K. Jain Rs. 200

CICIL-5 Dimensions of Library and Information Science: Kaula Festschrift
V. Venkatappaiah (Eds.) Rs. 600

CICIL-6 Book Numbers: Some Indian Methods
M.P. Satija and **S.P. Agrawal** Rs. 100

CICIL-7 National Policy for University Libraries in India: Problems and Perspectives
N.B. Inamdar and **L.S. Ramaiah** (Ed.) Rs. 250

CICIL-8 Media Utilisation for the Development of Women and Children
B.S. Thakur and **Binod C. Agrawal** Rs. 150

CICIL-9 Terrorism: An Annotated Bibliography
Susheela Bhan (Ed.) Rs. 275

CICIL-10 Transnational Library Relations: The Indo-American Experience
M.B. Konnur Rs. 175

CICIL-11 Geography of Marketing and Commercial Activities in India (Documentation on Research Information)
R.S. Dixit Rs. 130

CICIL-12 Information India 1988: Global View
S.P. Agrawal and **J.C. Aggarwal** Rs. 200

CICIL-13 Women's Education in India: Historical Review, Present Status and Perspective Plan
S.P. Agrawal and **J.C. Aggarwal** Rs. 360

CICIL-14 Cultural Communication in India: Role and Impact of Phonograms
J.M. Ojha Rs. 220

CICIL-15 Second Historical Survey of Educational Development in India: Select Documents 1985-1989
S.P. Agrawal and **J.C. Aggarwal** Rs. 490

CICIL-16 Documentation Encyclopaedia of UNESCO and Education
J.C. Aggarwal and **S.P. Agrawal** Rs. 800 (set of 2 parts)

CICIL-17 Attitude Towards Information: A Study of Post-Graduate Teachers and Researchers in Social Sciences
N.G. Satish (in press)

CICIL-18 Librarianship and Bureaucratic Organisation: A Study in the Sociology of Library Profession in India
P.K. Jayaswal Rs. 175

CICIL-19 Literature Search
K.A. Isaac Rs. 150

CICIL-20 Child Education in India: Index to Scholarly Writings in Indian Educational Journals and Newspapers since independence
S.P. Agrawal and **Naresh Kanta** Rs. 100

CICIL-21 Lok Sabha and Vidhan Sabha Elections in India 1989 & 1990: Process and Results with Comparative Study of Manifestos
S.P. Agrawal and **J.C. Aggarwal** Rs. 250

CICIL-22 Islamic Studies in India: A Survey of Human, Institutional and Documentary Sources
Mohamed Taher Rs. 180

CICIL-23 Panchayati Raj: An Annotated Bibliography
N.B. Inamdar, N.G. Satish and Anil Takalkar 290

CICIL-24 Information India 1989-90: Global View
S.P. Agrawal and **J.C. Aggarwal** Rs. 500

CICIL-25 First Handbook of Psychological and Social Instruments
Udai Pareek and **T. Venkateswara Rao** Rs. 500

CICIL-26 Educational and Social Uplift of Backward Classes: At What Cost and How? Mandal Commission and After
S.P. Agrawal and **J.C. Aggarwal** Rs. 275

CICIL-27 Mass Media and New Horizons: Impact of TV & Video an Urban Milieu
H.R. Trivedi Rs. 180

CICIL-28 Indian Writings on Education : An Indicator to Indian Educational Journals Grouped by Subject Deseriptors 1979 to 1986 (in two parts)
S.P. Agarwal Rs. 900 (per set)

CICIL-29 Nation in Crisis
S.P. Agrawal and **J.C. Aggarwal** Rs. 200

CICIL-30 Information India 1990-91: Global View
S.P. Agrawal and **J.C. Aggarwal** Rs. 500

CICIL-31 Development of University Libraries in India After Independence
O.P. Gupta Rs. 270

CICIL-32 Handbook on Child : With Historical Background
Pramila Pandit Barooah Rs. 320

CICIL-33 Weaker Section in Indian Society : Undiscovered Past, Uncertain Present and Unpredictable Future Index to Writings in Indian Scholarly Journals and 10 National Newspapers Classified under 1500 Descriptors 1886-1990
S.P. Agrawal and **Rajeev Kumar Sharma** Rs. 600

CICIL-34 Communication Informatics and Librarianship in India : An Introductory Guide to Publications Based on a Survey of Libraries in Capital City of India
S.P. Agrawal and **Pushpa Rani Sharma** Rs. 720

CICIL-35 Problems of Collection Development in Special Libraries
M.S. Sridhar Rs. 225

CICIL-36 National Information Resources for Social Sciences in India : Mobilisation, Dispersal and International Enhancement
S.P. Agrawal Rs. 225

CICIL-37 Modern History of Punjab : A Look Back into Ancient Peaceful Punjab Focusing Confrontation and Failures Leading to Present Punjab Problem, and a Peep Ahead : Relevant Select Documents
J.C. Aggarwal and **S.P. Agrawal** Rs. 400

CICIL-38 India Information Sources : Economics and Business
Kyllikki Ruokonen and **Manohar Lal** Rs.

CICIL-39 Educational Planning in India : With a Slant to Educational Financing and Administration, Vol. 1, Reports of Committees and Commissions, Five Year Plans, Statistical Tables
J.C. Aggarwal and **S.P. Agrawal** Rs. 650

CICIL-40 Integrated Library System : Two Case Studies : Latin America and India
Maria Luiza Rigo Pasquarelli, Rosaly Favero Krzyanowski, Ines Maria M. Imperatriz and S.P. Agrawal Rs. 160

CICIL-41 Social Science Information in India: Effort towards Bibliographical Control
S.D. Vyas Rs. 300

CICIL-42 Higher Education in India Since Independence: U.G.C. and its Approach
O.P. Gupta Rs. 360

CICIL-43 Government and Politics in India: A Bibliographical Study of Contemporary Scenario Chronicling Rajiv Gandhi Era
S.P. Agrawal and **Rajeev Kumar Sharma** Rs. 500

CICIL-44 Second Handbook of Psychological and Social Instruments
D.M. Pestonjee Rs. 300